CLOISONNÉ

Chilton
Book
Company/
Radnor,
Pennsylvania

Felicia Liban
and
Louise Mitchell

CLOISONNÉ

The
Art of
Cloisonné
Enameling
and
Jewelry
Making

FRONT COVER: *Trees* by Louise Mitchell.
Cloisonné enamel, 1¼″ (3.2 cm) diameter.
BACK COVER: *Country Scene* by Felicia Liban.
Cloisonné enamel set into a walnut box. Woodwork by Edward Lewand.
Pink Lady's Slipper by Felicia Liban.
Cloisonné enamel pendant set in 22- and 14-karat gold, 1⅛″ (2.9 cm) diameter.

Copyright © 1980 by Felicia Liban and Louise Mitchell
All Rights Reserved
Published in Radnor, Pennsylvania, by Chilton Book Company
and simultaneously in Don Mills, Ontario, Canada,
by Nelson Canada Limited
Library of Congress Catalog Card No. 80–957
ISBN 0-8019-6900
Designed by Arl
Manufactured i
Photographs by Gerald Stoodley

1 2 3 4 5 6 7 8 9 0   9 8 7 6 5 4 3 2 1

To the living memory of Claudia,
Felicia's daughter.
She encouraged us,
drew many of the illustrations,
and looked forward
to this book's publication.

Contents

Acknowledgments

There are many talented people working in cloisonné and jewelry today, and we are pleased to have the opportunity to recognize their contributions. We met while studying cloisonné with Bob Kulicke and Jean Stark at the Kulicke-Stark Academy in New York City. They were instrumental in developing the silver enameling techniques described in this book. Other excellent teachers/artists we have had the pleasure of working with include Joseph English and Fredericka Kulicke at the Jewelry Workshop in New York; Jeanette Klineman at the Little Neck YM-YWHA; and Hansi Minnig, James Bennett, Tom Reardon, Gary Miller, John Cogswell, and Harold Helwig at the Brookfield Craft Center in Connecticut. (Harold Helwig not only taught us Limoges and grisaille enameling, but a good deal about color diagrams and keeping notebooks, as well.) And we cannot fail to mention the craftspeople who taught the useful workshops sponsored by the Long Island Craftsmen's Guild. Barbara Mail's workshop on jewelry mechanisms was especially valuable.

We also wish to thank Gerald Stoodley, our excellent photographer, Edward Lewand, who did the woodworking for several pieces, and Jennifer Place, who provided invaluable help in revising the final manuscript. The line drawings are the work of Claudia and Julia Liban, the color diagrams the work of Louise Mitchell. Thanks also to Doris Travas, Bernard Klausman, and Marie Wren for their many useful suggestions, and to Muriel Paige and Louise Boland for their help with manuscript preparation. Our husbands, Eric Liban and Paul Mitchell, provided much-appreciated support.

Introduction

If you walk through any major craft fair in the United States or visit any of the numerous galleries or shops that now feature high-quality crafts, chances are that among the jewelry you will spot small, brilliantly colored enamels in gold or silver settings featuring intricate wire work and depicting flowers, animals, miniature landscapes, or abstract forms. This is cloisonné enameling. Although the techniques for making a cloisonné enamel are ancient, they were practically forgotten until the craft renaissance of the past decade. Now cloisonné is on its way to becoming one of the most admired forms of jewelry making.

The first evidence of the use of enamels dates back to early dynastic times in Sumeria, Mesopotamia, and Egypt. Archeological digs in these areas have unearthed small pieces of jewelry with colored stones and bits of glass inlayed between metal wires. Six enameled gold rings dating from the 13th century B.C. were discovered in Cyprus, and in Greece there is evidence of jewelry from the 5th century B.C. bearing tiny bits of enamel decoration.

In most ancient cultures the development of enameling followed fast upon the discovery and use of glass. Enamel itself is made from ground glass colored with metal oxides. When the ground enamel is applied to a piece of metal and heated from 1290° to 1510°F (700° to 820°C), the glass melts and fuses to the metal base.

Six historically recognized forms of multicolor enameling developed over the centuries: champlevé, cloisonné, Limoges, plique-à-jour, basse-taille, and grisaille.

The name *champlevé* comes from the French word for "raised plane." In this technique, the enamel colors are applied to depressed areas in the base metal. The depressions are created by etching or engraving into the metal, or by sawing areas out of a second metal sheet and fusing this to a base sheet. The process was first worked by the Celts in the British Isles during the 3rd century A.D.

Cloisonné is a multicolor enameling process in which each enamel color is separated by thin metal wires that form tiny cups or cells. (The word *cloisonné* comes from the French *cloison*, meaning "cell.") The wires not only contain the different colors, but they also act as a decorative element in the design, help anchor the enamel to

Figure I—1 An example of champlevé enamel by Felicia Liban.

the base, and share the stress of the intense heat required to melt the enamel.

Examples of early cloisonné enamels date from the 6th century A.D. in the Byzantine Empire and in Japan. The Byzantine enamels were fired on gold and used gold wires to form the designs. They portrayed a Christian empire: figures of Christ and the cross, various saints, and animals such as peacocks, the symbol for paradise. Japanese enamels from the same period were detailed in design and much more "painterly." They showed naturalistic scenes of flowers, birds, and landscapes.

The history of cloisonné in China is more obscure but probably dates around the 13th century A.D. Designs were far more patterned and ornamental than the Japanese, and colors were primarily opaque rather than transparent or shaded. Japan has a continous tradition of enameling, which reached a peak during the 19th century. Chinese arts and crafts, however, disappeared during the 1800s due to political strife and were not to flourish again until modern times. Now both cultures have export business in enamel wares.

Limoges enameling, also known as painted enameling, was developed by the Penicaud family of Limoges, France in about 1500 A.D. Moistened, ground enamels are applied freely onto the metal base with fine brushes and inlay tools. Areas of colored enamels are laid side by side in a thin, uniform layer, and when fired they do not intermingle. Further effects can be gained by using transparent, opaque, or opalescent enamels as well as gold or silver foils.

Plique-à-jour, or backless enameling, is another technique. In one method small openings are cut in a metal sheet, or wires formed in a pattern, but no base sheet is used. Instead, transparent enamels are placed in the openings and the piece is fired on a sheet of mica (enamel does not stick to mica). The result is a miniature stained-glass window, because light can pass through the transparent enamel.

Figure I–2 These pieces from the Liban collection show Chinese cloisonné work of the early 20th century. From left to right: black and white plate with a carved jade center, 4″ (10 cm) high; vase with a multicolored dragon on a white background, 7″ (18 cm) high; black casket with multicolored dragons, 4″ × 6″ (10 cm × 15 cm).

Basse-taille (literally, ''low cutting'') enameling uses a sheet of etched, engraved, or impressed metal covered with a thin layer of transparent enamel so the design of the metal can show through.

In grisaille (gray) enameling, fine opaque white enamel is sifted onto a prefired opaque black or dark enamel base. A design is scratched through the unfired white enamel to reveal the dark base. Additional areas of white can be built over the first layer in subsequent firings to improve the details of the design.

Modern enameling often makes use of several techniques within the same piece. For example, cloisonné wire designs may contain Limoges-type shading in certain areas. Therefore the instructions in this book include techniques for cloisonné and Limoges enameling.

We assume that you either have had some previous jewelry-making or enameling experience or are taking or planning to take a course in cloisonné. Fine jewelry making requires some expensive equipment, and it is much better if the beginner has access to a professional workshop or classroom before making the substantial investment needed to make cloisonné at home. The more experienced

xiii

Figure I–3 An example of grisaille enamel by Felicia Liban.

jeweler, however, will easily be able to add the necessary tools for enameling to a workshop or studio.

The book is structured so that the reader will first learn to make a cloisonné enamel, then how to make a jewelry setting for it. Since making the enamel itself requires some metalworking techniques, such as soldering and cutting metal sheet, these are taught in the enameling section. Later in the book the reader will learn some more sophisticated processes, such as fusing, gold and silver granulation, chain making, and how to make boxes from silver or copper.

The process for making an enamel is, briefly, as follows: create a design, make an enamel cup (base) by soldering a ring of wire (bezel) to a metal sheet, shape the wires to form the cloisons, prepare the enamels, fill the cloisons with layers of enamel, fire each layer of enamel in the kiln so it melts, and finally grind and polish the enamel until it is smooth and shining. After that you can transform this small "jewel" into a ring, pendant, or whatever it had been designed for by creating a setting that will highlight the special qualities of the piece.

The results of your efforts will be gemlike works of lasting quality and beauty. You will find cloisonné enamels are well received and salable items in galleries and shops, and that your efforts in mastering this time-honored and intricate craft will be rewarded well beyond your expectations.

ONE/
CLOISONNÉ
ENAMELING

Tools,
Equipment,
and
Studio

1

To begin cloisonné enameling, you must first have access to the necessary tools and equipment and a proper work space. Your equipment needs will depend upon your circumstances. The beginner who will be taking a class in cloisonné and has no tools will want to buy only the tools required to supplement the classroom or workshop equipment. If you have had some experience in cloisonné, however, you may now be ready to set up a simple home workshop. Other jewelers may wish to set up a more complete jewelry-making studio or add equipment to an existing studio.

This chapter lists the tools needed for each of these situations; each tool is described later in the text when it is actually put to use. The Sources of Supplies suggests where to purchase the tools and materials.

We will also describe two studio setups, a simple home workshop and a sophisticated teaching studio. In any situation, wear comfortable clothing. Jeans, work shirts, and low-heeled shoes are traditional craftsmen's clothing. Avoid loose sleeves that could catch on fire, and especially avoid wearing anything made of acetate, which will melt when heated and cause burns. If your hair is long, keep it tied back and out of the way.

It is also important to keep all your tools clean and orderly. Accidents should not happen if you take the time to set up all the tools you need before you begin working and if you clean up carefully after each session.

CLOISONNÉ IN THE CLASSROOM

In a classroom situation the student usually has access to a full line of jewelry-making equipment. Most classes, however, ask that you purchase the tools that are used individually, such as pliers and tweezers, as well as the silver or other metal you will be using. The classroom will probagbly have worktables, enamels, kilns, and the necessary soldering, grinding, and polishing equipment.

Here is a list of the tools a student is generally asked to buy and bring to class:

Chain-nosed watchmaker's pliers
Round-nosed watchmaker's pliers
Flat-nosed pliers
Two pairs of fine watchmaker's tweezers
Firing tweezers—7" long (18 cm) soldering tweezers for kiln use only
Small metal ruler, inch and metric
Bezel shears
Needle files, #2 cut
Curved burnisher

Soldering pick
Hard silver solder flux and small brush
Solder—IT, hard, medium, easy, and extra easy, 1 pennyweight (dwt) each
3" × 4" (8 × 10 cm) charcoal block
Stone or rocker pusher
Set-screw dividers
000 sable brush for enameling
Silver or copper for your projects

THE BASIC HOME SETUP

Once the student has had some enameling experience and has purchased some tools and silver, the next step is to set up a small workshop at home. One definite advantage to cloisonné is that it needs very little space. Most of the equipment needed for enameling and the jewelry fabricating described in this book can fit on one large worktable.

A kitchen or basement is probably the best location for a home studio. The equipment should be out of the reach of young children, and it is helpful if there is a supply of running water. At least one electrical outlet and a good light are essential. Keep a small fire extinguisher close at hand, or a box of baking soda, in case anything catches on fire. Make sure everything is neatly and properly stored and labeled.

The following list (in addition to the tools listed for the classroom) will complete a basic setup needed to make cloisonné enamels at home:

Enamels
Agate mortar and pestle
Small beakers or shot glasses
$\frac{1}{4}$ to $\frac{1}{2}$ teaspoon-sized (1 to 2.5 ml) spoon
Small bowls for washing enamels
Micrometer or wire gauge
Manicure scissors
Soldering torch (propane or acetylene) and starter
Tripod with wire mesh top
Iron binding wire
Chasing hammer
Steel pan filled with Carborundum grains
Firebrick (small)

Hard silver solder flux and small brush
Heat lamp
Yellow ochre or typist's nonflammable white correction fluid
A "third arm" and lock-tweezer
Pumice chunks
Sparex #2 pickle
Pickle pot or slow cooker
Copper or wooden tongs
Baking soda
Detergent for cleaning
Glass brush and old toothbrush
Two steel blocks, $2\frac{1}{2}$" (6 cm) square and $\frac{3}{4}$" (2 cm) high

Figure 1–1 The basic tools for enameling and soldering include, clockwise from far left: a magnifier; pickle pot and copper tongs; enamels; the kiln and spatula; torch; tripod with charcoal block and bowl of Carborundum grains underneath; torch starter; a black tile on which stand liquid flux, binding wire, bezel shears, and two sheets of solder; rouge and a polishing stick; two steel blocks; large tweezers; brushes; and a circle template.

Table-top kiln
Ceramic tile or Transite, 12″ (30 cm) square
Mica or high fire unglazed porcelain tile
Metal spatula for kiln
Plastic circle templates
Pencil
Ring or bezel mandrel
Felt buffing sticks
Bobbing and white diamond polishing compounds
Wood or steel dapping block and punches
Wet/dry Carborundum paper in 220 to 600 grits

150-grit dry aluminum oxide sandpaper
Magnifying glass or magnifier
Matte salt
Scotch stone
Butcher's wax
Dop cement
Wooden dowels
Single-edged razor blade
Small tin cans (such as tuna-fish cans)
Tin oxide
Suede leather block—4″ (10 cm) square wood block to which a piece of suede is stapled
Tracing paper

Kiln. The only kiln needed for small cloisonné work is a small electric hobby kiln, sometimes called a trinket kiln (see Sources of

Supplies). It has a 3″ (7.6 cm) diameter ceramic floor in which a heating element is encased. It turns on when plugged in and heats to about 1500° F (816° C). The largest size enamel that the trinket kiln will hold is about 2½″ (6 cm) in diameter. All the examples in this book are within this practical range. The next largest table-top kiln is 6″ (15 cm) in diameter and will hold an enamel about 4″ (10 cm) in diameter. Its coils are concealed in the ceramic floor as in the smaller model. It gives off quite a bit of heat, so unless a rheostat is connected to it, it must be unplugged between firings. This kiln is somewhat more expensive than the smaller one. Both kilns must be placed on a ceramic tile or Transite pad for safety.

If such trinket kilns are not available, chamber kilns with exposed heating coils may be used if they are fitted with a nichrome mesh screen. The mesh should rest on the outer ceramic edge and cover the coils so the coils do not touch the mesh, spatula, tweezers, or the enammel piece. Chamber kilns are more expensive to operate than the trinket kilns, but if you have one, you can use it for cloisonné enameling.

Trivets (stilts). A trivet or stilt is occasionally used to support the enamel piece in the kiln during firing. The trivet keeps the enamel off the floor of the kiln and also keeps the counter enamel on the back surface neat. Trivets or stilts are made of stainless steel or nichrome wire and are available from enameling suppliers in a variety of shapes and sizes. You can also buy nichrome wire and make a stilt of the size and shape you need.

Enamels and metals. This book uses Thomas Thompson enamel colors. The beginner can purchase a special kit of these enamels, consisting of 2 ounces (57 grams) of any eight colors. For metals, it is sufficient to begin with a supply of cloisonné wire, a sheet of 30- and 26-gauge fine silver, and a complete selection of silver solder. Chapters 2 and 3 will tell you much more about the enamels and metals used for cloisonné.

Soldering torch. A Benzomatic Bantam torch is a small propane torch that is adequate for the beginner. You may wish later to add a Benzomatic Master torch, which has two other tips for flame variation. A larger and more costly, but better, torch is an acetylene gas tank, combined with a regulator, hose, handle, and tips. This is the type of torch used in most classrooms and workshops. Chapter 4 gives more information about torches and soldering equipment.

THE COMPLETE JEWELRY STUDIO

The serious jewelry maker will want to invest in (or may already have) some of the more expensive and complex pieces of equipment. These are not necessary for making enamels, but they make jewelry fabrication faster and easier. They can be purchased as needed:

Vise	Metal polisher with dust collector
Rolling mill	Lapidary polisher
Draw plates and tongs	Ultrasonic cleaner

Flexible shaft	Drill press
Acetylene torch	Bench shear
Polishing tumbler	Circle cutter
Various size mandrels	Planishing hammer
Balance scale	Rivet hammer

WORKSHOPS AND STUDIOS

As mentioned earlier, a studio can range from a small, compact workshop to a large, professional teaching studio. Here we will describe and show our own setups.

The Mitchell studio is in a cheerful 9 × 17-foot (3 × 5 meter) sunroom that is well ventilated and large enough to accommodate all the equipment needed to do the projects in this book. (See figure 1–2.) There is no running water in the studio, so the enamels are carried on a tray to the kitchen to be washed.Extra electrical outlets were added, including a multiple outlet with individual switches that is handy for kilns and tumblers because they are turned on and off frequently. An extension-arm lamp can be moved into the best position for seeing the work. The worktables were made from 2 × 4s and plywood, and they have fireproof Transite tops. They are heavy and immobile.

Figure 1–2 Louise Mitchell's one-person studio.

The Liban studio takes up an entire basement and is equipped for teaching classes. The walls are painted white and the ceiling is loaded with fluorescent lights, which make it bright and cheerful. Electrical outlets are everywhere, including on the worktable top. The studio includes a sink, bench shear, drill press, and polishing equipment. The tools, enamels, books and catalogs are easily accessible and well organized. (See figures 1–3 and 1–4.)

YOUR NOTEBOOK AND FILES

Notebooks and files are an essential part of any workshop. You will want to keep records of your design ideas, a file of design sources, and careful records of each finished piece so you can duplicate your successes and avoid repeating mistakes.

The Clipping File

Although we have provided a number of designs for cloisonné enamels in Chapters 9 and 10, you will undoubtedly want to design some of your own. You cannot beat a sketch that you have drawn from real life as the basis of a design. It will have a freshness and originality that you cannot get any other way. The next best thing is taking a photograph yourself. You can focus on exactly the details you want in a particular subject.

Unfortunately, it is not always possible to sketch or photograph a subject from life, and here is where a clipping file comes into use. Most designers keep files of newspaper and magazine clippings on every subject they might want to use in a design. They use the clippings both as information sources and as the basis for stylized drawings or tracings. A library near you may also keep files of photographs that are available for people to borrow.

Some magazines such as *National Geographic* and *Smithsonian* should be saved intact because of the wealth of pictures they contain. There are also numerous sourcebooks available on the market that contain uncopyrighted designs from past eras and from different countries. These can be helpful for finding motifs. Worth collecting, too, are books about jewelry throughout history. Often an ancient piece can inspire a modern design.

Working Up Your Own Design

Once you have chosen an idea for your enamel from a sketch, photograph, or clipping, it is easy to transform that idea into a workable design. Some of the design aids that are available on the market are very helpful, especially plastic templates of various shapes and French curves.

Tracing paper is also an invaluable design aid. You can use it to adapt and vary photographs, sketches, or other illustrations to achieve a workable design you like. First, trace the original picture. Then draw an outline of the perimeter of the proposed enamel. Then make a sandwich of the tracing paper with the outline of your

Figure 1–3 A view of Felicia Liban's studio showing the polishing machines, lapidary machine, rolling mill, and reference library.

Figure 1–4 A second view of the Liban studio shows the soldering bench, kiln bench, sink, and shelves of enamels.

enamel on the bottom, the tracing of the artwork in the middle, and a clean sheet of tracing paper on top. On the top sheet, retrace the best elements of the design underneath. You can vary or simplify the lines or add new elements, always keeping in mind the shape of the outline underneath. Now, remove the middle drawing and add a clean sheet of paper on top. Redraw the image again, incorporating whatever new adjustments you think it needs. Keep going this way until you have the best possible design for your enamel. The final drawing will be clean and neat, and you won't have erased any ideas that you might want to refer to later.

With any design, try to keep the lines interesting and lively, remembering that they will eventually be gold or silver embedded in enamel.

Scaling Down Artwork

Cloisonné enamels are very small, and you will probably have to scale down and simplify most artwork for a design. You can have photographs reduced at a local photocopying service, or you can use the grid method to scale down the art yourself.

To use the grid method, simply draw a grid of squares on tracing paper over your original design (secure the grid to the design with tape "hinges" or paperclips). Next draw a smaller grid with the same number of squares over an outline of the proposed enamel. (This outline is the same size you want the finished piece to be.) Wherever an important line in the original design crosses the grid line, make a dot on the same spot on the small grid over the enamel outline. Using the original as a guide, connect the dots on the small grid freehand. (See figure 1–5)

Keeping a Notebook

A carefully kept notebook is an indispensable tool for the designer/craftsman. Good records will enable you to reproduce a successful enamel design at another time, and it can help ensure that you don't repeat your mistakes. For each enamel that you do, include in your notebook a pencil sketch, a rough color sketch for ready identification, color diagrams, wirework diagrams, notes on any special procedures, and any additional comments you wish to make.

(To make the illustrations and diagrams in chapters 9 and 10, we used a black fine-point marker for the outlines and wire lines, and Letratone dot film to represent the different colors. You could also use colored markers or pencils in your notebook.)

The Slide Portfolio

We recommend that you take color slides of every piece you make before you let it out of your hands. The slides will coordinate with your notebook and will automatically provide you with a portfolio of your work. If you do not know how to take 35 mm slides yourself, there are books available on how to photograph crafts, or it might be worthwhile to hire a professional photographer who specializes in

10

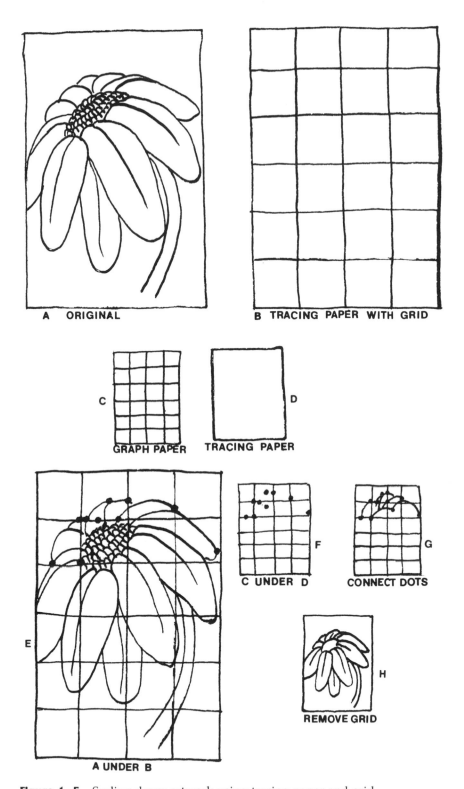

A   ORIGINAL

B   TRACING PAPER WITH GRID

C   **GRAPH PAPER**   D   **TRACING PAPER**

E

A UNDER B

F   **C UNDER D**

G   **CONNECT DOTS**

H   **REMOVE GRID**

Figure 1—5   Scaling down artwork using tracing paper and grid.

11

craft photography. Enamels are difficult to photograph because of the reflections from the enamels and the metal.

You should always try to present your work in its best light, whether it is in photographs or on display. Taking the time to put your work in a pretty box or jewelry pouch if you are showing it to an eventual buyer is very important. Having good photographs to show is just as important, especially if you are trying to create sales.

ENAMELS

2

Enamel is basically ground glass and, like all glass, it has a base of silica or sand. The amount of borax and lead oxide added to the silica determines the hardness of the enamel. Potash enhances the color, and the amount of soda and borax added affects the elasticity. Borax also helps the various metal oxides used to color the enamels mix together more easily. Different metal oxides produce different colors. For instance, red enamels are made from gold oxides, which is why they are more expensive than other colors. The addition of tin oxide will make an enamel opalescent or pearly.

To make enamel, all the ingredients are melted together in a furnace for about fifteen hours. Then the molten glass is poured from the furnace and quenched with water. This produces cool, coarse chunks. These are ground and sifted through graded sieves to a particular mesh size, or they are reprocessed to make specific shapes such as threads or ribbons. (The ribbons and threads are most often used in copper enameling, not in cloisonné.)

Enamel colors for cloisonné are available in chunks or in pulverized form. If you buy chunks, you must grind the enamel by hand using an agate mortar and pestle. It is far more convenient to buy small jars of pre-ground enamel. Although they do not keep indefinitely as do the chunks, they have a shelf life of several years. For most cloisonné enameling, an 80 mesh size is best. You can grind the 80 mesh to an even finer size by using an agate mortar and pestle. The finer grind can be helpful for occasional tiny details.

TYPES OF ENAMELS

There are three different types of enamels: transparent, opaque, and opalescent. A wide variety of colors are available in each type. The effect of each type of enamel in the finished piece is different. A transparent enamel has a jewel-like depth, an opaque is solid looking, and an opalescent looks like pale milk glass. Many different colors and effects can be achieved by firing one color over another or by using different types of enamels next to each other.

The color of opaque enamels is not affected by anything lying underneath since you cannot see through them. The final effect can only be slightly influenced by the way the enamel is finished. (Grinding and polishing methods can give different amounts of shine.)

The appearance of transparent enamels, however, is affected by the depth of the enamel and by the material that lies underneath it. The latter can include another transparent color, an opaque color, the metal base, the reflections from silver or gold cloisonné wire, and foils or decals. The many effects possible with transparent enamels are the basis of shaded enamel designs.

Since they are only semitransparent, opalescent enamels are only somewhat affected by what is underneath them.

Different enamels fuse (melt) at different firing temperatures. Thus enamels can be described as soft (low firing), medium, or hard (high firing). (See "Firing Temperatures," later in this chapter.)

Thomas Thompson enamels are the ones most commonly used in studios and workshops, and they are readily available at suppliers. The company manufactures 86 opaque colors, 58 transparent colors, 13 opalescent colors, and 18 crackle colors. (The crackle enamels are rarely, if ever, used in cloisonné.) Each color has a name and a number (see the back of the book for a list). The designs in this book call for Thomas Thompson enamels. When referring to a particular color we will use both name and number, as in Goldenrod 459.

SOFT-FUSING FLUX

Soft-Fusing Flux 426 is essential to cloisonné enameling. It is a transparent, colorless enamel that can be mixed with colored enamels or used instead of colored enamels in building up the final layers in the cloisons.

If you are using hard, high-firing enamels in the same piece with soft enamels, adding soft-fusing flux to the hard colors will help equalize the firing temperatures. Otherwise the softer enamels are in danger of overfiring and losing their color before the hard enamel has had a chance to fire properly. You can also use soft-fusing flux to lighten the color of a transparent enamel. It has the same effect as adding water to watercolor paint.

The most common use of soft-fusing flux is to fill the cloisons in the final firings to bring the enamel to the top of the cloisonné wires. These final layers of flux will protect a soft color from overfiring, keep a color from turning darker if another layer of color were added, or maintain a hard-firing enamel color at its full intensity, since adding flux to it would dilute or lighten the color.

COLOR SAMPLES

If you need to check a color, or if you need to find an enamel to match a particular color in your design, you can begin by ordering a color chart from Thomas Thompson. It reproduces each color along with the color name and number. Beware, however, because these printed colors only approximate the actual color of the fired enamel.

16

A better test for color is to fire a small sample of each enamel that you intend to use. Fire a tiny amount on a small scrap of the metal you will be using for the piece, and then glue or tape the sample to the top of the enamel jar.

A more complete color sample can be made on a rectangle of 18-gauge copper with strips of gold and silver foil and a layer of flux fired on it. This will show the appearance of a transparent enamel over fluxed copper, silver, and gold. The samples of opaque or opalescent enamels will give a fairly accurate idea of how the final color will look. Transparents, as mentioned, can be affected by many other factors.

The best way to judge color is to become familiar with the varieties of effects through practice. Keep good notes, and in time you will not need the aid of charts or samples.

WASHING ENAMELS

Enamels must be washed thoroughly before each use. The purpose of washing is to remove the very tiny powderlike grains, called fines, and leave the larger grains of enamel. If the fines are not removed, the fired enamels can appear dirty or cloudy. More fines occur when the enamel is exposed to air, which causes the grains to decompose, so it is necessary to wash the enamels right before use, and, for certain enamels, during the working process as well.

Tap water is ideal for washing enamels since it is readily available and its adjustable force will help stir the enamels. However, the tap water should be mineral free. Enamels washed in hard water should be rinsed with distilled water. Impurities and minerals can be removed from tap water, if necessary, by pouring the water through a coffee filter or by installing a water filter on the faucet. You can also wash the enamels with distilled water purchased from a hardware store or supermarket, or with water collected from a dehumidifier. This water should be put in a plastic squeeze bottle so that the water can be added forcefully when washing the enamels.

Wash only the colors you need immediately before filling the cloisons. (It is best to use fresh enamels from the jar rather than previously washed and stored enamels.) Enamels should be washed until the rinse water appears clear. Clean enamel grains will sink to the bottom of the flask, and then the cloudy water containing the fines is poured off. This is repeated until the water is clear. Opaque enamels should be washed four to six times. Transparents should be washed ten to fifteen times because the tiniest grain of decomposed enamel can spoil the transparency. Opalescents should be washed only once since they are meant to be milky looking and washing thoroughly would make them more transparent.

Here are the steps for washing enamels.

1. Set out the enamels needed for your project, a small beaker or shot glass for each color, a tiny spoon (¼ or ½ teaspoon or 1 to 2 ml), a large bowl, plastic wrap, and rubber bands. Have these near your sink or other water source.

Figure 2–1 Wash enamels in a small beaker or cup using water directly from the tap if it is relatively mineral free.

Figure 2–2 Let the enamel settle on the bottom, then pour off the water and residue.

2. Measure the amount of enamel needed and spoon into the beaker. Usually $\frac{1}{2}$ teaspoon (2 ml) is more than enough.

3. Pour cold water from the tap or jar directly into the beaker until it is two-thirds full. The force of the pouring water will stir up the enamel grains. (See figure 2–1.)

4. Let the enamel settle. You will see the decomposed grains floating on top of the water.

5. Slowly pour the water into the large bowl. As you pour, use a twisting motion so the good enamel stays on the bottom of the beaker. (See figure 2–2.)

6. Wash opaque colors about four to six times, and transparents at least ten times. It is best to judge by looking carefully at the enamel and washing until the rinse water is perfectly clear and there are no visible "dead" grains.

7. After washing, the enamels should be kept wet in the beakers for working. Cover the beaker with plastic wrap secured by a rubber band for short-term storage.

8. Allow the decomposed enamel in the large bowl to settle, then pour off the water. Never pour enamel grains into the sink, because they may clog the drain. Instead, wait until the leftover enamel grains

18

have dried, and save residue for use as counter-enamel (enamel on the back of each piece).

If filling the cloisons and firing takes a long time, the air can further decompose transparent enamels, so they should be rewashed several times during your work. Flux especially should be washed several times between firings to keep it absolutely clear.

If you must store washed enamels for a day or two, dry the enamel rapidly and put it in an airtight container, or store it under water in a small lidded jar. Rewash the enamel before using it.

FIRING TEMPERATURES

Enamels do not all fire at the same temperature. They are either soft (low firing, 1290°–1350° F, 700°–730 C), medium (medium firing, 1350°–1420° F, 730°–770° C), or hard (high firing, 1420°–1510° F, 770°–820° C). The harder the enamel, the longer it must be left in the kiln before it melts. The temperature of the kiln, therefore, must be higher than the melting point of the hardest enamel used. When an enamel has reached maturity, the kiln will glow with a bright red color (1550° F, 843° C). Heated further, the kiln will glow orange red (1650° F, 895° C). An enamel will fire faster if it is a finer mesh.

There is no specific length of time to leave an enamel in a kiln. It needs to be heated until it melts enough to fuse with the layer or metal underneath, but not so much that the color overfires and darkens cr the enamel layers break up.

Generally, the first layer of enamel is heated until it is smooth in texture. Subsequent layers are fired just until the surface texture is that of an orange peel.

If some enamel colors in your design are hard firing and others soft or medium, you run the risk of overfiring the soft enamels while bringing the hard ones to maturity. To avoid this, you can lower the firing temperature of the hard enamel by adding soft-fusing flux. Adding flux will lighten the color, however. Another way around the problem is to bring the lower firing enamels to maturity but let the hard enamels remain slightly underfired. Then use soft-fusing flux as the final thin layer over the entire surface. Firing a very hard enamel over a very soft one can cause cracks in the final piece.

Melting Temperatures of Enamels

Soft-firing colors: 1290°–1350° F (700°–730° C)
    Reds (opaque, opalescent, and transparent)
    Oranges (opaque, opalescent, and transparent)
    Pinks (opaque)
    Purples (opaque)
Medium-firing colors: 1350°–1420° F (730°–770° C)
    Yellows (transparent)
    Tans (transparent)
    Pinks (opalescent and transparent)
    Purples (opalescent and transparent)

Blues and greens (opaque, opalescent, and transparent)
Yellow-greens (opaque, opalescent, and transparent)
Browns and grays (opaque, opalescent, and transparent)
Hard-firing colors: 1420°–1510° F (770°–820° C)
Whites (opaque and opalescent)
Light yellows (opaque and opalescent)
Cream and ivory (opaque)
Beige (opaque)
Pastel blues and greens (opaque)

Black opaques, white opaques, and fluxes are all manufactured in soft, medium, and hard temperatures so each can be mixed with any of the enamel colors listed above.

Sheet
Metal
and
Wire

3

Making a cloisonné enamel involves three different gauges of metal: thin wire to form the lines of the cloisonné design, flat sheet metal for the enamel base, and slightly thicker sheet metal to make a rim or bezel. Bezel and base together are called an enameling cup. The cup contains and supports the cloisonné wires and the layers of enamel. (Enameling on bases without a bezel is discussed in Chapter 8).

Only certain metals are compatible with enamels: silver, gold, copper, some specially treated steel and aluminum, and special zinc-free brass and bronze. (The jewelry settings for your enamels can, on the other hand, be made from many types of metals or other materials.)

GOLD

The relative purity of gold is measured in karats (not to be confused with *carat*, which is the unit of weight of precious stones). There are 24 karats in pure gold, which is described as 24/24 gold. 20-karat gold is an alloy containing 20/24 pure gold and 4/24 of another metal; 18-karat gold contains 18/24 pure gold and 6/24 of another metal; and 14-karat gold contains 14/24 pure gold and 10/24 of another metal.

The color, melting point, and other characteristics of an alloy depend on what other metals have been added. Pure gold has a melting point of 1945°F (1063°C), and the melting points of gold alloys range down to 1580°F (860°C). White gold contains platinum or palladium and is very hard. Green gold contains silver, cadmium, and zinc and is quite soft. Yellow gold contains silver, copper, and zinc, and it is widely used in jewelry settings.

Gold cloisonné wire must be made from 24 karat gold because it is pure (so it will not oxidize), soft, and malleable. But these very characteristics make it unsuitable for most jewelry settings. A gold enameling cup can be made from 24- or 22-karat gold, alloyed only with pure silver to avoid problems of oxidation. Gold alloyed with copper or other metal will oxidize during firing. However, it is possible to enamel on gold alloyed with metals other than fine silver if it is specially treated to increase the purity of the surface to 22 or 24 karats. This is done by fluxing, annealing, and pickling six to eight

23

times. (These procedures are described in Chapter 4.) Enamel will not adhere to a gold alloy containing zinc.

SILVER

Pure silver is called "fine silver." It is the primary metal of choice for cloisonné enameling. It melts at 1761° F (961°C), it is similar to gold in its softness and ductility, and, like gold, it does not oxidize during firing. It is also considerably less expensive than gold.

Sterling silver is the alloy most commonly used in jewelry making. Made from 925 parts silver and 75 parts copper, it has a melting point of 1640°F (893°C). The copper makes the alloy tougher and more resistant to denting, but it oxidizes rapidly upon heating. Sterling silver can be used for enameling, but, like some of the gold alloys mentioned above, it must be properly prepared by fluxing, annealing, and pickling six to eight times to create a surface of pure silver that will not oxidize.

COPPER

Enamel adheres well to copper, and copper is often used in large enameling projects, such as plaques, trays, or bowls, where the cost of using silver or gold would be prohibitive. Copper is also used successfully for small cloisonné work, but it requires special handling.

Copper melts at 1981°F (1083°C), which is higher than the melting point of silver. When using copper wire on a silver base or silver wire on a copper base, there is a danger of melting the two metals together, because any mixture of metals will melt at a lower temperature than either pure metal. To prevent this, a protective coat of enamel must be fired on the base first, before the wires are positioned.

Also, copper oxidizes when heated, developing a black coating called firescale. Firescale flakes off during cooling and will contaminate the enamel. So copper cloisonné wire must be cleaned off after each firing. The special procedures described in Chapter 8 will help assure getting a successful piece of cloisonné on copper with jewel-like quality.

ALUMINUM, STEEL, BRASS, AND BRONZE

Aluminum can now be successfully used in enameling projects since the development, by Harold Helwig, of lead-free, low-fire vitreous enamels, manufactured by Vitrearc, a division of the Ceramic Coating Company. The aluminum must be a special alloy, called aluminum 3003, which is available from American Metalcraft and from Vitrearc. More information on enameling on aluminum is found in Chapter 8.

Steel is marvelous metal on which to enamel (witness your kitchen sinks, pots, stoves, and refrigerators), but the quantities of heat and acid used in preparing steel for enameling are hardly within the reach of most craftsmen. Fortunately, you can now buy pieces of steel that have either been silver-plated or covered with enamel on both sides ("ground-coated" steel). Silver-plated or enameled steel works well as an enameling base. Procedures for cloisonné enameling on ground-coated and silver-plated steel are given in Chapter 8.

Enameling on brass and bronze is rather difficult because the firing temperature must be very accurately controlled or else the zinc, an ingredient in both brass and bronze, will bleed through and prevent the enamel from adhering to the metal. When the piece cools, the enamel will simply pop right off. Chinese enamelers do use brass, but it is brass with a high copper content and a low zinc content.

Although brass cannot be used for the enameling cup, it can be used for the cloisonné wire because it will be held on all sides by enamel that has fused to the non-brass base. Brass wire must be handmade since it is not yet available commercially.

SHEET METAL FOR CLOISONNÉ

Although cloisonné wire can be relatively thin, the metal used for the base must be thick enough to support the layers of enamel. The size of the finished piece must also be taken into consideration; the larger the piece, the thicker the sheet metal should be. Otherwise warping or cracking may occur in the finished piece.

For all the projects in this book and for any piece whose finished size does not exceed 2″ (5 cm) in diameter, the base sheet should be made from 30-gauge fine (pure) silver. The rim of the enameling cup, called a bezel, should be made from 26-gauge fine silver.

CLOISONNÉ WIRE

Commercial cloisonné wire can be purchased in 24-karat gold and in fine silver. Local suppliers usually carry only one size, which is .010″ wide and $\frac{1}{32}$″ high (.25 × .8 mm). Hauser and Miller will supply cloisonné wire in any thickness and height you request. Brass and copper wire, and gold or silver wire of other dimensions, can be made yourself, as described later in this chapter.

Color

Color is an important consideration when choosing wire for cloisonné. Silver, gold, copper, and brass all vary in color: silver has a gray color, gold and brass are yellowish, and copper is pinkish. Each metal also has a different effect when viewed through transparent enamel. Silver tends to have a cool reflection, whereas gold casts a warm glow. Copper and brass, which oxidize during firing, cast a dark shadow into the enamel. Choosing which to use depends on the colors of enamel in the design, as well as preference. You can use different colored wires to achieve different effects in enamels that have the same design, and you can combine different metals within a design. For example, a bird could be made of silver and the branch it perches on from copper.

Height and Thickness

The higher a cloisonné wire is, the more reflective surface it has and the greater the shadow it will produce when used with transparent colors. Also, the higher the wire is, the greater the number of enamel layers that can be fired. This is especially important with shaded enamel designs.

Most projects in this book call for higher and thinner wire than is routinely available commercially. The higher, thinner wire permits intricate designs and numerous layers of enamel. An ideal size to work with is wire that is .005″ thick and about $\frac{1}{16}$″ high (.13 × 1.6 mm). The wire can be thinned by hand, although it is far easier to thin it in a rolling mill if one is available.

A very effective design variation is to use different thicknesses of wire within the same design. (Our bird, for example, could be done in fine wire, and the branch could be made of thicker wire.) Thick, smooth wire creates a strong linear pattern and is especialy suited to geometric designs. Thin, crinkled cloisonné wire, on the other hand, is delicate and creates more of a ''painterly'' look. It lends itself better to intricate designs such as landscapes or portraits.

MAKING CLOISONNÉ WIRE

There will be times when you will want to make your own cloisonné wire out of flat metal sheet, either for design or cost considerations, or for convenience. You may want thicker-than-normal wire, or wire made from copper or brass. You may feel that buying commercial cloisonné wire in gold is too expensive, and that making your own represents a saving. For some shaded designs you may need wire the same thickness as, but higher than, most commercial wire.

To make your own wire you will need metal sheet the same thickness as the desired wire, set-screw dividers, bezel shears, kiln, and firing tweezers.

1. Set the dividers to $\frac{1}{32}$″ or $\frac{1}{16}$″ (.8 or 1.6 mm) depending on the desired wire height. Run one point of the dividers along one of the long edges of the metal sheet. The other point will simultaneously score a parallel line on the metal itself.

2. Cut along the scored line with bezel shears.

3. Using tweezers, anneal the cut wire in a hot kiln for 20 seconds.

THINNING WIRE WITH A ROLLING MILL

To thin commercial cloisonné wire, 30-gauge sheet metal strips, or regular round or square wire, you will need the kiln, firing tweezers, bezel shears, and a micrometer or wire gauge. And, of course, you must have access to a rolling mill, which can often be found in larger workshops or studios.

1. Plug in the kiln. With bezel shears, cut a piece of commercial cloisonné wire about a yard long.

2. Wrap the piece of wire around several fingers and lightly circle the bundle with one end of the wire and tie. Using tweezers, place the wire bundle in the hot kiln for 30 seconds to anneal (soften) it. Leave the kiln plugged in.

3. Remove the wire from the kiln and let it cool for a few minutes on a fireproof tile or pad, untie, and place one end of the wire between the rollers of the rolling mill. Lower the movable roller until it just grabs the end of the wire. Do not make it too tight.

4. As you feed the wire through the mill, keep tension on it by holding it firmly with one hand. This will also keep the wire straight. Then turn the handle of the mill with the other hand until all the wire has gone through. (See figure 3–1.)

5. Check the thickness of the wire with the micrometer or wire gauge. If it is not yet as thin or high as desired, anneal the wire again, change the setting on the rolling mill to a lower one, and repeat the process.

6. Continue to anneal the wire and put it through the rolling mill at successively lower settings until the desired size has been reached. Then anneal a final time. Unplug the kiln.

7. You can straighten any kinks in the wire by gently running the wire over the edge of a table or some other smooth surface. Anneal again.

Figure 3–1 Thinning wire in a rolling mill.

THINNING WIRE BY HAND

Thinning wire by hand is considerably more troublesome than using a rolling mill, but the results are just as satisfactory. The wire can be commercial cloisonné wire, strips cut from 30-gauge sheet, or round or square wire. You will need a steel block, a small planishing hammer, a micrometer or wire gauge, bezel shears, the kiln, and firing tweezers (7" or 18 cm long nickel-plated tweezers used only for enameling, not for soldering).

1. Plug in the kiln. With bezel shears, cut a piece of cloisonné wire about a yard long.

2. Wrap the piece of wire around several fingers and lightly circle the bundle with one end of the wire and tie. Using tweezers, place the wire bundle in the hot kiln for 30 seconds to anneal it. Leave the kiln plugged in.

3. Remove the wire and let it cool for a few minutes on a heatproof surface, untie, and place one end on the steel block. With either end of the planishing hammer, tap the wire slowly and evenly along its length. (See figure 3–2.) Check the size with a micrometer or wire gauge.

4. Anneal and repeat the process each time you reach the end of the wire with the hammer. When the wire has reached the desired thickness, anneal a final time. Unplug the kiln.

CRINKLED CLOISONNÉ WIRE

Enamelists sometimes prefer wire to have an irregular, textured effect rather than being perfectly smooth. It is especially pleasing in a design that is very delicate. Making crinkled cloisonné wire requires already thinned cloisonné wire, the kiln, firing tweezers, and a pair of fine tweezers.

1. Anneal a length of thinned wire in a hot kiln for about 15 seconds. Let the wire cool for a few minutes.

2. Hold one end of the wire between the thumb and forefinger of your left hand. Grip the wire about $\frac{1}{2}$" (1.3 cm) from the end you are holding with the thumb and forefinger of your right hand.

3. Press the two sets of fingers together. The wire will be squeezed between them like the folds of an accordion.

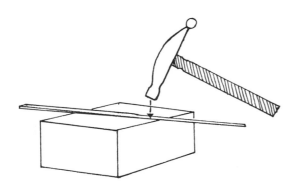

Figure 3–2 Wire can be thinned by hand using a planishing hammer and steel block.

28

Figure 3–3 Tweezers manipulate thinned wire to get a crinkled effect.

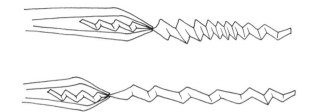

4. Continue this process along the whole length of the wire. Then gently pull the wire open.

5. Squeeze the wire along its entire length with a pair of small tweezers to straighten it out further, as in figure 3–3. The final effect will be a straight wire with irregular edges.

6. Repeat the process if necessary, annealing the wire first. Anneal a final time and the wire is ready for use.

Soldering, Annealing, and Cleaning

4

Several jewelry-making techniques are needed to make cloisonné enamels. In order to make an enameling cup to hold your wire design (the cloisons) and enamel, you must be familiar with soldering (permanently joining pieces of metal), annealing (softening metal with heat), and pickling (cleaning). All three of these processes are used throughout most jewelry fabrication. This chapter will describe the general equipment and techniques necessary for all three processes.

SOLDERING TOOLS AND EQUIPMENT

Soldering is the most common method of permanently joining two or more pieces of metal. Solder is usually a low-melting alloy of the same metal being joined. When the metal pieces being joined are placed together, a seam is created. Solder is placed on the seam and is heated with a torch. The solder melts and flows along the seam and, when it cools, it binds the metal pieces together. The joint will be invisible once smoothed and polished.

Set aside a particular area of your studio or home where you can solder safely without danger of fire. The work surface should be clean and covered with a fireproof material such as Transite. All flammable material should be stored well away from the working area. Adequate ventilation is important, and a venting fan should be installed if possible. All equipment should be readily available so you do not have to leave the area unattended while working.

For soldering you will need the following equipment: a torch, torch starter, flux, solder, charcoal block, Carborundum grains, a "third arm" and lock-tweezer, soldering pick, tripod and wire mesh, yellow ochre or typist's white correction fluid, a small brush, soldering tweezers, and bezel shears.

The Soldering Torch

Professional jewelers use a torch that works with a combination of compressed air and acetylene gas, or compressed air and natural gas. These provide a very hot flame and are the ideal equipment, but they are also the most expensive.

31

Figure 4–1 Soldering equipment includes, clockwise from left: water; two steel blocks; a "third arm"; the kiln and spatula; a bowl of Carborundum grains; a tripod with mesh top; charcoal block; the torch and torch tips; liquid flux; binding wire; bezel shears; two sheets of solder; a black tile; torch starter; tweezers; firebrick; and a magnifier.

A torch using acetylene gas alone is widely used by many jewelers and in most workshops. It is certainly adequate for most projects in this book. Purchased from a craft supplier or plumbing supply house, this type of torch comes with a tank of gas that is about 2 feet (60 cm) high and 6 inches (15 cm) in diameter (figure 4–2). When you buy the first tank of gas you pay for the tank and the gas inside. When the tank is empty, the supplier will replace it with a full tank, but you pay only for the gas. In theory you own your own tank.

You also initially purchase a regulator, hose, handle, and three tips (#1, #2, and #3) to make different size flames. A #1 torch tip is used only to get a very fine flame for smaller jobs. See figure 4–3 (1). Larger jobs call for at least a #2 torch tip and a strong, direct flame as in figure 4–3 (2). In both flames (1) and (2), the hottest part of the flame is at the tip of the light blue cone and slightly beyond it into the purple or lavender area. This part is used for soldering. At least a #2 torch tip is used to get a soft and bushy warming flame, as in figure 4–3 (3) for jobs like fusing, annealing, and melting flux. The cooler yellow end of the flame is used.

Figure 4–2 An acetylene tank can be equipped with a Y connection so that two different torch handles can be used. The small wire device hanging from the board is a torch starter.

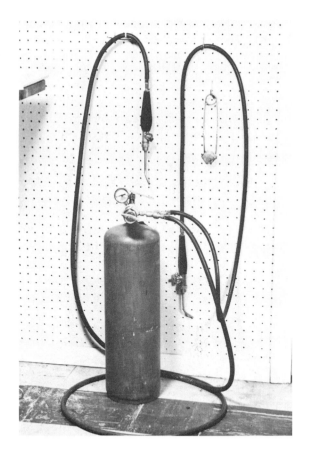

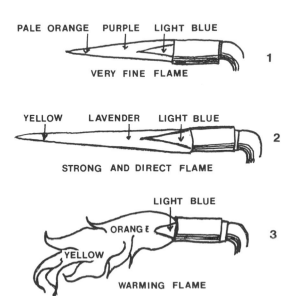

Figure 4–3 Torch flames. (1) A fine flame for small jobs, from a #1 tip; (2) a strong, direct flame, from a #2 tip or larger; (3) a warming flame, from a #2 tip or larger.

Most projects in this book suggest which torch tip to use. But a general rule of thumb to follow is this: The thicker the metal and the larger the piece, the larger the torch tip that should be used. If too much heat is applied too fast, the metal may melt. But if too little heat is used the solder will not melt, or it may take so long that the metal oxidizes too much. When overheated, silver can become pitted or brittle, and is called "tired silver." A bit of practice using a soldering torch and you should be able to tell which tip to use.

With a bit of care, the torch and tank are perfectly safe. Always store the tank in an upright position. A set of expanding belts with hooks on each end, available from an auto supply store, is ideal for strapping the tank to the worktable. Always keep the tank turned off when not in use, and never leave the handle without a tip screwed into it. After turning the tank off, let the torch burn until it goes out to leave the hose free of gas.

Small tanks of propane gas are also readily available and are adequate for most purposes. Two types of propane torches are available. The Benzomatic Master Torch has a nose and handle and two different tips equivalent to acetylene #2 and #3 tips. The Benzomatic Bantam Torch has a handle and one tip, which is equivalent to an acetylene #1 tip. If you wish to have all the flexibility of an acetylene torch, then you should purchase both types of propane torches. Always make sure to unscrew the nozzle from the propane tank when not in use; otherwise the gas will escape.

You will probably find it easiest to use a starting device for lighting the torch instead of matches, as a starter is used one-handed.

Soldering Flux

Upon heating, metals that contain copper (including silver solder and sterling silver) develop a coating of copper oxide called firescale, which impedes the solder flow. Firescale can be prevented by first brushing any areas to be soldered with a substance called soldering flux. Soldering flux can be purchased in paste, liquid, or powder form, and is made either from borax or fluoride. Handy Flux is a paste flux with a borax base that is good for pieces that require intense heat or intricate construction. For small pieces requiring less heat, however, paste flux tends to be too thick. A liquid flux, such as Battern's Self-Pickling Flux (Hard Solder Flux) is easier to use. It has a fluoride base and helps to clean the metal as well.

For prolonged heating or for fusing metals, we recommend making your own flux, called Prip's flux. It is not as bubbly as paste flux, and it protects the metal from melting during operations requiring prolonged heating. The ingredients can be purchased from a hardware store or pharmacy. Mix $\frac{1}{2}$ cup (120 ml) trisodium phosphate, $1\frac{1}{2}$ cups (360 ml) boric acid, $\frac{1}{2}$ cup (120 ml) borax, and 5 cups (1.2l) water. Bring all the ingredients to a boil in a glass saucepan and simmer on low heat for 20 to 30 minutes. Store in a glass jar and label.

Soldering flux is applied to the metal seam with a small inexpensive brush kept just for that purpose. Excess melted flux, called flux glass when cooled, must be removed by pickling before you continue working. Pickling is described later in this chapter.

Solder

Solder is purchased in .010″ (.25 mm) thick wire or sheet form. Solder should be pickled before using to remove any oxides or grease. It is then cut into tiny pieces for placing on the seam or joint. These small squares are called "paillons." Cut only as much solder as you will use at one time, and cut onto a black surface so the pieces can be seen easily. Paillons $\frac{1}{16}$″ or 2 mm square can be purchased precut.

Silver solders are alloys containing varying proportions of silver, copper, and zinc. They are available in several hardnesses and are called IT, hard, medium, easy, and extra easy. The harder the solder, the higher the temperature at which it melts. All five hardnesses should be purchased, because each has a different melting point and therefore a different use. For example, when a piece must be soldered more than once, you would make the first join with a hard solder and each successive join with softer solders. This way the previous joins will not melt and come apart. With a little practice you will get a feeling for which solder to use in which situation.

A substance called yellow ochre can be brushed on to protect previously soldered spots. You can also use typist's white nonflammable correction fluid for the same purpose. When brushed on a soldered seam, either one will inhibit the solder flow to that area, enabling you to do further soldering on other parts of the piece. We have found that the white correction fluid is more easily removed than is the yellow ochre.

IT solder is often needed when a lot of soldering must be done on one piece, or when the piece will be enameled after soldering. The melting point of IT solder is 1490°F (810°C), so there is no problem in using it on fine silver, which melts at 1760°F (960°C). Traditionally, IT solder has not been used on sterling silver, which melts at 1640°F (893°C), a melting point above that of IT solder, but a little too close for comfort. But, as metalsmith Jamie Bennett has demonstrated, IT solder can be used on sterling if reasonable care is exercised.

Silver solder melting points are as follows:

IT	1490°F	(810°C)
Hard	1460°F	(793°C)
Medium	1390°F	(754°C)
Easy	1325°F	(718°C)
Extra easy	1170° to 1270°F	(632° to 688°C)

Gold solder is graded by color and karat, and by hard, medium, and easy. In general, use solder that is the same karat as the gold being soldered. A solder two karats lower will flow a little faster (the lower the karat, the lower its melting point). According to a commercial jeweler we talked to, a good guideline is the following: the less gold to be soldered, the lower the karat of solder; the larger and thicker the piece, the higher the karat of solder. The procedures are the same as for silver soldering.

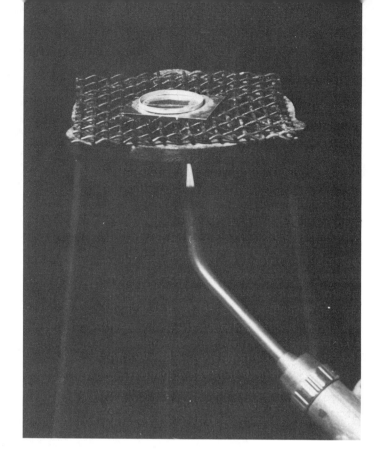

Figure 4–4 Using the tripod and wire mesh permits access to all parts of the piece.

Figure 4–5 A piece to be soldered can be positioned in a bowl of Carborundum grains and in a "third arm."

The Soldering Setup

The correct setup is as important to successful soldering as the actual soldering process itself. The piece must be positioned so that the heat can be properly applied, and there are a variety of ways to do this. You can set the piece on a charcoal block, on a piece of firebrick, in a steel bowl of Carborundum grains or pumice chunks. All are fireproof, and all retain heat to make the soldering go faster.

A charcoal block is exactly that—a lightweight block of compressed charcoal. Firebrick is made of fired clay. Generally used to line ceramic kilns, it can be purchased from most suppliers of soldering or jewelry making equipment, and it costs much less than charcoal. Carborundum grains placed in a small metal dish (a tunafish tin would do) is a useful setup because your work can be partially buried in the grains, thereby limiting the amount of metal surface exposed to heat. It also permits you to place the work at an odd angle. Pumice chunks, although larger, serve the same purpose.

To heat a piece from underneath, as is required in some soldering, it is set on a tripod covered with a sheet of wire mesh (figure 4–4). This arrangement allows the torch to heat almost any part of the metal. For very small pieces, however, a "third arm" permits greater ease of working. This is a self-locking tweezer in a jointed stand that will hold a piece in any position (figure 4–5).

The work must be set up so that the surfaces to be soldered are held together securely and all points along the seam are touching. This is done in various ways such as springing the ends of a metal ring or using binding wire. It is very important to remember that solder flows toward heat.

SOLDERING TECHNIQUES

It will take a bit of practice before you know which of the various methods of soldering is best for a particular project. We will suggest which technique to use for each project in this book, and eventually you will get a feeling for it. For example, to solder together the ends of a small ring of metal such as a bezel, you would flux the seam and place the ring on a charcoal block with a piece of solder directly underneath the seam. The heat is played over the seam, from above, and the solder melts and flows upward along the seam toward the heat. To join a seam when it is difficult to place the solder on the joint, as on a chain link, you would use the point soldering method. A third technique is sweat soldering, which is most often used to join two flat pieces of metal. Train yourself to hold the torch in your weaker hand, so you will have more control of the soldering pick in your stronger hand.

Regular soldering

When we use the term "soldering" in this book, the intended technique is as follows:

1. Place the metal to be joined on a charcoal block or firebrick. The edges of the metal should be touching tightly.

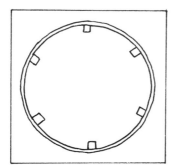

Figure 4–6 Solder paillons are placed around a seam for regular soldering.

2. Brush flux on the seam. Brush flux on the rest of the metal if it needs protection from firescale or overheating. Place small paillons of solder on one side of the seam, touching the seam. (See figure 4–6.) Be careful not to use too much solder; use just enough to join the seam.

3. With a torch, heat the entire piece, and then concentrate the flame on the side of the seam opposite the solder. The solder will flow into the seam in the direction of the heat source. A soldering pick can be run along the seam to aid the solder flow. (A soldering pick is a pointed tool with an insulated handle used for directing solder along a seam or in a difficult spot.)

4. When the seam is completely filled, remove the heat and let the piece cool. The seam should be firmly joined.

Point soldering

In point soldering, the solder is first melted into small balls, called shot, and then placed along the seam with a soldering pick.

1. Place the pieces to be joined on a charcoal block or firebrick. The edges of the metal should be touching tightly. Flux the seam.

2. Put a paillon of solder on the charcoal block and heat it with the torch until it forms a red-hot ball. Touch the ball with the tip of the soldering pick (still heating the ball) and the ball will adhere to the pick (figure 4–7).

3. Heat the seam with the torch until the flux turns glassy and slightly brown in color. This indicates that the metal has reached a high enough temperature for the solder to melt and flow. Touch the

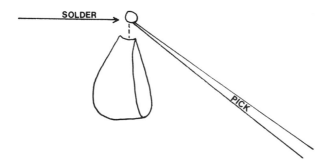

SOLDER

PICK

Figure 4–7 Point soldering uses a bead of melted solder placed with a soldering pick.

seam with the ball of solder on the pick, and the solder will flow into the seam. If you touch the solder to the seam before the seam is hot enough, the pick will conduct too much heat away from the seam and the solder will not flow.

4. When the seam is filled, remove the heat and let the piece cool.

Sweat soldering

Sweat soldering is used to join two flat pieces of metal, or to solder small pieces or wire to a larger piece. To sweat solder two flat pieces:

1. Flux both pieces and let them dry. Place the upper piece, flux side up, on a wire mesh and tripod or in a third arm.

2. Put paillons of solder all over the surface, at least $\frac{1}{8}''$ (3 mm) apart.

3. Heat the metal from underneath until the solder melts. Flux again.

4. Place the second piece on top of the melted solder to make a sandwich. Flip the two pieces over and heat again from underneath until a thin silver line appears between the metal sheets, indicating that the solder has flowed completely. (See figure 4–8) (Sometimes pressing with soldering tweezers is necessary if the sandwich does not meet well.) Remove the torch and let cool.

To solder a very small piece of metal or wire to a larger one (such as an earring post to the earring, or a bail to a pendant), a bit of solder is first melted (or "sweated down") on the tip of the small piece, which is held in a lock tweezer. It is then placed, solder down, on the larger piece, which is heated so the solder reflows and seals the joint. Always sweat the solder down on the smaller piece because the solder tends to stay on the tip of it, whereas on the larger piece the solder tends to flow where you don't want it, leaving solder scars. The only exception is when attaching pin backings. These findings are so tiny they might melt or the solder might interfere with the mechanisms, so the solder should be sweated down on the larger piece of metal.

This technique requires a lock tweezer and third arm.

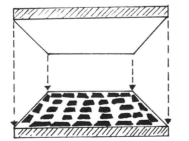

Figure 4–8 Two flat pieces of metal are sweat soldered by sandwiching the solder between them.

1. Place the small piece to be attached in a lock tweezer with the tip to be soldered facing up. Add a drop of flux to the tip. Place the larger piece on a charcoal block or in a bowl of Carborundum grains.

2. Put a paillon of solder on the charcoal block and heat it with the torch until it forms a red-hot ball. Pick up the ball with the soldering pick.

3. Run the torch flame (#1 tip) gently up and down the fluxed piece of metal. The tip of the metal will become white, indicating the flux has melted and is almost ready to receive the solder.

4. With the soldering pick in the stronger hand and the torch in the other, touch the solder to the fluxed tip. Concentrate the flame on the tip of the metal, but move the flame gently all the time. The flux will turn brown and the solder will flow suddenly. Remove the pick and the flame immediately.

5. Turn the lock tweezer so the soldered tip is facing down and let it touch the point where it is to attach to the larger piece. Add a drop of flux to the area to be joined.

6. Play the torch over the larger piece. (For anything larger than an earring, use a #2 tip.) As soon as the solder flows, remove the heat and let the piece cool.

Solder Scars

Solder scars are small lumps of solder visible at a joint after the piece has cooled. They occur when too much solder has been used or when the solder has been improperly placed along the seam. If soldering is properly done, there should be no visual residue along the seam or joint, but if scars or lumps do happen, they can be removed by filing or sanding.

ANNEALING

Metal becomes stiffer and brittle when hammered, bent, forged, twisted, or polished, and this can cause cracking or breakage. To prevent this and to keep the metal malleable, you need to anneal (heat and soften) the metal before you begin working it and throughout the working process.

Every metal has a specific annealing temperature that is considerably lower than its melting point. Annealing occurs automatically when you solder, but with other metalworking processes, annealing must be done periodically as you work, usually done with a torch. Small pieces of silver or gold can be put in a hot trinket kiln 15 to 30 seconds to anneal them. After annealing, let the metal cool.

There are three ways to control the heat while annealing:

1. Soldering flux can be used as a heat indicator. Brush the flux on the metal and heat with the torch or in the kiln. The flux will look glassy when heated to about the same temperature at which the metal anneals. After annealing, remove any excess flux by pickling.

2. Color is also a good indicator. If you anneal with a torch in semi-darkness, you will see the metal give off a cherry-red glow when it has been annealed.

3. If you anneal small pieces of metal or wire in the kiln, the number of seconds to leave the metal in the kiln depends on the volume of the metal. A small coil of thin wire, for example, should be left in the kiln about 30 seconds.

PICKLING

Any alloy that contains copper, such as sterling silver, gold of 22 karats or lower, as well as silver or gold solder, will oxidize upon heating. This oxidation must be removed before work continues. This is done by immersing the piece, after it has been soldered or annealed, in an acid solution called pickle. Metals were once cleaned with sulphuric and nitric acid, but fortunately today we have a milder acid to work with. It is called Sparex #2, and it is made from sodium bisulfate and other chemicals.

Sparex #2 comes in granular form and is mixed with water. It works best when heated. Do not let it boil, though, because it will give off harmful fumes. Pickle can be heated in a special pickle pot,

Figure 4–9 For pickling and cleaning you need detergent, old toothbrushes, an ultrasonic cleaner (optional), a glass brush, a pickle pot, and copper or wooden tongs.

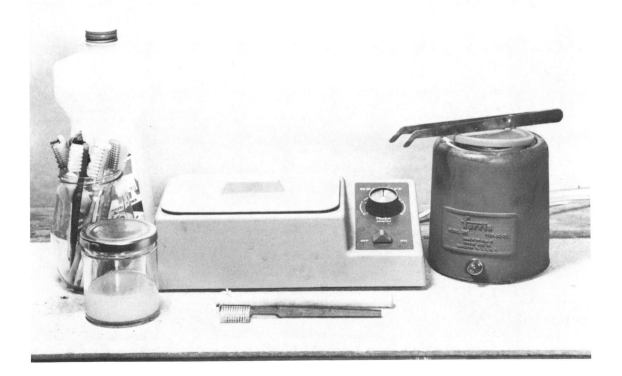

in a Pyrex saucepan, or in a Crock-Pot or slow cooker. The slow cooker is an excellent alternative because it keeps the pickle at a constant warm temperature without letting it boil, and it is much more reasonable in cost than a commercial pickle pot.

Place the metal in the warm pickle solution with copper or wooden tongs. Never put steel or iron tweezers or wire in the pickle, because these metals will react with the acid solution, resulting in copper plating of your metal. Let the metal remain in the pickle for 2 to 5 minutes. Remove it, again with the copper or wooden tongs, and rinse thoroughly with cold water.

To neutralize the acid, rinse the piece in a solution of water and baking soda for a few minutes and then rinse in plain water. This neutralizing rinse is essential if the metal is to be enameled, and it will help protect your tools. Any unneutralized acid on the metal can eat through the metal and solder, resulting in holes (which may appear years later).

Pickle can be left in the pot, covered, from day to day. With use, it will gradually lose its effectiveness and you must make up a fresh solution. Do not throw the old pickle down your drain because it may damage the pipes. Pour it into the ground instead.

CLEANING

Jewelery can be further cleaned by using a warm mild solution of dishwashing detergent and ammonia. Scrub the piece in the solution using a soft toothbrush or glass brush to remove most grease, buffing compounds, or dirt. An ultrasonic cleaner is an added luxury. This machine uses a solution of detergent, ammonia and water, and it removes even the most stubborn dirt hidden in crevices. After cleaning, rinse the piece in cold water.

The
Silver
Enameling
Cup
and
Wirework
5

The first step in cloisonné enameling is to make the enameling base that holds the wires and layers of enamel. The sturdiest and most versatile is an enameling cup, which is a base of sheet metal with a bezel (rim) soldered around it. The bezel helps to contain the wires and enamel during the firings. In fact, with a relatively complex wire pattern or a design that involves many layers of enamel, it is essential to use an enameling cup (see figure 8-1). For small enamels that will not require great enamel depth, simple domed discs may be used instead. Enameling on domed silver discs and other metals is described in Chapter 8.

Your design will determine the size of your enameling cup. If you are a beginner, you might start with the simple design shown in figure 5–1. It has an easy-to-follow wire pattern and uses only two colors, one for the background and one for the clover. Make your enamel exactly the same size as the diagram.

If you are not a beginner, or if you are more adventurous, you can begin with any one of the examples in Chapter 9, Unshaded Enamels. The designs in Chapter 9 use single colors in each cloison and are therefore easier to manage than the shaded enamels of Chapter 10. Each design gives a wirework and color diagram to follow.

If you really want to start out making your own designs, then get out your paper and pencil. You will need to make your own wirework and color diagrams just like those shown in Chapter 9. Keep your first efforts simple so your concentration is focused on the enameling process rather than on a complicated design.

No matter how you have arrived at your first design for cloisonné, you should be prepared with a pattern the exact size of your finished piece, showing the wirework, the outline for your enamel, and the colors you will use.

The various steps in enameling, including making the cup and firing and finishing the enamel, may be done all at once, or in stages. If you do stop and put the work away, put your work in a dust-free container until you are ready to begin again.

Figure 5–1 A wirework diagram shows the design with the wires in position (left), and separated to indicate how the individual wires should be cut (right).

MAKING AN ENAMELING CUP

You will need 26-gauge and 30-gauge fine silver sheet, bezel shears, metal shears, a circle template and pencil, flat-nosed and round-nosed pliers, a ruler, set-screw dividers, the kiln, firing tweezers, torch, soldering equipment, bowl of Carborundum grains, charcoal block, needle files, a ring mandrel, two steel blocks, pickle, copper tongs, baking soda solution, glass brush or old toothbrush, burnisher, and 150-grit dry sandpaper.

Determining the Length of the Bezel

Before you can cut a strip of metal for a bezel, you need to determine its length by measuring the circumference of the circle or shape you have used for your design. Circle templates usually indicate the diameters of the circles, but not the circumferences. You can determine the circumference by multiplying the diameter by 3.1416. To save you this trouble, however, we have provided tables that give the circumferences of circles found on most templates, in inches and in millimeters. It is a good idea to have templates in both inches and

Table 5–1 Circle Circumferences in Inches

DIAMETER (inches)	CIRCUMFERENCE (rounded up to nearest $\frac{1}{32}$ inch)	DIAMETER (inches)	CIRCUMFERENCE (rounded up to nearest $\frac{1}{32}$ inch)
$\frac{1}{4}$	$\frac{25}{32}$	$\frac{7}{8}$	$2\frac{3}{4}$
$\frac{5}{16}$	1	$\frac{15}{16}$	$2\frac{15}{16}$
$\frac{11}{32}$	$1\frac{3}{32}$	1	$3\frac{5}{32}$
$\frac{3}{8}$	$1\frac{3}{16}$	$1\frac{1}{8}$	$3\frac{17}{32}$
$\frac{13}{32}$	$1\frac{9}{32}$	$1\frac{1}{4}$	4
$\frac{6}{16}$	$1\frac{3}{8}$	$1\frac{3}{8}$	$4\frac{5}{16}$
$\frac{15}{32}$	$1\frac{15}{32}$	$1\frac{1}{2}$	$4\frac{21}{32}$
$\frac{1}{2}$	$1\frac{19}{32}$	$1\frac{5}{8}$	$5\frac{1}{8}$
$\frac{17}{32}$	$1\frac{21}{32}$	$1\frac{3}{4}$	$5\frac{1}{2}$
$\frac{9}{16}$	$1\frac{25}{32}$	$1\frac{7}{8}$	$5\frac{29}{32}$
$\frac{19}{32}$	$1\frac{7}{8}$	2	$6\frac{9}{32}$
$\frac{5}{8}$	2	$2\frac{1}{8}$	$6\frac{11}{16}$
$\frac{21}{32}$	$2\frac{1}{16}$	$2\frac{1}{4}$	$7\frac{1}{16}$
$\frac{11}{16}$	$2\frac{5}{32}$	$2\frac{3}{8}$	$7\frac{15}{32}$
$\frac{23}{32}$	$2\frac{1}{4}$	$2\frac{1}{2}$	$7\frac{3}{4}$
$\frac{3}{4}$	$2\frac{3}{8}$	$2\frac{5}{8}$	$8\frac{1}{4}$
$\frac{3}{16}$	$2\frac{9}{16}$	$2\frac{3}{4}$	$8\frac{21}{32}$
		$2\frac{7}{8}$	$9\frac{1}{32}$
		3	$9\frac{7}{16}$

Table 5–2   Circle Circumference in Millimeters

DIAMETER (mm)	CIRCUMFERENCE (rounded up to nearest mm)	DIAMETER (mm)	CIRCUMFERENCE (rounded up to nearest mm)
5	16	19	60
5.5	18	20	63
6	19	21	66
6.5	21	22	70
7	22	23	73
7.5	24	24	76
8	25	25	79
8.5	27	26	82
9	29	27	85
9.5	30	28	88
10	32	29	91
11	35	30	94
12	38	32	101
13	41	35	110
14	44	38	120
15	48	40	126
16	51	42	132
17	54	45	142
18	57	50	157

millimeters since the circles are not exactly the same sizes and this offers more design possibilities.

If your design is not a circle, measure the perimeter of the shape using flexible wire or plastic (garbage bag ties work well). Fit the wire or plastic inside the template opening or around the shape, and cut it off where the two ends overlap. Flatten the wire out and measure. This will be the length of your bezel.

Cutting the Bezel

1. Measure along one edge of the 26-gauge silver and mark it with a pencil or score with the dividers at a point $\frac{1}{16}$" (1.6 mm) longer than your bezel measurement.

2. With the dividers, measure the height of the cloisonné wire you plan to use (see figure 5–2). Then set the dividers so they measure $\frac{1}{32}$" (.8 mm) more than the height of the wire. Run one arm of the dividers along the edge of the silver, letting the other arm score a parallel line on the silver itself (figure 5–3).

3. Cut the bezel along the scored line with shears.

4. Anneal the bezel in a hot kiln for 20 seconds. Cool.

5. Using flat-nosed pliers and your fingers, form the bezel inside the template opening for your circle or shape (see figure 5–4). Now check the formed bezel with your wirework diagram to make sure it is the right size. You can change the dimensions at this stage for a perfect fit.

Figure 5–2 The height of the bezel is determined by measuring the height of the cloisonné wire with the dividers.

Figure 5–3 Use the dividers to score the silver sheet at the right height for the bezel.

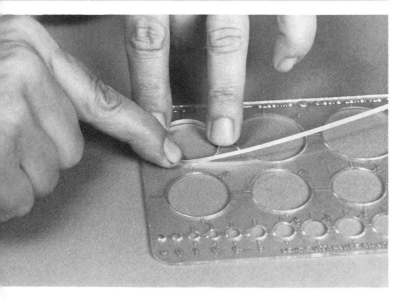

Figure 5–4 The cut bezel is formed inside the template.

6. Trim off any excess from the bezel, and make sure the two ends butt up against one another smoothly to make a perfect seam. Then, with flat-nosed pliers, flatten out the joining point so the ends meet head on and not on an angle. The rest of the bezel need not be perfectly formed now because it will be reshaped after the joint is soldered.

Soldering the Bezel Joint

1. Cut a $\frac{1}{16}''$ (1.6 mm) square of IT solder. Place the solder on a charcoal block that has been set on a bowl of Carborundum grains. Place the bezel on top of the piece of solder so the joint is touching directly in the center of the solder square, as illustrated in figure 5–5.

2. Put one drop of flux on the bezel joint, using the squeeze bottle or the brush if necessary.

3. Light the #1 tip on the torch. Using the feathery yellowish tip of the flame, circle quickly around the bezel until the solder runs up the joint. Let the bezel cool for a few minutes.

4. Pull on the joint to make sure it is firmly soldered. If it isn't, solder again. Using a half-round needle file, file off any excess solder on the inside of the joint.

5. To smooth out the bezel, place it on a ring mandrel. (A ring mandrel is a length of steel used for shaping and measuring ring size.) Then roll the mandrel on a steel block. Remove the bezel and reverse it on the mandrel, then roll again. This gets all the kinks out of the bezel and work hardens it. (See figure 5–6)

6. Place a piece of 150-grit dry sandpaper on a table or steel block and sand the edges of the bezel using a rotating motion. Turn the bezel over and sand the other edge.

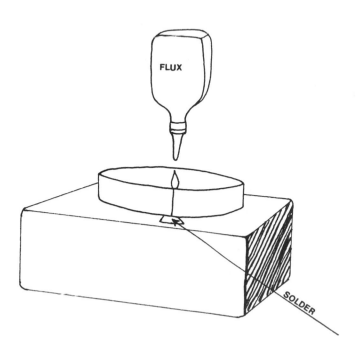

Figure 5–5 Place one drop of flux on the joint to be soldered.

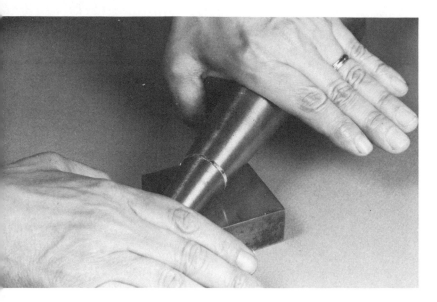

Figure 5–6 Roll the soldered bezel on a ring mandrel to smooth and shape it.

7. Anneal in a hot kiln for 10 seconds. Reshape the bezel once again on the ring mandrel as in step 5.

8. If the bezel is not a circle, shape it by pressing it against the sides of the template opening. Use a burnisher (a smooth pointed metal rod with a wooden handle) as a shaping aid if necessary.

9. To make sure the bezel is level and straight, place it between two steel blocks and press the top and bottom edges gently.

Cutting the Base

1. With a pencil, draw around the inside of the template opening that corresponds to your design size on the 30-gauge fine silver sheet. Using a ruler, draw a square (or rectangle) around the circle

Figure 5–7 Flatten the silver for the base by squeezing it between two steel blocks.

(or shape) about $\frac{1}{8}''$ (3mm) larger all around. Cut along this square outline with metal shears.

2. Anneal the square in a hot kiln for 20 seconds.

3. Flatten the square by placing it between two steel blocks and pressing gently (figure 5–7).

Soldering the Bezel to the Base

1. Place the flattened square of silver sheet on the tripod. Set the bezel on top, using the penciled outline as a guide.

2. Brush a drop of flux around the top edge of the bezel. Don't use much or it will be difficult to clean off. Dry the flux by heating it gently with the torch flame directed from underneath the tripod. When the flux is dry it will look glassy.

3. Cut small squares ($\frac{1}{16}''$ or 2 mm) of medium solder and place them about $\frac{1}{4}''$ to $\frac{1}{2}''$ (6 to 13mm) apart around the outside of the bezel. It is important to place the solder on the outside so solder marks or scars do not appear inside the cup to mar the appearance of any transparent enamel.

4. Using the #2 torch tip, hold the torch in one hand and a soldering pick in the other. Use the feather tip of the flame and run it in a circular motion around the bezel from underneath the tripod (figure 5–8). When the solder flows, it will make a bright shiny line around the bezel. If the shiny line is not visible in some spots, press

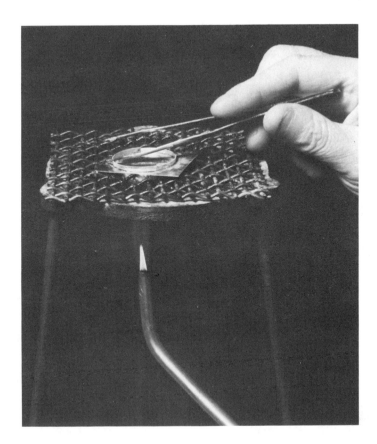

Figure 5–8 Solder the bezel to the base as shown.

51

Figure 5–9 Trim the excess silver from the base, leaving a small tab to use as a handle.

Figure 5–10 Turn the cup upside down and dome the cup by pressing gently with your thumb.

lightly on the top of the bezel in that area with the soldering pick to make sure the bezel has been soldered to the base at all points.

5. After the bezel has cooled, pickle and clean in baking soda and water solution.

6. With bezel shears, trim the excess silver from the square or rectangle surrounding the bezel. Leave a tiny tab that can be used as a handle (figure 5–9).

7. Reshape the bezel if necessary using pliers.

8. Clean the inside of the cup with a glass brush and a detergent containing a degreaser (Whisk or Fantastik, for example). Rinse thoroughly and avoid touching the inside of the cup.

9. The last thing to do is to dome the cup. Place the enameling cup upside down on a soft surface (a piece of cloth or paper towel). Press down on the base with your thumb (figure 5–10). Make a depression in the center of the cup about $\frac{1}{8}$" (3mm) deep. The enameling cup is now ready to use.

SHAPING THE CLOISONNÉ WIRES

You are now ready to cut the cloisonné wires into small sections and bend them to conform to your wirework diagram. Translating the linear pattern of your design into a wirework diagram is fairly easy, but there are two basic problems you may run into: First of all, wires cannot intersect or cross one another. Secondly, wires forming a straight line will fall over.

The first problem is solved by dividing the lines in your design into small segments of wire that can be easily manipulated and that meet but do not cross. There is usually more than one solution for most designs. Usually it is best to keep the wire segments about equal in length rather than having one long wire and several short ones in the same piece.

The second problem can also be solved (thanks to Jamie Bennett's ingenuity). To make a very straight line in a cloisonné enamel, first straighten a piece of annealed wire by putting one end in a vise and pulling on the other end with pliers. Cut the length of wire that you need. Then snip into the wire about $\frac{1}{16}''$ (2mm) from one end and bend the resulting tab down so it will rest on the base and act as an anchor. The wire will not fall over now.

Aside from the design and diagram, you will need thinned cloisonné wire, the kiln, a good light, a magnifying glass, two pairs of fine watchmaker's tweezers, flat and round-nosed pliers, bezel shears, and your enameling cup. You will also find that a black tile or paper and double-stick tape are useful.

1. Anneal the cloisonné wire in a hot kiln for 15 seconds. Then cut off about 2″ (5 cm) of the annealed wire to work with.

2. With one of the tweezers in your weaker hand, hold one end of the wire over the wirework diagram. Hold the second pair of tweezers in your stronger hand and use these to shape the wire. The wire should be cut and a new piece begun whenever there is a logical break in the design.

Figure 5–11 The cloisonné wires are shaped with tweezers and pliers to match the lines of the design.

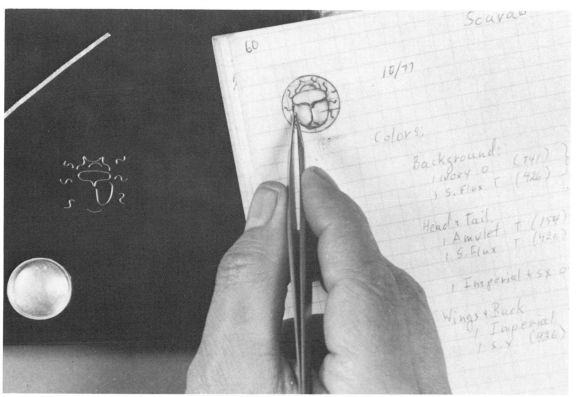

3. Different types of pliers can also be used to shape wires. Use round-nosed pliers to shape a curved turn or circle. To get a teardrop or circle shape to close tightly, squeeze it with flat-nosed pliers on the side opposite the joint rather than on the joint itself. Use flat-nosed pliers to make square shapes and corners. To make a sharp point, bend the wire in half and squeeze the bend tightly with flat-nosed pliers. Insert the tip of the tweezers, and open as far as needed for the design.

4. Place the small sections of shaped wire on a black tile or paper. When all are cut, check to make sure each shape exactly conforms to the lines in the drawing, using a magnifying glass if necessary (figure 5–11).

5. When all the wires have been formed, check to make sure they fit properly in the enameling cup. Lift the wires into the cup using tweezers and position them properly. Trim any wires that don't fit with bezel shears. Place the wires back on the tile or paper.

6. If you are not going to add the enamel right away, a good way to store the wires is to attach them in the proper position on double-stick tape placed over a copy of your drawing. Then place this in a small box or other covered container.

Enameling
Techniques
6

This chapter describes procedures for making unshaded and shaded enamels. Unshaded enamels are simpler because in each firing you use only one color per cloison. In shaded enamels, two or more colors may be used in a single cloison. Using layers of transparent enamels permits you to see not only the enamel colors beneath, but also the reflections of the silver base and wires, the shadows cast by the wires, and anything else that can be successfully applied underneath, such as gold foil or decals. Using one transparent color over either a transparent or opaque color creates a new effect because the undercoat will show through and influence the final color.

When planning your designs, it is important to keep in mind that firing any transparent enamel, even a light one, over another color will make the color underneath appear darker since less light will be refracted through it. Also, any single transparent enamel color will become darker with each successive layer that is applied. Once a color has reached the desired tone, use soft-fusing flux in subsequent layers instead of more color. A typical enamel might require eight to ten layers of enamel.

Whether you are making shaded or unshaded designs, you will first fire a layer of soft-fusing flux in the enameling cup to fix the wires in position.

THE FLUX FIRING

The first layer of enamel added to the enameling cup is called the flux firing. It is a very fine layer of enamel, generally Soft-Fusing Flux 426 or Vitrearc's LF-302 flux for silver, into which you will set the cloisonné wires. You will need ¼ teaspoon (1 ml) of either flux, freshly washed at least ten times, a fine sable brush, the completed enameling cup, the shaped wires, fine tweezers, the kiln, a heat lamp (or electric bulb or tensor lamp), and firing tweezers.

PLEASE NOTE: Figure 6–1 shows a small piece of asbestos on top of the kiln, used to dry enamels. Now that we know about the hazards of asbestos, we have replaced it with an ordinary heat lamp for drying (figure 6–2). See Sources of supplies, page 233.

1. Heat up the kiln. Using the fine brush, "haze" a very fine coat of enamel flux into the bottom of the enameling cup. The enamel

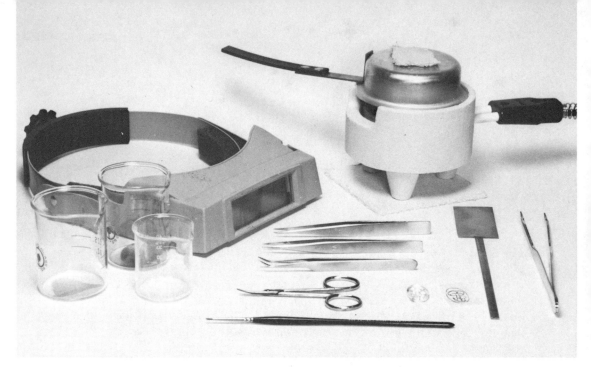

Figure 6–1 The equipment needed for enameling includes the washed enamels, a magnifier, the kiln and spatula, tweezers, bezel shears, a fine brush, and the enamel design, wires, and enameling cup.

should be very wet, and the coat very thin, so that the grains are next to each other rather than on top of each other.

2. Using fine tweezers, transfer the wires to the enameling cup. Make sure the wires are properly positioned and that they touch each other. The wires will stay in place because of the moisture in the enamel. Once the enamel is fired the wires cannot be moved.

3. With tweezers, carefully pick up the enameling cup by the tab and move it under the heat lamp to dry. The enamel should dry very slowly (it can spatter from heating up too fast). You can also dry the enamel by putting it on the lid of a cold kiln. Turn the kiln on to dry the enamel gradually. When the enamel appears dry, it is ready to be fired inside the kiln.

4. Lift off the kiln lid. The wires are easily disturbed at this point, so lift the enameling cup straight up very carefully by its tab using firing tweezers. Now lower the cup onto the coils of the kiln (figure 6–3). Return the lid.

5. Keep lifting the lid every few seconds to check the progress of the melting enamel flux. When the surface looks partially melted (it should be pebbly-shiny, like an orange peel) press gently where needed with the firing tweezers on the tops of the wires to make sure they are in contact with the enamel. At this point the enamel will be smooth.

6. Remove the enameling cup from the kiln using firing tweezers. Place the cup near the kiln to cool slowly. Check the wires against

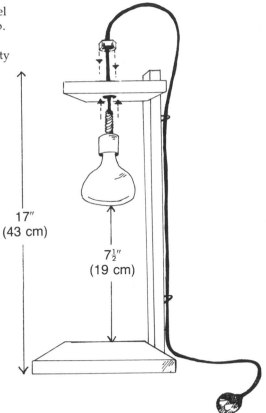

Figure 6–2 Eleanor Silk Schogel designed this infrared heat lamp. It uses a 250-watt bulb and 115-125 volts, and it has a heavy-duty ceramic socket.

17"
(43 cm)

7½"
(19 cm)

Figure 6–3 The enameling cup containing the wires and a layer of soft-fusing flux is placed in the kiln for the first firing.

the design once more, as they can be adjusted slightly with fine tweezers before the enamel cools and hardens. Once cooled (about 2 minutes) the wires will be firmly set in the cup.

UNSHADED ENAMELS

There are slightly different procedures for filling the cloisons in shaded and unshaded enamels. This chapter describes both, but your first project will most likely be an unshaded design, so begin by following the instructions below.

Prepare all the necessary enamel colors for your design by washing them according to the instructions in Chapter 2. You will also need the kiln, firing tweezers, a glass of water, a fine sable brush, a small wood block, some toilet paper or facial tissue, the heat lamp if available, 180-grit sandpaper, your enameling cup, and your design or color diagram. Work in good light and keep a magnifying glass nearby to use if necessary.

1. *The First Color Firing.* Set up your enamels in front of you, all washed and labeled. Put the enameling cup on a small block of wood that can be turned without touching the enamel while you are filling the cloisons. Have the cup of water, brush, and tissue nearby.

2. For each color, fill the smallest cloison that receives that color first and work toward the largest. Fill in the background last. To add enamel to a cloison, put a tiny drop of water in it with a fine sable brush. The water will draw the tiny amount of enamel off the tip of the brush into the cloison by capillary action. Continue to add more color bit by bit until the cloison is about one-third full. You want a nice even layer of enamel. Do not mound the enamel.

Because enamel tends to climb up the walls of the cloisons during firing, it is important to compensate for that and make sure that no enamel is clinging to the wires. If you are not careful, the enamel may even reach the top of the wires upon firing. When the piece is ground and polished, the color of the undercoat will be exposed, ruining the intended effect.

3. Continue to fill each cloison so there is a thin even coating of enamel over the whole surface of the enameling cup. Wipe the brush on the tissue from time to time to help keep it pointed.

4. When all the cloisons and the background are filled about one-third full, gently tap the edge of the enameling base with the wooden end of your brush to level the enamel and release any air that might be trapped. Remove excess moisture from each cloison by touching the edge of the enamel gently with tissue. Take care not to disturb the evenness of the enamel layer.

5. Plug in the kiln.

6. Dry the enamel under the heat lamp. Then place it on the lid of the hot kiln for a bit more heating before firing.

7. Place the enamel, using firing tweezers, in the hot kiln. For

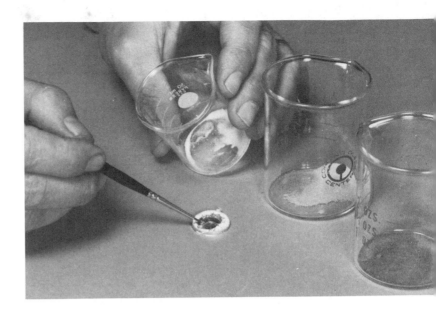

Figure 6–4 Enamels are added using a fine sable brush.

the first firing, leave the enamel in the kiln just until the surface becomes shiny and liquid looking, then remove it from the kiln. Do not overfire or the wires can collapse. When fired, the enamel layer will have shrunk to about one-third of its original depth. Unplugging the kiln between firings will help prolong the life of your kiln.

8. *The Second Firing.* Add another layer of enamel to each cloison and the background, as described for the first firing. Dry the enamel as before.

9. For the second and subsequent firings, fire the enamels only until they turn pebbly-shiny, like the texture of an orange peel. They should not get completely liquid looking. Then remove the cup from the kiln and let it cool.

10. *Subsequent Firings.* After the second firing, fill all red, pink, or orange cloisons with Soft-Fusing Flux 426 or Vitreac LF 302, instead of color, as these colors tend to burn out and darken. The flux will protect them. Wash the soft-fusing flux before each use to make sure it stays completely clear.

11. Continue to fill the cloisons, dry, and fire to a shiny-pebbly texture until the enamel reaches the top of the wires.

A typical enamel might require eight to ten layers of enamel. It is important that each layer be applied thinly and the color checked carefully after firing so you can switch to flux once the desired tone is reached. Also, thin layers are less likely to trap air, which causes pits. As the enamel layers get closer to the top, be very careful not to jiggle the cup or disturb the enamel grains when drying and lifting the cup into the kiln. The enamel grains could jump from one cloison to another and contaminate your colors.

12. After all layers are fired, your enamel is now ready for

counter enameling, which is simply adding a layer of enamel to the back of the enameling cup. Instructions are given later in this chapter.

SHADED ENAMELS: LIMOGES TECHNIQUE

Making shaded enamel designs like the one shown in figure 6–5 and the examples in Chapter 10 depends on the use of Limoges or "painterly" enameling techniques to create variations of color within a cloison. The basics are the same as for unshaded enamels, of course. You begin with your enameling cup in which the wires have been fired in position in soft-fusing flux. Since Thomas Thompson's flux for silver (757) turns brown, we use their Soft-Fusing Flux 426, even though it has a very slight yellow cast. Absolute clarity can be obtained with Vitrearc's flux for silver (LF-302).

The first color coat (base coat) in shaded enamels can be transparent, opalescent, or opaque. It will influence the colors of the enamels laid on top of it. All shading is done in the second and third layers after the base coat has been fired. If you shade layers after that, you are in danger of losing some of the shading in the grinding and polishing stages. After the shaded layers are fired, continue to fill shaded cloisons with soft-fusing flux or opalescents. Unshaded areas, such as the background, are built up with color or flux.

A number of techniques are used to achieve variety of color and shading within the cloisons:

1. Transparent enamels can be mixed and washed together to create new colors. The new colors can be used in unshaded enamels, of course, but the delicate differences in hue that are possible are especially useful in creating lovely effects in shaded enamels.

2. Dark to light shading can be created by manipulating the thickness of the enamel. By piling the enamel against a wire and letting it taper off toward the center of the cloison, firing it, and using soft-fusing flux in subsequent firings, the color will appear to fade gradually from dark to light. The "pile" should be only a couple of grains deep.

3. You can also vary color tones by blending and feathering the edge between two colors. Very subtle tones can be built up over the base coat in this way.

4. Lines can be made between two colors within a cloison by arranging the grains of enamel very close to one another in a straight line, like soldiers, using the tip of your brush to align them. If you want a finer line, you can grind the enamels to a finer mesh with a mortar and pestle.

5. Firing a transparent color over a shaded layer will alter the effect of the color and shading. The lighter the color of the transparent top layer, the better the lower layer can be seen. Nevertheless, a light color on top will make the lower layer seem darker. This can be put to good effect. Even a very distinct pattern under a dark transparent covering will appear vague and mysterious.

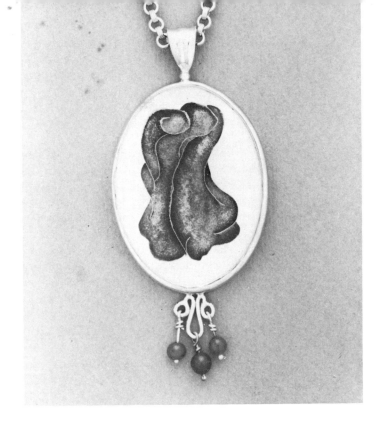

Figure 6–5 A shaded enamel pendant by Felicia Liban.

6. Opaque enamels can also be used in a painterly manner if they are added very thinly and then covered with soft-fusing flux in subsequent layers. You can simulate veins in a leaf, feathers, and other delicate patterns. Opaque enamels mixed and washed together give a salt-and-pepper effect.

Chapter 10 has numerous examples of shaded enamels with color diagrams that will serve as a guide to shading. You might like to make some of those examples to gain some experience with these techniques and see some of the possible effects. Stick to the simpler designs, such as "Mushrooms" and "Mountain Landscape," for your first attempts. Here is an outline of the steps to follow in creating shaded enamels. You will need your color diagrams, washed enamels, the enameling cup with wires in place, the kiln, firing tweezers, a heat lamp if available, a cup of clean water, a fine sable brush, a small wood block, some toilet paper or tissue, and a magnifying glass to use if necessary.

1. *The First Color Firing.* Put the enameling cup on the wood block so you can turn it without disturbing the enamel while you are filling the cloisons.

2. Fill all the cloisons and the background with enamel, starting with the smallest cloison. To fill a cloison, first put a tiny drop of water in it with the sable brush. Then pick up a tiny amount of enamel on the tip of the brush and place it in the cloison. The water

will draw off the enamel. Add more color bit by bit until the cloison is about one-third full. The enamel should be in an even layer.

3. When all the cloisons and the background are filled about one-third full, remove excess moisture from each cloison by touching the edge of the enamel gently with tissue. Take care not to disturb the evenness of the enamel layer.

4. Plug in the kiln.

5. Dry the enamel under the heat lamp. Then place it on the lid of the hot kiln to dry further before firing.

6. Place the enamel, using firing tweezers, on the coils of the hot kiln. For this first firing, leave the enamel in the kiln just until the surface becomes shiny and liquid looking, then remove it from the kiln. Be sure not to overfire.

7. Make sure the base color has covered the bottom of the enameling cup completely. Use the magnifying glass to check if necessary. If it hasn't, fire another base-color coat, filling the empty spaces with enamel but only hazing the enamel in a very thin layer over the rest.

8. *Second and Third Firings.* The enamel is now ready for the "painting" stages, where you will use a variety of transparent colors in successive layers to create the shading and blending of colors in your cloisons. Follow the color diagram for each layer of enamel, blending the colors with a fine brush to keep the edges between them soft and feathered rather than harsh. Rinse the brush well before touching it to a new color. Fill all areas of the enameling cup evenly with each layer or the uneven pressure might cause the wires to move during firing.

9. Dry each layer and fire it until the enamel becomes pebbly-shiny. Remember to cover the entire enameling cup with at least a hazing of enamel or else the previous layer might overfire. If any color seems to be getting too dark, switch to soft-fusing flux or Vitreac LF 302 (wash it before each use!). After the second color firing, switch to flux over reds, pinks, and oranges, which will begin to darken.

10. *Subsequent Layers.* After the shaded layers are filled and fired, continue to fill and fire the shaded cloisons with flux until the enamel reaches the top of the wires. This may require eight to ten layers. (Unplug the kiln between firings to prolong the life of your kiln.) Nonshaded cloisons can be filled to the top with layers of color. Remember, though, that a transparent enamel color will become darker with each successive layer that is applied. Once a color has reached the desired tone, flux should be used instead of colored enamel. Fire each layer until it is pebbly-shiny.

11. After the piece is filled and fired to the top of the wires, it is ready for counter enameling.

COUNTER ENAMELING

If only the top of the enameling cup were covered with enamel, it would eventually crack due to the different expansion rates for enamel and metal. This problem is eliminated by counter enameling, which is adding an equal thickness of enamel to the back of the enameling cup. Thus the silver will actually be sandwiched between two layers of enamel. We do the counter enameling as the last firing only when an enameling cup is used as the base for the cloisonné. The discs described in Chapter 8 are always counter enameled first.

When the enamel is to be encased in a setting, you do not have to consider the aesthetic qualities of the counter enamel as you would if the back were to be exposed to view. When the back will not be visible, a tweedy mixture of enamels makes a good counter enamel because it does a good job of equalizing the stresses on the enamel.

You can purchase fresh enamel called "counter" or "backing" enamel. You can also use surplus enamels that you have washed for a project but not used. Before using, always rewash counter enamel that has been stored in a jar. We recommend using the residue from washing your enamels as counter if it has been thoroughly washed to avoid pitting.

To add the layer of counter enamel, you will need enamel, mica or small porcelain tile (see discussion which follows the numbered steps), shears, a tiny spoon, toilet paper or tissue, soft-fusing flux, brush, kiln, spatula, firing tweezers, and 180-grit dry sandpaper, and 120-grit wet Carborundum paper.

1. Cut off the tab on the enameling cup with bezel shears. Wash the counter enamel several times.

2. If using mica, cut a piece approximately $\frac{1}{2}$" (13 mm) wider than the enameling cup.

3. Put the enameling cup face down on your work surface. Using a tiny spoon, gradually pile dampened counter enamel on the back of the cup until it is three times the height of the enamel on the front. (It will shrink to $\frac{1}{3}$ its height upon firing.) If the enamel is not added slowly, air bubbles can occur and holes will appear after firing.

4. Absorb extra moisture from the enamel by gently touching the surface with tissue.

5. Turn the cup over onto the piece of mica so the counter enamel is on the mica. Press the cup down slightly to flatten the bottom of the counter enamel. The enamel may protrude slightly from the edges; if it does, push it closer to the cup with a flat tool.

6. Make sure there is no counter enamel on the surface of the fired enamel. If there is, wipe it off. Then haze the top of the enamel with freshly washed Soft-Fusing Flux 426 or Vitreac LF 302.

7. Fold a section of tissue in quarters. Hold it against the cup so it will absorb moisture from both the top and bottom layers of enamel without disturbing the thin coat of flux. Move the paper all around the rim of the cup.

8. With a small spatula and firing tweezers, transfer the cup and mica to a wire mesh stand under the heat lamp. Let it dry. Plug in the kiln. When the enamel seems dry, transfer the cup and mica to the kiln lid and let the enamel dry further.

9. When there is no further evidence of moisture evaporating, use the spatula and firing tweezers to transfer the enamel and mica to the floor of the hot kiln. Check the firing process every few

seconds. Remove the enamel when the surface looks shiny and smooth. Unplug the kiln.

10. Place the enamel close to the kiln or on top of the hot kiln lid so it cools slowly. When completely cool, remove the mica by peeling it away from the counter enamel.

11. Hold the enamel sideways and, with a swiveling motion of the wrist, grind off any edges of counter enamel or excess silver that stick out beyond the enameling cup on 120-grit wet Carborundum paper by hand or on a lapidary machine.

12. Check the counter enamel for holes, pits, or unevenness that could later cause cracking. Repair any flaws by adding more counter enamel to the back, flux to the top, and repeating the whole firing process as just described.

Mica Substitute

Mica is not necessarily the ideal material on which to fire counter enamel. It gets brittle, flakes, and it can warp, resulting in an uneven layer of counter enamel. A very good alternative has been worked out by our friend Bernard Klausman. He uses a 2" (5 cm) square high-fire, unglazed porcelain tile, which can be purchased at a ceramic shop (see Sources of Supplies). First coat the tile with kiln wash and let it dry. Add counter enamel to the bottom of the enameling cup, blot with tissue, put the piece counter side down on the tile, and flux the front. Thorough drying is essential. Absolutely no moisture can exist on or in the tile when it goes into the kiln. After drying under a heat lamp, place the tile on the hot kiln top for further drying before firing.

After firing, remove the tile with a warm spatula (so it does not crack the tile) and place the tile on top of the kiln and let it cool very slowly. This method, although slower because of the long drying and cooling periods, produces very nice results, and the tile can be used over and over again (mica must often be replaced).

COMMON PROBLEMS

From time to time you will undoubtedly run into problems. Fortunately, most can be resolved, and you can rescue most pieces from all but the worst disasters. Here are several of the most common problems and how to prevent or solve them.

Gaps between wires. On occasion you may inadvertently leave open spaces at the intersection of two cloisonné wires. The wet enamel can flow through the gap into a cloison where it does not belong. If this happens, dry the enamel with tissue and, using a damp brush, lift the enamel from the contaminated area before continuing to fill and fire.

Filling tiny corners. Tiny crevices and corners must be completely filled with enamel or else holes and cracks can appear after the piece has been fired. To prevent this, use the tip of the brush or a sharp instrument like a needle or dental tool to push the enamel grains into tight spaces.

Collapsed or misshapen wires. Each cloison must receive an even, thin layer of enamel with each firing. Otherwise the wires can get pushed out of shape or collapse during firing due to uneven pressure from the enamel.

Pinholes. Pores in the enamel surface are sometimes due to improper filling of the cloison. They may also be the result of poorly cleaned or old enamels. Make sure all impurities have been removed from your enamels and that you store your unused enamels in airtight containers to prevent dust, moisture, and air from seeping in. If pinholes do occur, you can fix them as described in the section on repair in Chapter 7, or you can drill out a larger hole, then add more enamel to the surface and refire.

Jumping enamel grains. Always make sure the enamels are dried very slowly and thoroughly. Otherwise the enamel grains can "spit" and jump around during the firing. The only real cure is prevention, because once the enamel is fired it cannot be removed except by grinding. So take care to dry slowly and completely each time before firing.

APPLYING FOIL AND DECALS

Gold and silver foils used under transparent enamels yield an iridescent effect. Gold foil is generally used under warm transparent colors and silver under cool colors. Gold foil under opalescent white enamel gives the effect of an opal gem. Cutting the foil into small squares (paillons) makes it easier to apply and increases the iridescence.

Ceramic decals are applied basically the same way as foils except that they are used in one piece rather than small squares. Decals available include flowers, insects, birds, and landscapes. The smallest decals are most useful for cloisonné, but you can also cut a segment out of a large decal.

Foils and decals are applied after firing the initial layer of soft-fusing flux. You will need some Klyr Fire (a plastic-based liquid that adheres to but does not contaminate the enamels), a small container such as a jar lid, small scissors, 2 fine brushes, freshly washed soft-fusing flux, the kiln and firing tweezers, and a small burnishing tool (a dental tool with a smooth rounded end is ideal).

1. Foil comes sandwiched between paper that is impregnated with rouge to keep the metal from tarnishing. Keep the sandwich intact when cutting the foil, using paperclips if necessary. Cut off only what you think you will need. Using small scissors, cut the foil into paillons that are about ⅛" (3 mm) square. With a decal, cut it into a shape that will fit the cloison.

2. Dip a moistened brush into Klyr Fire and sparingly paint it on the bottom of the cloison.

3. Pick up the paillons, one at a time, with a fine brush premoistened with Klyr Fire. Place them in the cloison so they overlap (or, simply place the decal). Smooth with the brush.

4. With a dry brush, press down on the paillons or decal to mop up any excess Klyr Fire and remove any air pockets. Then dry the enameling cup under the heat lamp.

5. Place the enameling cup in a hot kiln for no more than 10 seconds. (Gold foil will darken, but the luster will return when covered with enamel on the *next* firing.) Decals are fired to maturity. Remove the cup from the kiln and, while still hot, burnish the foil (but not a decal) gently with the small burnishing tool.

6. If any foil does not stick, remove that piece, glue a new one down with a tiny amount of Klyr Fire, dry under the heat lamp, and refire. Then burnish again. You are now ready to add enamels on top of the foils or decals.

VARIATION OF TEXTURE

There are several ways to vary the surface texture of a cloisonné enamel. One way is to mix two opaque colors together. Each grain of enamel will fire separately, and the result is a salt and pepper effect. Depending on the colors used, the effect can be either subtle or quite contrasting.

In concave cloisonné, the enamel is built up higher around the cloisonné wires and left low in the middle of the cloisons. When fired, the enamel retains this gentle ridge and valley effect. In polishing concave cloisonné, only the wires need to be cleaned and polished, using Scotch Stone and a felt polishing stick (see Chapter 7).

Concave cloisonné is a fast procedure compared to traditional cloisonné because it normally requires only two to three layers of enamel and you don't have to polish the piece, which is very time consuming. Concave cloisonné is especially appropriate for enameling on discs or larger panels. These bases usually utilize fewer layers of enamel than enameling cups, and they have no bezel that requires the enamel to be a certain height. Also, since concave cloisonné requires the enamel to be piled high against the wires, you don't have to worry about enamel "climbing the walls," which it has a natural tendency to do. In traditional cloisonné, this tendency can spoil the effect of the finished piece.

"Feathered" cloisonné wire, made by clipping or fringing the wire after it has been secured in the first layer of enamel, imitates the fuzzy appearance of fur or feathers. After the wires have been set and fired in place, clip and fringe the top edge of the wire with manicure scissors or with a single-edge razor blade, making the cuts as close together as possible. After the edge has been fringed, straighten the wire again by running fine tweezers along the length of the wire. Continue to fill and fire the enamel.

Another surface variation is achieved by using gold or silver balls, called shot. The shot should be the same height as the cloisonné wire. They are set into the second color coat before firing. Short pieces of round wire can be used the same way. They will appear as flat solid circles in the finished piece.

Another way to vary the surface texture is through choice of finish. For example, a wax finish is more subtle than a polished finish. Part or all of the enamel can be given a matte finish, or the enamel can be polished to a high gloss. Several finishes are described in the next chapter.

Finishing
and
Polishing
7

The next step in making an enamel into a "jewel" is to grind and polish. The face of the enamel must be ground down to the point where all the wires are showing and the surface is flat. The surface is then sanded until it is very smooth and even, and then the piece is polished. This process can take several hours, especially when working by hand.

Most people choose the traditional high-polish finish that gives a gemlike appearance to the enamel. This is the finish described below. Variations on this finish are given later in the chapter.

DOPPING

In order to handle the enamel with ease during the sanding process, it is attached to a short wooden handle called a dop stick. It is made from a 2″ to 3″ (5 to 8 cm) length of wooden dowel that is somewhat smaller in diameter than the enamel. The diameter of the dowel should be big enough to support the back of the enamel but small enough to allow room for the dop cement.

You will need your enamel, dop cement (broken in small chunks with a hammer and chisel), a dop stick, the tripod with wire mesh, the torch, Transite surface, a small cup of water, a small tin can, and a single-edge razor blade.

1. Dop cement comes in a solid bar. To use it, break off a few small chunks with a hammer and chisel. Place the chunks in a small tin can (such as a tuna or cat food can). Set the can on the tripod and heat it from underneath with the torch until the cement melts. Add a few more chunks until the can is about $\frac{1}{3}$ full. This supply will last for a number of polishing sessions, so you can simply leave the cement in it and store the can, reheating the cement before each use.

2. Dip the dop stick in the heated cement and scoop as much as you can onto the end of the stick.

3. Place the enamel face down on the Transite surface. Now heat the dop cement on the stick for a few seconds while holding the stick over the enamel back (figure 7–1). The cement will drip a bit onto the enamel. As soon as it does, press the dop stick down onto the back of the enamel and remove the heat (figure 7–2). Turn right side up and center the enamel at a 90° angle to the stick.

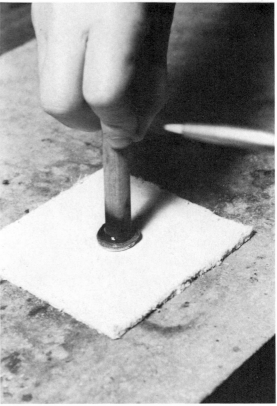

Figure 7–1 Heat the dop cement until it is molten and drips onto the enamel. (Caution: A soft asbestos pad is now recognized as a health hazard. Use a firebrick or transite instead.)

Figure 7–2 The heated dop stick is pressed onto the back of the enameling cup.

Figure 7–3 The still-warm dop cement is shaped with wet fingers.

4. Using wet fingers (so they don't burn), shape the still-hot dop cement around the base of the dop stick so the cement covers most of the enamel back (figure 7–3). Try not to get any dop cement on the sides of the cup.

5. Make sure the dop stick is secure on the enamel once it has cooled. If not, reheat the dop cement with the torch and reshape the cement with wet fingers. If any dop cement is on the sides of the cup, remove it using a single-edge razor blade.

GRINDING

Once the enamel is secure on a dop stick, the next step is to grind the enamel down to a surface level with the wires. Work on a flat surface or countertop near a sink. You will need the enamel on its dop stick, a piece of 220-grit wet/dry Carborundum paper, and several pieces of paper towel. You can also grind an enamel on a lapidary machine.

1. Hold the enamel by the dop stick. Wet the Carborundum paper under running water and place it on the paper towels. Move the enamel back and forth over the Carborundum paper in one direction. Periodically turn the enamel 180° to keep the top surface level. The scratches will still be going in one direction. They will be removed on finer grits of paper. Do not change the direction of sanding or else you will have all sorts of scratches on the surface. Make sure there is plenty of water on the paper for lubrication, and rewash the paper from time to time as you see deposits of ground enamel build up on it.

2. Occasionally blot the surface of the enamel with a dry paper towel to check your progress. The enamel should be completely level with no low spots that appear shiny, and all the wires should be showing.

3. To repair a deep scratch while sanding (or later when polishing), go back to the preceding grade of Carborundum paper and sand in the opposite direction until the scratch is removed. If this process removes *all* the sanding lines from the old direction, continue grinding and polishing in the new direction. Otherwise return to the first direction.

POLISHING

The enamel now has an even but dull surface. As it is polished it will gradually begin to shine again. Polish near the sink so water is available. Get out new and worn wet/dry Carborumdum paper, from 320 to 600 grit. If you want a high gloss, fine finish, you will also need tin oxide and a suede block (see step 4).

1. Move the enamel over the wet 320-grit Carborundum paper in the same direction you used for grinding. Hold the enamel level and use even pressure. Wash the paper frequently.

2. Check the progress from time to time by drying the enamel and looking at it under light. When a new shine appears and no further progress is made, it is time to shift to the next grade of paper, from 320 grit to 400 grit. After polishing with the 400 grit, you can give the enamel a fire finish or matte finish (see below), or you can continue to polish to a high gloss.

3. Continue the same process using first worn 400 grit, then 500, then worn 500, and finally 600 and worn 600. The reason for using old paper after new is to get a finer and finer sanding each time. Remember to keep washing off the paper and checking your progress.

4. Give the enamel a final polish by using tin oxide on a suede block. (Make a suede block by stapling a piece of suede onto a wood block.) Make a paste out of $\frac{1}{2}$ teaspoon (2 ml) tin oxide with water. Rotate the enamel in this paste on the suede for about a minute. Rinse in clean water and dry. The enamel should have a jewel-like finish.

5. Remove the dop stick by putting the enamel and dop stick in the freezer for five minutes. While still cold press against the back and side of the enamel with the thumb of your stronger hand. Hold the weaker hand under the enamel to catch it as it pops off. Any dop cement that remains on the enamel can be scraped off with a single-edge razor blade.

6. Check the enamel for cracks that may have developed during polishing, usually from uneven counter enamel. If you do find one (which is rare), do not panic. It is easy to fix if done right away while the enamel is still clean. Instructions for how to repair a broken enamel are given at the end of the chapter.

7. Put a small dab of clear wax shoe polish on a cotton ball and wax and buff the enamel.

8. The enamel is now ready for a setting. Put your enamel away in a dust-free container until you have fabricated and polished a setting for it.

OTHER FINISHES

Most enamels are given a high polish as described above, but there are a number of other surface treatments that can be used.

Fire finish. The enamel is fired to the top of the wires, ground flat, and polished through the 400-grit stage (as described above). Then it is cleaned with a glass brush, rinsed off well, and refired until the surface is shiny.

Matte finish. There are several ways to obtain a matte finish. The simplest is to polish the enamel through the 400-grit stage and leave it with this dull finish. After polishing to a high gloss, it is possible to achieve a matte finish on selected areas of the enamel by coating the desired areas with a product called Matte Salt. The salt is removed by rinsing, and then the piece is given a wax finish. A matte surface can also be obtained by rubbing with the finest grade of

Scotch Stone. Scotch Stone, which is made of Carborundum, is a common jeweler's polishing tool.

Wax finish. For a wax finish, the enamel is polished as far as using 400-grit Carborundum paper. Then a thin coat of butcher's wax or clear shoe wax is applied with your thumb. The heat of your finger will melt the wax slightly so it can be rubbed in. Then the surface is buffed with a soft cloth or piece of felt. The result is a semi-matte, rubbed look.

REPAIRING A BROKEN ENAMEL

If an enamel becomes cracked or chipped while being ground and polished or while being set, it should be repaired as soon as possible. Otherwise dirt can become embedded in the crack. If you cannot get an enamel clean, or cannot remove it from the setting, then there is really nothing that can be done to repair a crack. You can try to disguise a small crack or hole by filling it with colored wax crayon. Or you can mix oil paint with epoxy glue and fill the hole with that mixture.

If you can remove the enamel from the setting, however, and the surface and fault are clean, you can refire the piece so it is as good as new. Follow this procedure:

1. Remove all traces of dirt by scrubbing with a glass brush or old toothbrush under warm running water for two to three minutes. You can also use an ultrasonic cleaner if you have one. (Don't use detergent, because soap residue can cause just as much trouble as dirt.)

2. If there are any pits in the counter enamel, fill them first. Then put the enamel face up on a small piece of mica or on a porcelain tile (see page 66). If there are tiny holes, fill them with enamel that has been ground in an agate mortar and pestle to 150 or 200 mesh. Wash the enamel grains before grinding, but not after. If there are cracks in the enamel, haze the top with freshly washed soft-fusing flux.

3. Dry the enamel under a heat lamp. Then fire in the hot kiln until the surface looks glassy and smooth.

4. Repolish the enamel starting with 400-grit wet/dry Carborundum paper and go all the way to 600 grit for a high gloss. The enamel should then be as good as new.

Alternate
Enameling
Cups
and
Bases

The basic procedure described in this book calls for making a fine silver enameling cup as a base for cloisonné enameling. This base offers the greatest design flexibility since it is possible to position your cloisonne wires right up to the rim. The cup is sturdy and can be made in different shapes. The finished enamel can be placed in a wide variety of settings. Silver is the most trouble-free base, since the pure silver circumvents the problems of firescale.

There are times, however, when you may wish to use a different base, especially when you want to make a very large piece, to minimize the cost of the metal, to increase the piece's rigidity, or to eliminate the need for soldering.

This chapter gives instructions for enameling on domed silver discs, silver-plated steel dics, copper discs, ground-coated steel tiles, copper enameling cups, and aluminum sheet. Each has its own advantages and disadvantages. The regular Thomas Thompson vitreous enamels will adhere to all of them except aluminum, for which one needs special low-fire enamels. These are described in the aluminum enameling section.

All of these bases, except aluminum, require more heat than silver and so must be fired in a 6″ (15 cm) trinket kiln or in a chamber kiln. If they are fired on a trivet, the back can be kept nice-looking; if the back will not be seen in the finished piece, they can be fired on mica or on a porcelain tile.

Most of the techniques described in this chapter use Klyr Fire to hold wires or the enamel to the base. Commonly used in copper enameling, Klyr Fire is a water-soluble, plastic-based adhesive that burns out in the kiln with no flame. Since it is water soluble, wet enamel can dissolve it, so if your wires are glued in place with it, be very careful when laying in the enamel because the wires may move.

DOMED SILVER DISCS
If the intended design is very simple, such as the first few designs shown in Chapter 9 or the design in figure 5-1, you can use an enameling base that is simply a domed disc of fine silver sheet. (A sterling silver disc will oxidize like copper; to enamel on sterling,

follow the directions for enameling on copper discs.) Domed discs are used convex side up, and, when fired, the enamel will taper off and be quite thin along the edge. Therefore it is necessary to plan a simple design with the wire pattern in the center.

The wires are shaped as described in Chapter 5, but the wires cannot be as high as when using an enameling cup. This is because there will be a thinner coat of enamel on a disc than in a bezeled cup. Hauser and Miller supplies cloisonné wire in any height needed. You can also make your own, of course.

To make a domed silver disc, you will need a circle cutter or circle template and jeweler's saw or bezel shears, 20-gauge fine silver sheet, a wooden or steel dapping block and punch, a nichrome wire or stainless steel trivet, a rawhide mallet, medium-grade Carborundum stone, a kiln, and a pencil.

1. With a pencil and the circle template, mark the silver sheet with the enamel outline. Cut along the outline with a jeweler's saw or shears, or cut with a circle cutter. Anneal the disc for 30 seconds.

Figure 8—1 Fine silver enameling cup.

Figure 8—2 Copper discs that have been domed in preparation for enameling.

2. Select the depression in the dapping block and the corresponding punch that is the closest in size to your metal disc. The disc should just slightly overlap the depression. Place the disc over the depression, and with the round end of the punch facing down, lightly tap the punch with the rawhide mallet until the silver is formed to the dapping block. The disc should now rise in a gentle curve.

3. Anneal the disc in the kiln for 30 seconds. Cool.

4. Counter enameling is done first, so clean the back (concave) side and paint or spray on a coating of Klyr Fire. Using an 80-mesh sifter of the type used in copper enameling, sift on a generous amount of hard-firing enamel or counter enamel. Sift a heavier concentration on the edges to minimize crawling (enamel tends to pull away from the edges of the disc).

5. Dry under a heat lamp and fire in a preheated kiln on a trivet, concave side up, until the enamel is smooth. Cool.

6. Repeat the above procedure on the convex (top) side using the enamel color of your choice or Soft-Fusing Flux 426 or Vitreac LF 302. Place on mica or a trivet, counter-enameled side down, dry under a heat lamp, and fire until smooth. Rub the surface gently with medium-grade Carborundum stone under running water. The wires adhere better to this matte finish. Clean with a glass brush under running water.

7. Place a few drops of Klyr Fire in a shallow dish. Dip the wires in the Klyr Fire and place them in position on the disc. Carefully fill the cloisons and background with a layer of enamel. Dry.

8. Fire on mica or a trivet in a preheated kiln until the wires are fired in position. A good indicator is when the matte finish of the pre-enameled disc appears shiny. Cool and clean off the oxidation on copper and brass wires with a glass brush under running water. Silver or gold wires need no cleaning.

9. Continue to fill the cloisons as described in Chapter 6 and fire each time on mica or a trivet. The copper and brass wires must be cleaned between each firing. No further counter enameling is necessary because the domed shape itself helps prevent cracking and warping. Grind and polish the piece as described in Chapter 7.

SILVER-PLATED STEEL DISCS

Pre-domed, silver-plated steel discs are available in a variety of shapes from Immerman's Crafts, Inc. They are made of a special enameling steel coated with a heavy layer of silver. The surface of the disc has a crinkled appearance that reflects light through transparent enamels. The surface appears identical to that of fine silver at a fraction of fine silver's cost. Pre-enamel both the convex (top) and concave (bottom) sides. Either opaque or transparent enamels can be used; however, transparent enamels in cool colors produce the most beautiful effects over the silver.

A kiln with a pyrometer is preferable, but, because the discs are thin and do not require especially high temperatures to fire, a trinket kiln can be used. Watch the enamel carefully to avoid overfiring.

1. If the disc is tarnished, rub it with a paste of baking soda and water. Do not use abrasive household cleansers or a brush because you may scratch the silver plating.

2. Counter enameling is done first, so paint or spray Klyr Fire on the concave side of the disc. This will be the back or counter enameled side. If the Klyr Fire runs or pulls, it indicates an oily surface. To burn off any oily residue, wipe off the Klyr Fire and prefire the disc in the kiln for about 15 seconds at 1350°F (732°C). Then reapply the Klyr Fire.

3. Sift counter enamel over the concave side of the disc. Sift a heavier concentration of enamel on the edges. Dry and fire in a preheated kiln until smooth. Remove and cool.

4. Repeat the procedure on the convex side of the disc using soft-fusing flux, but this time place the disc on mica or a trivet before firing in a hot kiln. Do not overfire or the silver plating may turn brown. Rub the enameled convex surface gently with medium-grade Carborundum stone under running water to achieve a matte finish. Clean with a glass brush under running water.

5. Dip each wire in Klyr Fire and place it on the convex side of the disc. The wirework may be silver, copper, brass, or a combination of all three. Dry. Place into a hot kiln and fire until the wires tack down on the enamel. (The matte finish will get smooth.) Remove and cool.

6. Fill the cloisons, fire, and finish as described in Chapters 6 and 7. Because of the added strength provided by the concave shape, no further counter enameling is necessary.

COPPER DISCS

Pieces of 18-gauge copper in many different shapes and sizes are available at most enameling hobby stores. More heat must be applied to copper than to silver of the same gauge before enamel applied to it will melt. Therefore you will need at least a 6" (15 cm) diameter trinket kiln to produce the required firing temperatures. Because silver wires may melt unless you are very careful, copper or brass wires are better choices.

1. Anneal the copper disc, pickle, and rinse in a solution of baking soda and water. Rinse again in plain water.

2. Dome the disc in a wooden dapping block. (See step 2 under "Domed Silver Discs," above.)

3. Anneal, pickle, rinse in baking soda and water, and then rinse in plain water. Dry.

4. Paint Klyr Fire on the back (concave) side of the disc and dust it generously with hard-firing counter enamel, using an 80-mesh sifter. Place the disc on mica or a trivet, enamel side up, and dry well under a heat lamp.

5. Place the counter enameled disc on mica or a trivet into a hot kiln. Fire until the enamel is smooth. Remove from the kiln and cool.

Frog with Wings pendant by Felicia Liban. Cloisonné enamel underlaid with gold foil, encased in 14- and 22-karat gold and embellished with amethyst stone. 2″ x 1¼″ (5 x 3 cm). Collection of Julia Walker.

Initial by Louise Mitchell. Cloisonné enamel pendant on handmade 22-karat gold, single loop-in-loop chain with fused clasp. ⅝″ (16 mm) diameter. Designed for the Rev. Roberta Mitchell.

Snail by Felicia Liban. Cloisonné enamel brooch/pendant, set in 22-and 14-karat gold. 2″ x ⁷⁄₁₆″ (50 x 11 mm) oval.

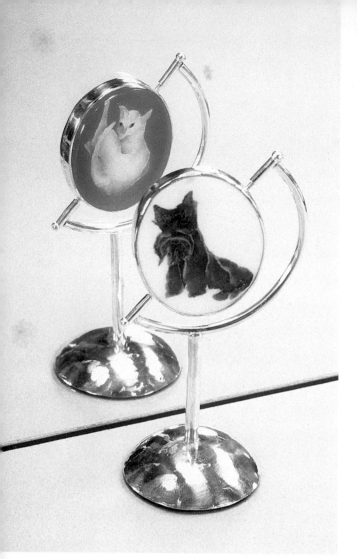

Snowdrop by Felicia Liban.
Pendant, cloisonné enamel set in
22- and 14-karat gold. 1⅛″ (29
mm) diameter.

Friends by Felicia Liban. Cloisonné
enamel portraits of the artist's pets are
set in a two-sided frame executed in
sterling silver and mounted on a
revolving stand. 5″ (12.5 cm) high.

Hairbrush by Felicia Liban. Cloisonné enamel of a griffin set in a handmade
rosewood brush. Woodwork by Edward Lewand.

The Golden Fish Necklace by Felicia Liban. Cloisonné enamel underlaid with gold foil. The piece contains gold, silver, and copper cloisons, and is encased in sterling silver and embellished with 14-karat gold with jelly opal stone. Hung on handmade fine silver chain. Collection of Mr. and Mrs. Harry Bigman.

Mountain Landscape by Louise Mitchell. Cloisonné enamel. 1⅛" (29 mm) diameter.

Flying Elephant pendant/brooch by Felicia Liban. Cloisonné enamel underlaid with gold foil, encased in sterling silver and 14-karat gold with seed pearls. 3" x 2½" (75 x 62 mm). Collection of Mr. and Mrs. Bernard Gotfryd.

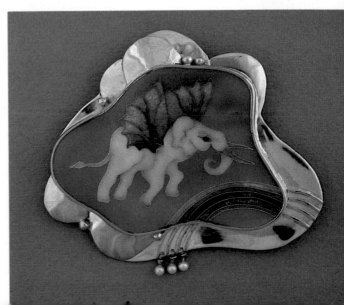

Earth Choker by Felicia Liban. Fine silver, hand-woven mesh chain, 15″ (38 cm) long, with 22-karat gold terminals embellished with gems and granulation. The clasp, depicting Earth, is cloisonné enamel encased in 22-karat and 14-karat gold, 1½″ x 2″ (38 x 50 mm).

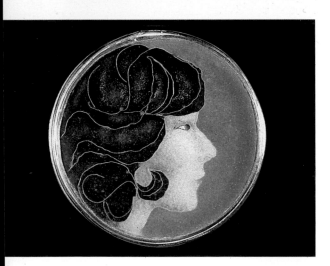

Julia by Felicia Liban. Cloisonné enamel box top depicting the artist's daughter. 1⅝″ (4 cm) diameter.

Flying Fish by Felicia Liban. Cloisonné enamel pendant underlaid with gold foil, encased in a 14-karat gold cast setting.

Jonquil by Felicia Liban. Cloisonné enamel pendant with jade and carnelian beads set in 22-karat and 14-karat gold, suspended on a handmade Sailor's Knot 22-karat gold chain. 1½" (4 cm) diameter.

Yellow Birds by Felicia Liban. Cloisonné enamel on the back of a hand mirror. 3" (7.5 cm) diameter.

Dandelion (Triptych) necklace by Felicia Liban. Cloisonné enamel encased in sterling silver, embellished with 14-karat gold hung on mother-of-pearl, jade, and silver beads. A small carnelian hangs from the center section. 5" x 1" (12.5 x 2.5 cm).

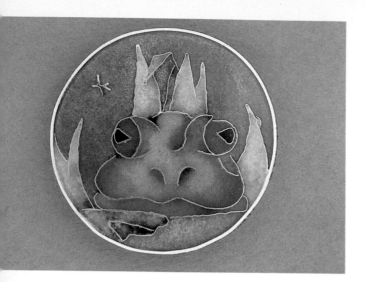

Frog by Louise Mitchell. Cloisonné enamel. 1⅛″ (29 mm) diameter.

Dragon by Louise Mitchell. Cloisonné enamel, 1½″ (4 cm) diameter. *Peacock Feather* by Felicia Liban. Cloisonné enamel on copper, set into a handmade silver box. 1″ x 2″ x 1″ (2.5 x 5 x 2.5 cm).

Jack-in-the-Pulpit by Felicia Liban. Cloisonné enamel pendant set in 22- and 14-karat gold. 1¼″ (32 mm) oval.

Unicorn by Felicia Liban. Cloisonné enamel pin/brooch set in 14-karat gold. 1¼″ x 2″ (3 x 5 cm).

Mushrooms by Felicia Liban. Cloisonné enamel pendant set in silver. ¹⁹/₃₂″ x 1″ (15 x 25 mm) oval.

Renaissance Portrait by Louise Mitchell and Jean Reist Stark. Cloisonné enamel. 1¼″ (3 cm) diameter.

Moonscape by Felicia Liban. Executed with the assistance of the staff of the Kulicke Stark Academy. Cloisonné and basse taille enamel set into sterling silver and hung on a hand-woven silver chain. 4″ x 2″ (10 cm x 5 cm).

Brooch by Felicia Liban. Copper pipe with carved ivory water pump, trimmed with silver and baroque pearl. Sweet-water pearl hangs as a droplet over a cloisonné enamel puddle stickpin set in silver. 3″ x 5″ (7.5 x 12.5 cm).

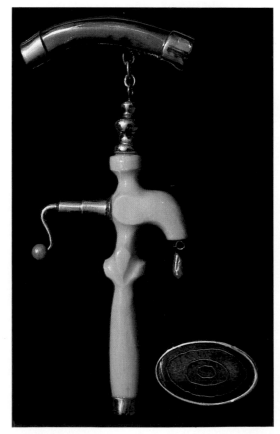

David by Felicia Liban. Cloisonné enamel portrait of the artist's son set on a sterling silver box lid.

Figure 8–3 Flower brooch by Felicia Liban, $1'' \times 1\frac{3}{4}''$ (2.5 × 4.5 cm), made with brass cloisonné wires on a copper disc, set in sterling silver. Silver foil gives brightness to the leaves; shaded flower is overlaid with opalescent white enamel.

6. Immerse in warm pickle for one minute. Rinse in a baking soda and water solution and clean the front and edges with a glass brush and household detergent. When all the firescale is off, rinse the disc well under water. Avoid touching the surface with your fingers so oil from your hands will not contaminate it. Dry. If you are using copper or brass wires, go to step 9.

7. If gold or silver wires are going to be used, they must be protected from the copper by a coat of enamel. Paint Klyr Fire on the front (convex) side of the disc and dust over it a generous coat of Undercoat White 621 for an opaque background or Hard Fusing Flux 333 for a transparent background. (Hard fusing flux will not only cover the copper, but it will result in a glowing gold color over which transparent enamel colors show up beautifully.

8. Dry the piece under a heat lamp and fire on mica or on a trivet in a hot kiln until the enamel is smooth. Rub the surface of the cooled piece under running water with a medium-grade Carborundum stone. Clean with a glass brush under running water.

9. Place a few drops of Klyr Fire into a shallow dish. Dip each shaped cloisonné wire into the Klyr Fire and place it in position on the copper disc. Silver and gold cloisonné wires must be glued to the enamel undercoat and tack-fired, but brass or copper wires could be glued directly to the copper base and then filled with enamel. Dry. Fire the wires in position in a hot kiln.

10. Continue to fill the cloisons, fire, and finish as described in Chapters 6 and 7. Brass and copper wires must be cleaned with a glass brush under running water between each firing. No further counter enameling is required.

GROUND-COATED STEEL TILES

Ground-coated steel tiles are pre-enameled and can be obtained from Thomas Thompson or Vitrearc, in sizes ranging from 3" (7.6 cm) square to large panels. Ground-coated steel is enameled white on the front and counter enameled gray on the back. It is thick and heavy and therefore not too useful as jewelry, but it works beautifully as plaques, pictures, boxes, and belt buckles.

Because of the thickness of the metal, you will need a chamber kiln with a pyrometer to obtain the higher firing temperatures needed for tiles over 2" (5 cm) in diameter.

1. Wash thoroughly with a degreaser (liquid household detergent will do), dry, and spray or paint the top with Klyr Fire.

2. Using an 80-mesh sifter of the type commonly used in copper enameling, sift on Opaque Undercoat White 621 for a white background or Opaque Hard Black 124A for a black background. Opaque enamels can be fired over either a white or black background since the background does not show through. A white background, however, gives you the option of using transparent enamels in later layers. A black enamel background prepares the tile for grisaille enameling.

3. Dry under a heat lamp; preheat the kiln to 1600°F (870°C) (red-orange).

4. Fire the tile on a trivet in a preheated kiln until the enamel is smooth. Remove from kiln and cool.

5. Dip each piece of shaped cloisonné wire into Klyr Fire and assemble your design on the tile front. Dry under a heat lamp.

6. Fire again at 1600°F (870°C), but peek into the kiln often so that you will not melt the wires. Because of their higher melting point, copper and brass wires are a lot safer to use than silver, which can simply melt away. When the trivet starts to glow, it is a good indication that the enamel has melted and the wires are tacked down. Remove from the kiln and cool.

Figure 8—4 Ground-coated steel tiles.

7. Now you are ready to do your wet inlay as described in Chapter 6. Because of the rigidity of the steel, there is no warping. Because it is pre-enameled, no counter enameling is required. Grind and polish the piece as described in Chapter 7.

COPPER ENAMELING CUPS

A $1\frac{1}{2}''$ (3.8 cm) diameter copper enameling cup is the largest size that can be successfully enameled on the small trinket kiln with a 4" (10 cm) diameter heating element. To achieve the higher temperatures necessary for a larger copper cup, we recommend using a kiln with a 6" (15 cm) diameter element.

Making the Cup

1. Cut a square out of 23-gauge copper that is at least $\frac{1}{8}''$ (3 mm) larger all around than your design. Anneal, pickle, rinse in baking soda and water, and then rinse in water. Press the square flat between two steel blocks.

2. To make the bezel, cut a strip of 23-gauge copper that is slightly longer than the perimeter of your design and $\frac{1}{32}''$ (1 mm) higher than the cloisonné wire you are using. File the ends so when they are butted together the bezel fits your design perfectly.

3. Solder the seam of the copper bezel with IT silver solder just as you would if the bezel were silver. (See Chapter 5.) Round the soldered bezel on a mandrel and sand both edges of the bezel so it will sit flat on the square copper base.

4. Solder the bezel to the sheet with hard silver solder using a #2 torch tip. Pickle, rinse in baking soda and water, and dry. Trim all around the bezel with shears.

5. Turn the cup upside down on a table and press it with your thumb to dome it slightly.

Counter Enameling

1. To prevent firescale from forming on the back that might subsequently contaminate the front, put down a $\frac{1}{8}''$ (3 mm) coat of wet counter enamel on the back (concave) side, and dry under a heat lamp.

2. Place the cup on mica or a trivet with the counter enamel up, and put it into a preheated kiln. Fire until the counter enamel is smooth.

3. Remove the cup from the kiln and cool. Pickle until the copper is free of oxidation. Rinse in baking soda and water, and clean the front and all exposed copper with a glass brush and household detergent. Rinse with water. Dry, but do not touch areas that are to be enameled. If brass or copper wires are to be used, go to "Adding the Wires and Enamels," below.

4. If silver or gold cloisonné wires are to be used, first fire a coat of Hard Fusing Flux 333 or White Undercoat 621 in the cup. (When fired over copper, Hard Fusing Flux 333 will result in a glowing gold

color over which warm transparent enamel colors will show up beautifully.) Dry under a heat lamp and fire the undercoat.

5. Rub the undercoat under running water with medium-grade Carborundum stone to create a matte surface. Clean with a glass brush under running water.

Adding the Wires and Enamels

1. Place a few drops of Klyr Fire into a shallow dish. Dip each shaped cloisonné wire into the Klyr Fire and place it in position in the copper cup. Silver and gold cloisonné wires are glued to the enamel undercoat and tack-fired, but brass or copper wires could be glued directly to the copper base and filled.

2. The first coat of enamel protects against firescale and establishes the base color. Gold or silver foils under transparent enamels will make them more vibrant where desired. Using the same procedure as in Chapter 6, fill all the cloisons evenly one third of the way up. Mop with toilet paper and dry under a heat lamp. When dry, place the cup on mica or a porcelain tile (not on a trivet), cloisonné side up, and place it into a hot kiln. Fire until smooth and shiny. Cool.

3. Clean all oxidized cloisonné wires and other areas with a glass brush under running water until no firescale flicks off. Leave the cup on the mica.

4. Continue to fill the cloisons, dry, and fire each layer. When cool, clean the oxidation off with a glass brush under running water.

5. When all the cloisons are filled and fired, the counter enamel and the enamel on the front of the cup will not be equally thick. Peel and sand off the mica. If you have used a porcelain tile, remove any kiln wash from the counter enamel. Rinse. Counter enamel again as described in Chapter 6. The piece is now ready for polishing.

ALUMINUM ALLOY SHEET

Aluminum has been enameled commercially for the last twenty years or so. The complicated metal preparation, narrow firing range, and other technical limitations have made enameling on aluminum impractical for the craftsman until the recent development of lead-free enamels and a special aluminum alloy.

Lead-Free Enamels

Developed by Harold Helwig, one of America's foremost enamelists, and manufactured by Vitrearc, a division of the Ceramic Coating Company in Newport, Kentucky, these new enamels are available in a wide range of colors and may be used on copper, silver, gold, and aluminum alloy 3003. (Harold Helwig is still experimenting with new colors and techniques, such as enameling on brass and bronze.)

These lead-free enamels are soft-fusing and melt between 950° to 1050° F (510° to 566°C), which is considerably lower than the 1450° to 1550°F (788° to 843°C) that conventional enamels melt at. To avoid overfiring them, you must use a chamber kiln that has a pyrometer. These enamels cannot be mixed or fired side-by-side with medium or hard-firing vitreous enamels because the firing temperatures are totally different. Vitrearc makes a line of preground lead-free enamels, with the same firing ranges as Thomas Thompson enamels, which can be used on glass, porcelain, and metals other than aluminum. (Only lead-free enamels can be used on anything that will contain food.) A catalog is available from Vitrearc, which would provide the most up-to-date information about their enamels.

The lead-free enamels for aluminum were shipped to us from Vitrearc in lump form. They had to be ground under water with a mortar and pestle to 150 mesh. This is much finer than the regular 80 mesh enamels of Thomas Thompson. If your tap water is hard, use distilled water to wash and prepare the enamels.

Aluminum 3003

Aluminum 3003 is an alloy developed by Vitrearc to be compatible with the low-firing enamels. It can be purchased in sheet form from Vitrearc, from American Metalcraft, or from a local metal supplier. The most satisfactory thickness for cloisonné enameling is either 18 or 16 gauge. If no cloisonné wires are to be used, and if the enamel layer on the front is kept thin, it is not necessary to counter enamel the back of the sheet. However, to do cloisonné enameling, you must also enamel the back of the piece.

A special cleaner is available from Vitrearc to clean the aluminum. Simply scour with the cleaner and a wet rag. Do not use household cleansers containing chlorine because the chlorine will cause the enamel to chip from the metal surface when it cools. The aluminum does not need to be cleaned between firings.

Procedure

1. Saw a disc, oval, rectangle, or other shape out of a sheet of 18 or 16 gauge aluminum 3003. The larger the piece, the thicker the metal should be.

2. Grind the enamels under distilled water with an agate or porcelain mortar and pestle to 150 mesh.

3. Prefire the aluminum for three to five minutes at 950° to 1050°F (510° to 566°C). Cool.

4. Spray distilled water on the back of the metal with a spray gun or plant mister. This fine spray will help to obtain a smooth surface after repeated firings at these low temperatures. Do not apply too much water or the enamel will run.

5. Any of the low-firing Vitrearc enamels can be used as counter enamel. Shake the ground dried enamel through a 150 mesh screen or sifter onto the back. Each coat of enamel should be no thicker than .002" to .004" (.05 to .1 mm) thick (i.e., very very thin!). Dry under a heat lamp.

6. Fire on a trivet at 950° to 1050°F (510° to 566°C) for five to seven minutes until the enamel is glossy. A long low heat is better

than a short high heat. Cool. This first firing will have a very noticeable orange peel surface texture. The surface will smooth out in later firings.

7. Repeat the above procedure to add more thin coats of enamel. If you want a thin coat with areas of the base coat showing through, add only one more coat; but if you want a solid coat of enamel that is completely smooth, two or three firings are necessary.

8. Repeat the above steps on the top surface of the aluminum piece.

9. You are now ready to attach your shaped cloisonné wires to the front of the piece. Dip the wires in Klyr Fire to "glue" them in place. The enamels should be mixed with distilled water and applied with a fine brush or spatula. Remove excess water by blotting with toilet paper. Dry under a heat lamp. Place on a trivet and fire each layer in the kiln at 950° to 1050°F (510° to 566°C) for five to seven minutes. Continue filling and firing to the top of the wirework.

10. Grind and polish the piece as described in Chapter 7.

Unshaded Enamel Designs

This chapter contains ten designs for cloisonné enamels that have no shading within the cloisons. The designs are shown in order of difficulty. The first three will be especially helpful in giving you experience with forming wires and working with enamels. You can copy the design exactly or use them as starting points for other designs.

Each example contains a small wirework diagram showing the exact size to which the wires should be cut and how they will look placed together in the cup. An enlarged wire diagram shows the separate wires. Color diagrams indicate where each enamel color will go. Usually two to three color firings are given; thereafter, the cloisons are filled with flux or with the last color.

All colors are listed by their Thomas Thompson name and number. A T indicates a transparent enamel, O an opaque enamel, and Opal an opalescent enamel. If two or more enamels are listed under a single heading, they should be combined and washed together, then used as a single color.

The color diagrams and firing instructions assume your wires are already fired in place in Soft-Fusing Flux 426 or Vitreac LF 302.

SIGNATURE

DIMENSIONS
Enameling cup: $\frac{5}{8}$" (16 mm) diameter circle.
Cloisonné wire: .010" (.25 mm) smooth fine silver or gold.

WIREWORK
Cut and shape 4 wires as shown in the diagram.

COLOR
Background, all layers: O Cocoa 813.

SPECIAL PROCEDURES
To make your own design, use a signature small enough to serve as a direct pattern for the wirework. This can be the signature of the wearer or of someone related to the wearer. The size and shape of the enameling cup can be adjusted to suit the handwriting.

Figure 9–1 *Signature* by Louise Mitchell, ⅝″ (16 mm) diameter. Simple wirework, taken directly from a signature, with a brown background.

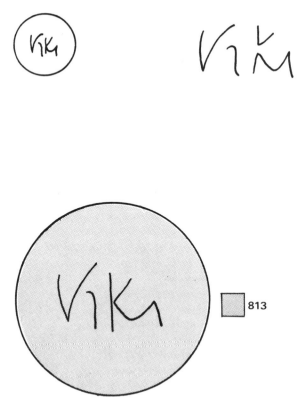

813

INITIAL

DIMENSIONS
Enameling cup: ⅝″ (16 mm) diameter circle.
Cloisonné wire: .003″ (.08 mm) gold or fine silver.

WIREWORK
Cut and shape 6 wires as shown in the diagram.

COLORS
Background, all layers: T Seal 191, T Cocoa 238, and T Soft-Fusing
    Flux 426.
Initial, all layers: T Chinchilla 313 and T Soft-Fusing Flux 426.

SPECIAL PROCEDURE
From your clipping file, find an interesting example of the needed
letter. In each style of lettering, one letter may be interesting while
another is not. Advertisements are a good source.

Figure 9–2 *Initial* by Louise Mitchell, ⅝″ (16 mm) diameter. Light blue initial on a medium brown background.

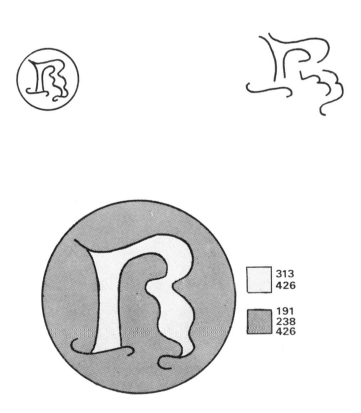

ABSTRACT

DIMENSIONS
Enameling cup: $\frac{5}{8}$" (16 mm) diameter circle.
Cloisonné wire: .010" (.25 mm) smooth fine silver.

WIREWORK
Cut and shape 10 wires as shown in the diagram.

COLORS
Area 1: O Elk 691.
Area 2: O Parchment 261.
Area 3, first layer: O Ivory 334; second layer: T Hazel 112.
Area 4, first layer: O Canary 1069; second layer: T Mikado 755.

SPECIAL PROCEDURES
Semicircles of wire are easily formed over a small ring mandrel. Many variations of this design are possible.

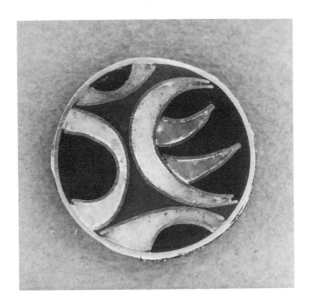

Figure 9–3 *Abstract* by Louise Mitchell, $\frac{5}{8}$″ (16 mm) diameter. A color scheme of four complementary colors, using unmilled wire.

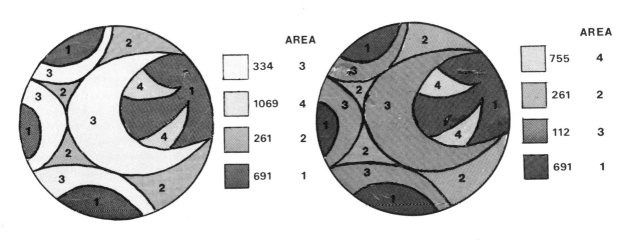

	AREA	
334	3	
1069	4	
261	2	
691	1	

first layer

	AREA	
755	4	
261	2	
112	3	
691	1	

second layer

SCARAB

DIMENSIONS
Enameling cup: $\frac{11}{16}$" (17 mm) diameter circle.
Cloisonné wire: .010" (.25 mm) smooth silver.

WIREWORK
Cut and shape 12 wires as shown in the diagram.

COLORS
Background, all layers: O Ivory 334 and T Soft-Fusing Flux 426.
Head and tail, first layer: T Amulet 154 and T Soft-Fusing Flux 426;
    second layer: T Imperial 122 and T Soft-Fusing Flux 426; third
    layer: T Soft-Fusing Flux 426.
Wings and back, first and second layers: T Imperial 122 and T Soft-
    Fusing Flux 426; third layer: T Soft-Fusing Flux 426.

SPECIAL PROCEDURES
Gold foil may be put in the cloisons of the wings and tail prior to
adding the first layer of color. (See Chapter 6.)

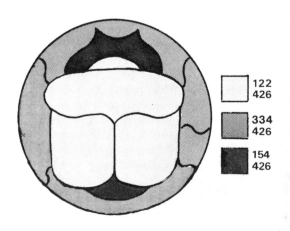

first layer

96

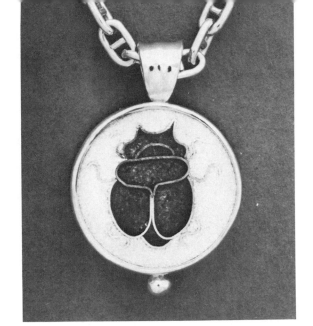

Figure 9—4 *Scarab* by Felicia Liban, $\frac{11}{16}''$ (17 mm) diameter. Gold foil used underneath transparent blue-green enamel gives the scarab an iridescent quality. It has an ivory background.

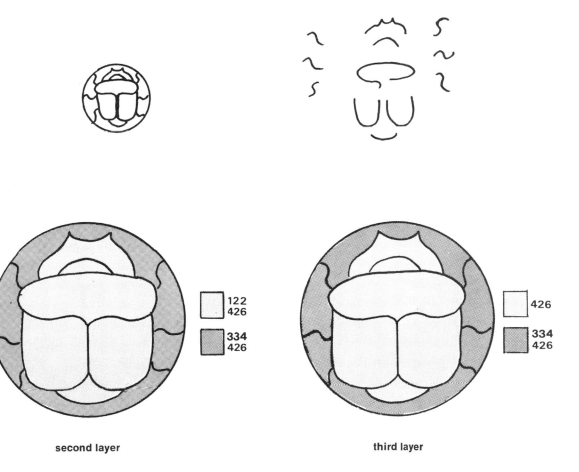

	122 426
	334 426

second layer

	426
	334 426

third layer

MEDIEVAL PORTRAIT

DIMENSIONS
Enameling cup: 1½" (3.8 cm) diameter circle.
Cloisonné wire: .006" (.15 mm) smooth fine silver or gold.

WIREWORK
Cut and shape 13 wires as shown in the diagram.

COLORS
Background: Opal Mauve 853.
Shadow areas, first layer: O Medium Fusing Black 124; second layer: T Smoke 834.
Highlight areas, first layer: O Ivory 334 and T Soft-Fusing Flux 426; second layer: T Gold 724.

Figure 9–5 *Medieval Portrait* by Louise Mitchell, 1½″ (3.8 cm) diameter. Deep wine, black, and gold enamels reflect the richness of the medieval period.

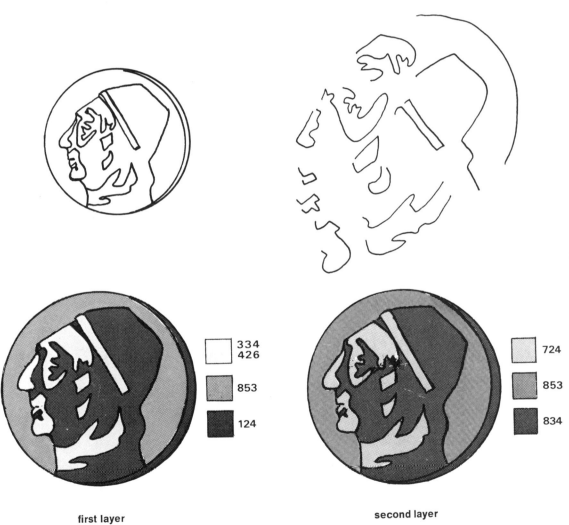

334	
426	
853	
124	

724	
853	
834	

first layer

second layer

COMPLEX ABSTRACT

Enameling cup: 1½″ (3.8 cm) diameter circle.
Cloisonné wire: .005″ (.13 mm) smooth fine silver.

WIREWORK
Cut and shape 29 wires as shown in the diagram.

COLORS
Area 1, first layer: O Soft-Fusing White 644; second layer: Opal White 835.
Area 2, both layers: O Ivory 334 and T Soft-Fusing Flux 426.
Area 3, first layer: O Canary 1069 and T Soft-Fusing Flux 426; second layer: T Amber 728.
Area 4, first layer: T Tan 131 and T Soft-Fusing Flux 426; second layer: T Soft-Fusing Flux 426.
Area 5, both layers: O Brick 707.
Area 6, both layers: O Elk 691.

Figure 9–6 *Complex Abstract* by Louise Mitchell, 1½″ (3.8 cm) diameter. A six-color design using shades of brown.

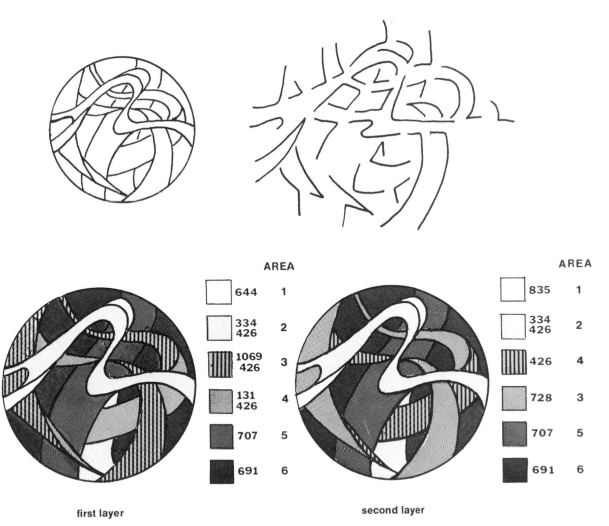

AREA

644	1
334 426	2
1069 426	3
131 426	4
707	5
691	6

first layer

AREA

835	1
334 426	2
426	4
728	3
707	5
691	6

second layer

DRAGON

DIMENSIONS
Enameling cup: 1½" (3.8 cm) diameter circle.
Cloisonné wire: .003" (.08 mm) crinkled fine silver or gold.

WIREWORK
Cut and shape 27 wires as shown in the diagram.

COLORS
Background: T Copen 604 and T Soft-Fusing Flux 426.
Body: T Gold 724.
Tongue, first layer: O Chinese 167; second layer: T Soft-Fusing Flux 426.
Eye center, first layer: O Medium-Fusing Black 124; second layer: T Smoke 834.
Eye outer circle, first layer: O Chinese 167; second layer: T Soft-Fusing Flux 426.
Mouth and comb: T Palm 997.
Teeth, whiskers, and horns, first layer: O Soft-Fusing White 644 and T Soft-Fusing Flux 426 (wash only twice); second layer: Opal White 835.

SPECIAL PROCEDURES
To make the eyes, set the wire circle for the centers on ½" (13 mm) squares of mica. Fill and fire them with O Black until the enamel reaches the top. Clean the mica off the back. Set each of the larger outer circles of the eyes on a ½" (13 mm) square of mica. Fire one layer of O Chinese. Place the black center into the wet layer of O Chinese. When it is fired it will be held in place. Clean the mica off the back and place the eyes into the wet second color layer in the dragon. Continue filling and firing the eyes with soft fusing flux to the top.

Gold foil is put in the cloison for the body prior to adding the first layer of T Gold 724.

Figure 9–7 *Dragon* by Louise Mitchell, 1½″ (3.8 cm) diameter. A golden, shimmering dragon created by using gold foil under the enamels. It has a green comb, a red mouth, and white teeth and whiskers.

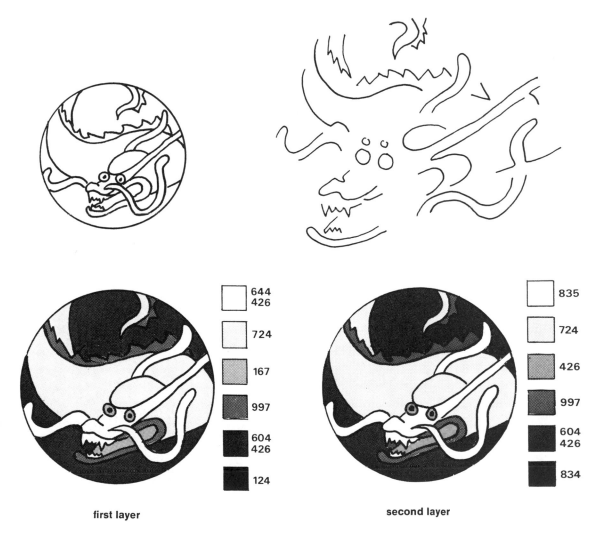

644	
426	
724	
167	
997	
604	
426	
124	

first layer

835	
724	
426	
997	
604	
426	
834	

second layer

TREES

DIMENSIONS
Enameling cup: 1½″ (3.8 cm) diameter circle.
Cloisonné wire: .003″ (.08 mm) crinkled fine silver or gold.

WIREWORK
Cut and shape 31 wires as shown in the diagram.

COLORS
Sky: O Pastel 487 and T Soft-Fusing Flux 426.
Grass and left tree leaves, first layer: O Ivory 334 and T Soft-Fusing Flux 426; second layer: T Dark Olive 839 (thin coat).
Left trunk: Opal Raisin 856.
Right trunk and vines on left tree: Opal Elephant 850.
Right tree leaves and shrubs: 2 parts O Evergreen 689 and 1 part T Soft-Fusing Flux 426.

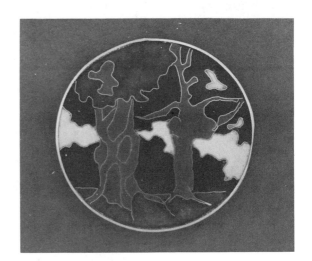

Figure 9–8 *Trees* by Louise Mitchell, 1½″ (3.8 cm) diameter. Tonal contrasts of various greens show a woodland scene with the light of the sky coming through the purple and gray trees.

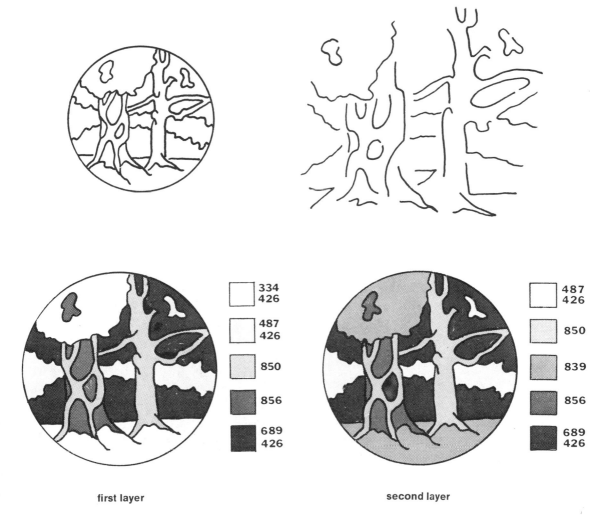

	334 426
	487 426
	850
	856
	689 426

first layer

	487 426
	850
	839
	856
	689 426

second layer

SNOWDROP

DIMENSIONS
Enameling cup: 1⅛″ (2.9 cm) or 1 1/16″ (2.7 cm) diameter circle.
Cloisonné wire: .003″ (.08 mm) crinkled gold or silver.

WIREWORK
Cut and shape 10 wires as shown in the diagram.

COLORS
Background: 1 part each of T Lawn 160, T Smoke 834, T Khaki 129,
    and Opal White 835, and 4 parts of T Soft-Fusing Flux 426.
Petals, first layer: O Ivory 334 and T Soft-Fusing Flux 426; second
    layer: (1) Opal White 835, (2) Opal Elephant 850, and (3) O
    Arcadian 326; third and subsequent layers: Opal White 835.
Leaf and stem, first layer: O Arcadian 326; second layer: (stem) T
    Khaki 129, (leaf) T Lawn 160; third and subsequent layers: T Soft-
    Fusing Flux 426.
Calyx, first layer: O Ivory 334 and T Soft-Fusing Flux 426; second
    layer: T Lawn 160; third and subsequent layers: T Soft-Fusing
    Flux 426.

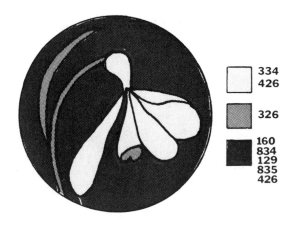

☐	334 426
▨	326
■	160 834 129 835 426

first layer

Figure 9–9 *Snowdrop* by Felicia Liban, 1⅛″ (2.9 cm) diameter. Pearl-white petals accented with green on a dull green background.

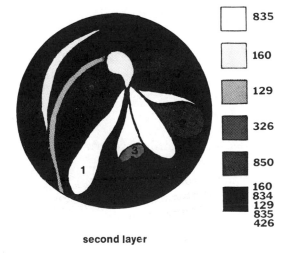

	835
	160
	129
	326
	850
	160 834 129 835 426

second layer

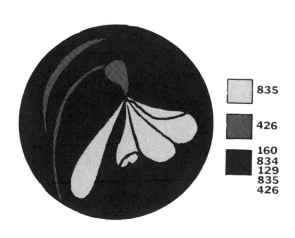

	835
	426
	160 834 129 835 426

third layer

SWAN

DIMENSIONS
Enameling cup: 2″ wide × 1⅛″ high (5.1 × 2.9 cm) oval.
Cloisonné wire: .002 (.05 mm) crinkled gold or silver.

WIREWORK
Cut and shape 10 wires as shown in the diagram.

COLORS
Background: 1 part each of Opal Periwinkle 851, T Old Silver 1013, and T Chinchilla 313, and 3 parts of Opal White 835.
Body, first layer: O Soft-Fusing White 644 and T Soft-Fusing Flux 426; second layer: Opal Petal 837, Opal Mauve 853, Opal Elephant 850, and Opal White 835; third and subsequent layers: Opal White 835.
Mask, first and second layers: O Charcoal 463; third and subsequent layers: T Soft-Fusing Flux 426.
Beak, first layer: O Marigold 226; second layer: T Mikado 755; third and subsequent layers: T Soft-Fusing Flux 426.

644	226	851	463
426		1013	
		835	
		313	

first layer

108

Figure 9–10 *Swan* by Felicia Liban, 2″ wide × 1⅛″ high (5.1 × 2.9 cm). The swan has opalescent white feathers, a black mask, and an orange bill on a background of dull blue.

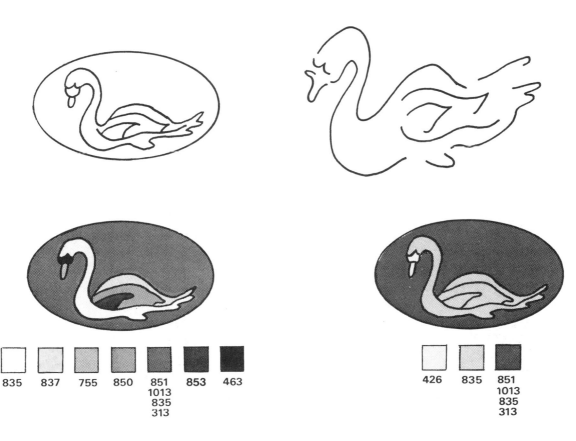

835	837	755	850	851 1013 835 313	853	463

second layer

426	835	851 1013 835 313

third layer

Shaded Enamel Designs

10

Here are ten enamel designs that are somewhat more complicated than those in the previous chapter. They use shadings of color to expand their imagery. Again, each example has a wirework diagram, an enlarged view of the wires, color diagrams, and a photograph of the finished piece.

All designs except "Mountain Landscape" assume the wires are already fired in place in a layer of Soft-Fusing Flux 426 or Vitreac LF 302. Use the colors listed in the last color diagram for all subsequent firings until the enamel has reached the top of the wires. Remember that all the shadings are done in the second and third layers of color or there is a danger of losing the design in the polishing stages.

MUSHROOMS

DIMENSIONS
1. Enameling cup: $\frac{1}{2}$" wide × 1" high (1.3 × 2.5 cm) oval.
2. Cloisonné wire: .004" (.10 mm) smooth gold or silver.

WIREWORK
Cut and shape 7 wires as shown in the diagram.

COLORS
Background: 1 part T Chestnut 308 and 3 parts T Soft-Fusing Flux 426.
Grass blade, first and second layers: T Lawn 160 and T Soft-Fusing Flux 426; third layer: T Soft-Fusing Flux 426.
Large stem, first layer: O Soft-Fusing White 644 and T Soft-Fusing Flux 426; second layer: (bottom) Opal White 835, (top) T Champagne 130; third layer: Opal White 835.
Small stem, first layer: O Soft-Fusing White 644 and T Soft-Fusing Flux 426; second layer: Opal White 835; third layer: Opal White 835.
Under the cap, first layer: O Soft-Fusing White 644 and T Soft-Fusing Flux 426; second layer: Opal Elephant 850; third layer: Opal White 835.
Cap, first layer: O Citron 1068 and T Soft-Fusing Flux 426; second layer: (outer area) T Mikado 755, (center highlight) T Burnt Orange 531; third layer: T Soft-Fusing Flux 426.

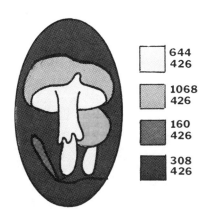

644	426
1068	426
160	426
308	426

first layer

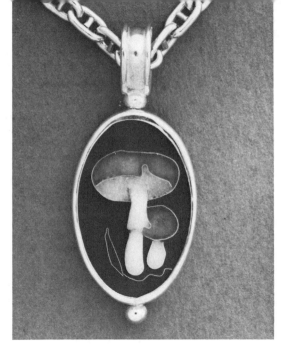

Figure 10–1 *Mushrooms* by Felicia Liban, $\frac{19}{32}''$ wide × 1″ high (1.3 × 2.5 cm). Yellow caps shaded with orange, white stems shaded with gray, and green grass on a brown transparent background.

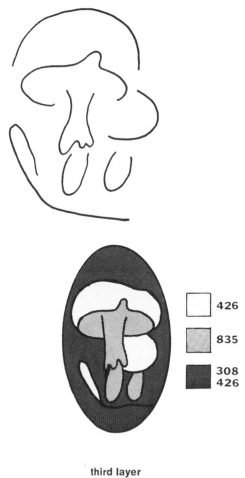

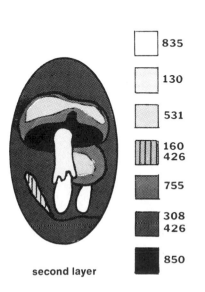

☐	835
☐	130
☐	531
▥	160 426
▨	755
▨	308 426
■	850

second layer

☐	426
▥	835
■	308 426

third layer

MOUNTAIN LANDSCAPE

Fire the wires in position using a mixture of O Ivory 334 and Soft-Fusing Flux 426 (instead of the flux alone).

DIMENSIONS

Enameling cup: 1⅛" (2.9 cm) diameter circle.
Cloisonné wire: .005" (.13 mm) crinkled fine silver or gold.

WIREWORK

Cut and shape 7 wires as shown in the diagram.

COLORS

Area 1: T Soft-Fusing Flux 426.
Area 2: T Pigeon 101.
Area 3: T Wineberry 150 and T Soft-Fusing Flux 426.
Area 4: T Pigeon 101 and T Wineberry 150.
Area 5: T Midnite 387.

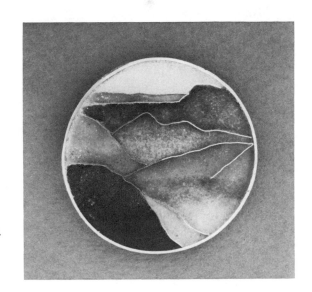

Figure 10–2 *Mountain Landscape* by Louise Mitchell, $1\frac{1}{8}''$ (2.9 cm) diameter. A special effect is used to reveal gradations of blue, mauve, and deep blue.

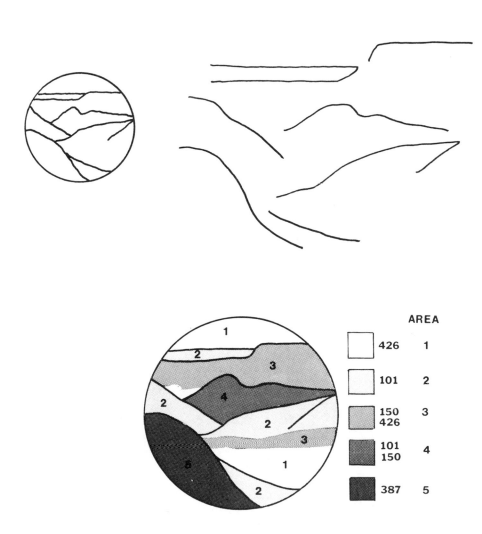

SNAIL

DIMENSIONS
Enameling cup: 2″ wide × 1½″ high (5.1 × 3.8 cm) oval.
Cloisonné wire: .002″ (.05 mm) smooth gold or silver.

WIREWORK
Cut and shape 8 wires as shown in the diagram.

COLORS
Background, first layer: O Carmel 301; second and subsequent layers:
    Opal Beige 852.
Shell, first layer: Opal White 835; second layer: (top) Opal White 835,
    (middle) Opal Petal 837, (bottom) Opal Elephant 850; third and
    subsequent layers: Opal White 835.
Rim of Shell, first layer: Opal White 835; second and subsequent
    layers: Opal Petal 837.
Head, all layers: T Toast 132 and T Soft-Fusing Flux 426.
Tail, all layers: T Tan 131 and T Soft-Fusing Flux 426.
Feelers, all layers: T Peach 750.

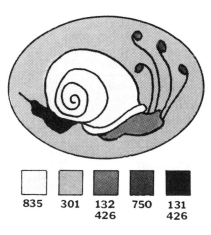

| 835 | 301 | 132 | 750 | 131 |
| | | 426 | | 426 |

first layer

116

Figure 10–3 *Snail* by Felicia Liban, 2″ wide × 1½″ high (5.1 × 3.8 cm high). Shaded soft pastels are used on an ivory background. The tips of the feelers are like rubies.

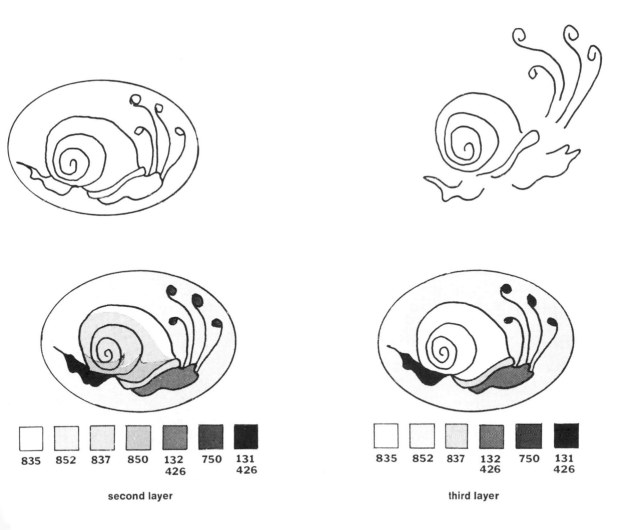

835	852	837	850	132 426	750	131 426

second layer

835	852	837	132 426	750	131 426

third layer

117

LOTUS

DIMENSIONS
Enameling cup: 1⅜″ (3.5 cm) diameter circle.
Cloisonné wire: .002″ (.05 mm) crinkled gold or silver.

WIREWORK
Cut and shape 26 wires as shown in the diagram.

COLORS
Background, first layer: O Ivory 334 and T Soft-Fusing Flux 426;
    second and subsequent layers: Opal Beige 852 and T Soft-Fusing
    Flux 426.
Petals, first layer: O Soft-Fusing White 644 and T Soft-Fusing Flux 426;
    second layer: (most petals) T Goldenrod 986, (some tips) T
    Forsythia 108; third layer: (around center) T Old Silver 1013,
    (some tips) T Tan 131, T Toast 132, and T Gold 724, (rest of
    petals) T Soft-Fusing Flux 426; fourth and subsequent firings: T
    Soft-Fusing Flux 426.
Center, first layer: O Lemon 1067 and T Soft-Fusing Flux 426; second
    layer: T Goldenrod 986; third layer: (tip of center) T Mikado 755,
    (rest of center) T Burnt Orange 531; fourth and subsequent layers:
    T Soft-Fusing Flux 426.
Leaves, first layer: O Ivory 334 and T Soft-Fusing Flux 426; second
    layer: T Emerald 121; third layer: (shadow) T Khaki 129, (rest of
    leaves) T Soft-Fusing Flux 426; fourth and subsequent layers: T
    Soft-Fusing Flux 426.
Stem, first layer: O Ivory 334 and T Soft-Fusing Flux 426; second
    layer: T Emerald 121; third and subsequent layers: T Soft-Fusing
    Flux 426.

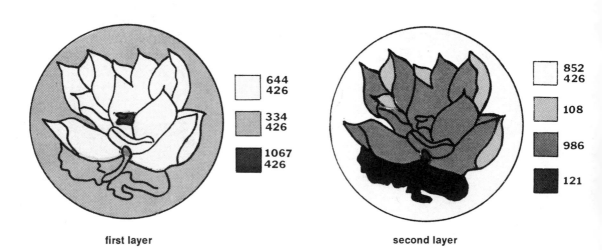

first layer

	644 426
	334 426
	1067 426

second layer

	852 426
	108
	986
	121

Figure 10—4 *Lotus* by Felicia Liban, 1⅜″ (3.5 cm) diameter. The flower is in soft shades of light yellow on a beige background.

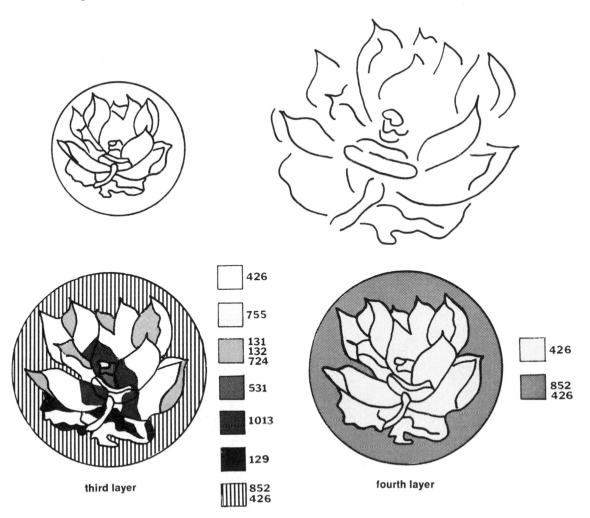

☐	426
☐	755
▨	131 132 724
▨	531
▨	1013
■	129
▥	852 426

third layer

☐	426
▨	852 426

fourth layer

FROG

DIMENSIONS
Enameling cup: 1⅛" (2.9 cm) diameter circle.
Cloisonné wire: .003" (.08 mm) crinkled fine silver or gold.

WIREWORK
Cut and shape 25 wires as shown in the diagram. The star is made by bending one wire into four or five points.

COLORS
Sky, all layers: T Pigeon 101, T Old Silver 1013, and T Soft-Fusing Flux 426.
Bullrushes, first layer: O Lemon 1067 and T Soft-Fusing Flux 426; second layer: T Palm 997, T Emerald 121, and T Shamrock 932; third and subsequent layers: T Soft-Fusing Flux 426.
Frog, first layer: O Canary 1069 and T Soft-Fusing Flux 426; second layer: (inner area) T Forsythia 108, (outer area) T Mikado 755; third and subsequent layers: T Soft-Fusing Flux 426.
Eyes, first layer: O Canary 1069 and T Soft-Fusing Flux 426; second layer: T Mikado 755; third and subsequent layers: T Soft-Fusing Flux 426.
Pupils, all layers: O Soft-Fusing Black W 10.
Nose, first layer: O Canary 1069 and T Soft-Fusing Flux 426; second layer: T Toast 132; third layer: T Chestnut 308.
Lily pad, first layer: O Arcadian 326; second layer: T Dark Olive 839 and T Evergreen 121; third and subsequent layers: T Soft-Fusing Flux 426.
Water, all layers: T Aquamarine 200, T Old Silver 1013, and T Soft-Fusing Flux 426.

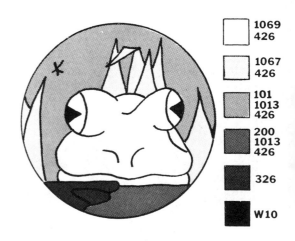

first layer

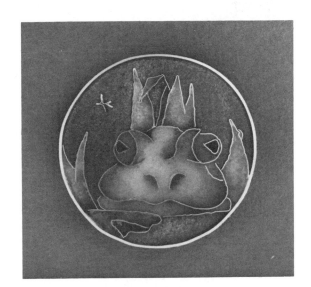

Figure 10–5 *Frog* by Louise Mitchell, $1\frac{1}{8}''$ (2.9 cm) diameter. An orange, yellow, and brown frog, shaded green bullrushes and lily pad, and turquoise water under a transparent blue-gray sky.

	101 1013 426
	108
	755
	132
	997 121 932
	200 1013 426
	839 121
	W10

second layer

	426
	101 1013 426
	308
	200 1013 426
	W10

third layer

JACK-IN-THE-PULPIT

DIMENSIONS
Enameling cup: 1¼" high × ¾" wide (3.2 × 1.9 cm) oval.
Cloisonné wire: .002" (.05 mm) crinkled gold or silver.

WIREWORK
Cut and shape 13 wires as shown in the diagram.

COLORS
Background, first layer: O Ivory 334 and T Soft-Fusing Flux 426;
    second and subsequent layers: 2 parts Opal Beige 852 and 1 part
    T Soft-Fusing Flux 426.
Petal, first layer: O Lemon 1067 and T Soft-Fusing Flux 426; second
    layer: (inner) T Palm 997, (outer) T Forsythia 108, T Amber 728,
    and T Tan (131); third layer: (highlight) O Medium-Fusing White
    118 of 150 mesh, (stamen) T Forsythia 108, T Amber 728, and T
    Tan 131; (rest of petal) T Soft-Fusing Flux 426, fourth and
    subsequent layers: T Soft-Fusing Flux 426.
Trumpet, first layer: O Lemon 1067 and T Soft-Fusing Flux 426;
    second layer: T palm 997; third layer: (top) T Burnt Orange 531,
    (bottom) T Mikado 755; fourth and subsequent layers: T Soft-
    Fusing Flux 426.
Leaves, first layer: O Lemon 1067 and T Soft-Fusing Flux 426; second
    layer: (top) T Lawn 160, (underside) T Emerald 121; third and
    subsequent layers: T Soft-Fusing Flux 426.
Stem, first layer: O Lemon 1067 and T Soft-Fusing Flux 426; second
    layer: T Khaki 129; third and subsequent layers: T Soft-Fusing
    Flux 426.

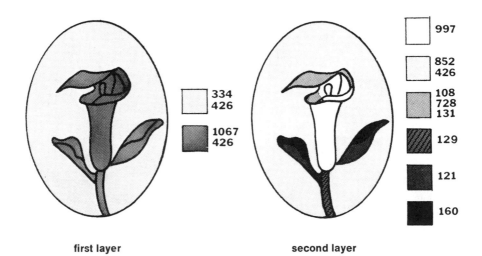

first layer

second layer

Figure 10–6 *Jack-in-the-Pulpit* by Felicia Liban, 1¼" (3.2 cm) oval. Greens, yellows, and light brown shaded delicately give a lifelike effect. The leaves are two tones of green, and the background is ivory.

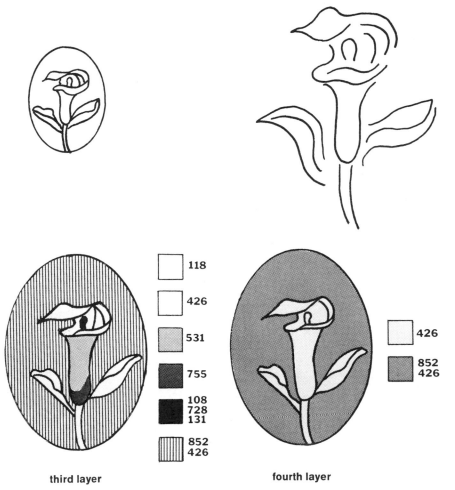

☐	118
☐	426
▨	531
■	755
■	108 728 131
▥	852 426

third layer

☐	426
▦	852 426

fourth layer

EPIDENDRUM ORCHID

DIMENSIONS
Enameling cup: $1\frac{3}{16}''$ wide $\times$ $1\frac{9}{16}''$ high (3 $\times$ 4 cm) oval.
Cloisonné wire: .002" (.05 mm) crinkled gold or silver.

WIREWORK
Cut and shape 11 wires as shown in the diagram.

COLORS
Background, first layer: O Medium-Fusing Black 124; second layer: T
    Smoke 834 and T Medium-Fusing Flux 1005; third and fourth
    layers: T Smoke 834 and T Medium-Fusing Flux 1005.
Leaves, first layer: O Arcadian 326; second layer: (highlights) T
    Shamrock 932, (highlight) T Goldenrod 986, (rest of leaves) T
    Soft-Fusing Flux 426; third layer: (highlights) T Palm 997, (rest of
    leaves) T Soft-Fusing Flux 426; fourth layer: T Soft-Fusing Flux
    426.
Stem, first layer: O Arcadian 326; second layer: T Soft-Fusing Flux
    426; third layer: T Palm 997, (highlight) T Soft-Fusing Flux 426;
    fourth and subsequent layers: T Soft-Fusing Flux 426.
Petals, first layer: O Soft-Fusing White 644 and T Soft-Fusing Flux 426;
    second layer: (highlights) T Shamrock 932, (highlights) T
    Goldenrod 986, (remaining petal) T Soft-Fusing Flux 426; third
    layer: (top) O Arcadian 326, (highlights) T Palm 997, (remaining
    petals) T Soft-Fusing Flux 426; fourth layer: (top) T Evergreen 234,
    (remaining petals) T Soft-Fusing Flux 426.

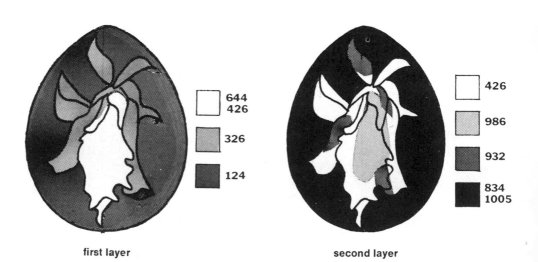

first layer

second layer

Figure 10–7 *Epidendrum Orchid* by Felicia Liban, 1 $\frac{3}{16}$″ wide × 1 $\frac{9}{16}$″ high (3 cm wide × 4 cm high) oval. Light and dark greens dominate the outside of the orchid. The white petals are shaded with green and the background is black.

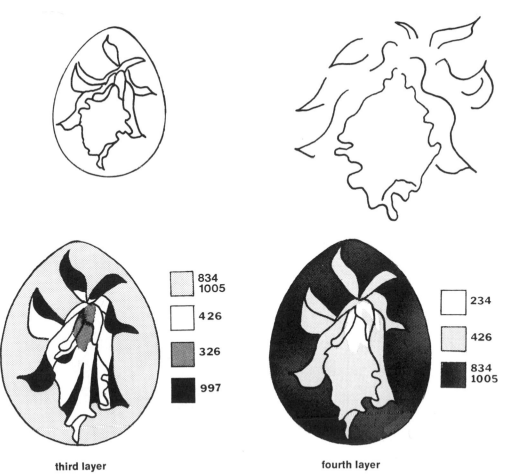

834 1005	
426	
326	
997	

third layer

234	
426	
834 1005	

fourth layer

PINK LADY'S SLIPPER

DIMENSIONS
Enameling cup: 1⅛″ (2.9 cm) diameter circle.
Cloisonné wire: .002″ (.05 mm) crinkled gold or silver.

WIREWORK
Cut and shape 20 wires as shown in the diagram.

COLORS
Background, all layers: 1 part each of T Lawn 160, T Smoke 834, T Khaki 129, and Opal White 835, and 4 parts T Soft-Fusing Flux 426.

Leaves, first layer: O Arcadian 326; second layer: (shadow) T Dark Olive 839, (highlights) T Emerald 121, (tips) T Ruby 674; third and subsequent layers: T Soft-Fusing Flux 426.

Stem, first layer: O Arcadian 326; second layer: T Dark Olive 839; third and subsequent layers: T Soft-Fusing Flux 426.

Pouch, first layer: (outside) O Petal 841, (inside) O Lemon 1067 and T Soft-Fusing Flux 426; second layer: (outside right and highlights left) T Ruby 674, (outside left) T Soft-Fusing Flux 426, (inside) T Forsythia 108, T Mikado 755, and T Amber 728, (inside top) T Dark Olive 839; third and subsequent layers: T Soft-Fusing Flux 426.

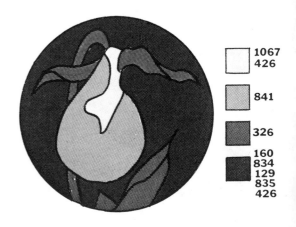

first layer

126

Figure 10–8 *Pink Lady's Slipper* by Felicia Liban, $1\frac{1}{8}''$ (2.9 cm) diameter. The pouch uses shades of pink and orange, with bright orange in the center. The leaves and stem are shaded in green and brown, and the background is dark green.

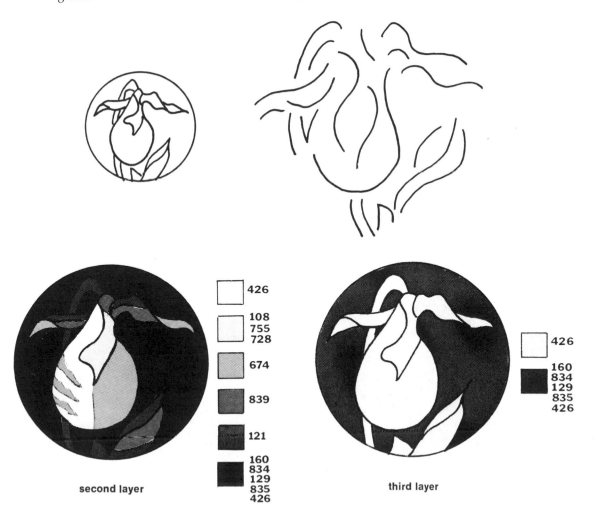

426	

108	
755	
728	

674

839

121

160
834
129
835
426

second layer

426

160
834
129
835
426

third layer

JONQUIL

DIMENSIONS
Enameling cup: 1½" (3.8 cm) diameter circle.
Cloisonné wire: .002" (.05 mm) crinkled gold or silver.

WIREWORK
Cut and shape 17 wires as shown in the diagram.

COLORS
Background, all layers: O Charcoal 463.
Petals, first layer: O Lemon 1067 and T Soft-Fusing Flux 426; second layer: (highlights) T Goldenrod 986, (shading) T Mikado 755, (center) T Burnt Orange 531; third layer: (highlights) T Goldenrod 986, (shading) T Toast 132, (remaining parts) T Soft-Fusing Flux 426; fourth and subsequent layers: T Soft-Fusing Flux 426.
Stem and leaf, first layer: O Emerald 478; second layer: T Palm 997; third layer: (stem highlight) T Mikado 755, (remaining parts) T Soft-Fusing Flux 426; fourth and subsequent layers: T Soft-Fusing Flux 426.

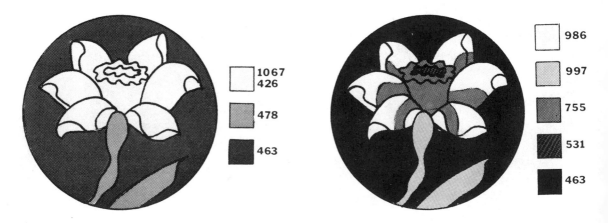

first layer

second layer

1067
426

478

463

986

997

755

531

463

128

Figure 10–9 *Jonquil* by Felicia Liban, $1\frac{1}{2}''$ (3.8 cm) diameter. Various yellows shaded with orange and light brown give the illusion of light and shadow. The stem and leaf are shaded green with brown, and the background is charcoal gray.

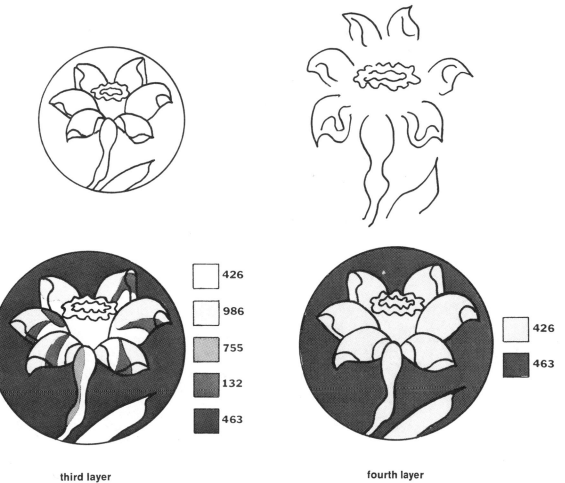

☐	426
☐	986
▨	755
▦	132
■	463

☐	426
■	463

third layer   **fourth layer**

129

RENAISSANCE PORTRAIT

DIMENSIONS
Enameling cup: 1¼" (3.2 cm) diameter circle.
Cloisonné wire: .002" (.05 mm) crinkled gold.

WIREWORK
Cut and shape 22 wires as shown in the diagram.

COLORS
Background, all layers: 1 part of T Chestnut 308 and 3 parts of T Soft-Fusing Flux 426.

Skin, first layer: O Nude 320 and T Soft-Fusing Flux 426; second layer: (highlights) T Soft-Fusing Flux 426, (medium shadow) T Toast 132 and T Soft-Fusing Flux 426, (dark shadow) T Toast 132; third layer: T Soft-Fusing Flux 426, (face highlights) O Soft-Fusing White 644, (neck) T Toast 132 and T Soft-Fusing Flux 426, (neck) T Toast 132; fourth layer and subsequent layers: T Soft-Fusing Flux 426.

Hair, first layer: O Ochre 664; second layer: T Mikado 755; third layer: (shadows) T Toast 132, (medium highlights) T Amber 728 and T Soft-Fusing Flux 426, (highlights) T Soft-Fusing Flux 426; fourth and subsequent layers: T Soft-Fusing Flux 426.

Eye, first, second, and third layers: (pupil) T Pigeon 101 of 150 mesh, (eyeball) O Soft-Fusing White 644 of 150 mesh, (eyelash) T Toast 132; fourth layer: T Soft-Fusing Flux 426.

Necklace and headband, first layer: O Soft-Fusing White 644, T Soft-Fusing Flux 426, and a pinch of T Champagne 130; second and subsequent layers: T Soft-Fusing Flux 426.

SPECIAL PROCEDURES
The same shading and highlighting techniques can be used to do portraits of real people. Be sure to select enamels that will most accurately portray your subject's coloring.

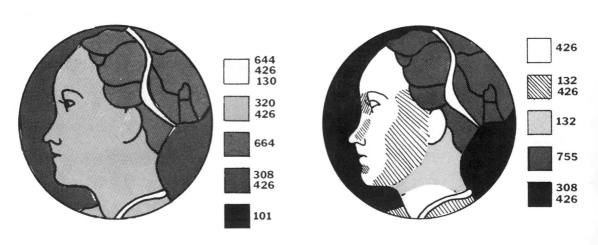

first layer

644
426
130

320
426

664

308
426

101

second layer

426

132
426

132

755

308
426

Figure 10–10 *Renaissance Portrait* by Louise Mitchell and Jean Reist Stark, 1¼″ (3.2 cm) diameter. A supple, delicate portrait inspired by Renaissance paintings.

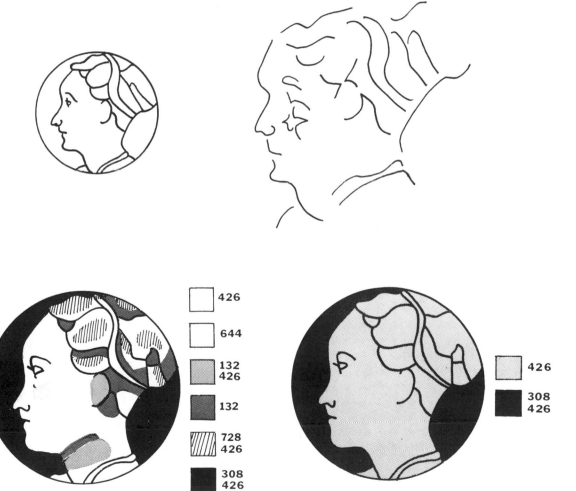

☐	426
☐	644
▨	132 426
▤	132
▨	728 426
■	308 426

third layer

☐	426
■	308 426

fourth layer

TWO/ JEWELRY SETTINGS FOR CLOISONNÉ ENAMELS

Silver
and
Gold
11

Practically any metal can be considered in making a jewelry setting. In addition to silver and gold, it is possible to use platinum, copper, aluminum, brass, pewter, and alloys or combinations of other metals. However, silver or gold are the traditional metals from which fine jewelry is made. They have the advantage of being strong and easy to work with, and they are the most compatible with cloisonné enamels since the wires used in a design are usually silver or gold.

There are several factors to consider when choosing between silver and gold for settings. If you are a beginner, it is best to begin with silver and leave gold for some small decorative touches. Silver is much less expensive than gold, and its lower cost also means that you can stock silver sheet and wire in a variety of gauges. Gold is easier to fuse than silver, and it is more malleable, ductile (capable of being drawn out or hammered thin), and resistant to corrosion. Silver, however, is almost as good in these respects. For a major piece, or a commissioned one, you might choose gold for your setting. Or, if the piece is very small, you might be able to afford to use gold. In some fine jewelry stores gold sells better than silver.

Most cloisonné enamels are made using fine (pure) silver for the wires and enameling cup, but a setting may require either fine silver or sterling silver. We will always indicate which to use for the projects in this book as they are not interchangeable and each has its own characteristics. For example, when annealed, fine silver sheet or wire can be easily bent or twisted into forms, and it lends itself especially well to bezels. However, fine silver dents quite easily, even when work hardened. Sterling silver is strong and resists denting, and therefore lends itself very well to settings.

Because pure gold is much too soft to use for settings, most settings made in gold use a gold alloy. Yellow gold is the best all-around alloy for jewelry making, and it is the one we normally use with our enamels.

Two other types of gold alloy are especially good for fusing and granulation. They are 22-karat alluvial gold and 18-karat "ancient" gold. Directions for fusing and granulation are given later in this chapter. Both alloys can be used in the same way as fine silver for items such as bezels or chains as they are quite malleable, but they are easily dented. Jewelry parts that need more strength, such as pin backs or hinges, must use 14-karat yellow gold, just as sterling silver must be used instead of fine silver.

BUYING SILVER AND GOLD

Metal suppliers can provide you with a wide range of metal sheet and wire gauges in fine silver and sterling, as well as base metals like copper and brass. Most suppliers can also provide a full range of karat golds. The Sources of Supplies in the back of the book lists several places that specialize in the needs of jewelry makers.

In the last few years the prices of precious metals have fluctuated widely. It pays to keep an eye on the price of metals. One way is to check the *New York Times,* which lists the prices at Handy & Harman and at Englehard in New York, as well as in other select world markets.

Metals for jewelry come in flat sheets, wire, and tubes. Wires are available in many shapes, including round, half-round, square, triangular, oval, and flat. Hollow tubing can either be round or square.

When you buy base metals, you need to specify the length, width, and gauge of the metal. Silver, however, is often ordered by weight rather than size. For example, you might ask for 20 pennyweight (dwt) of 18-gauge fine silver round wire. When buying gold you need to specify the color and karat as well—for example, 3 feet of 18-gauge, 14-karat yellow gold round wire.

The system of drams, ounces, and pounds in everyday use at the grocery store is called avoirdupois weight. Gold and silver, however, are weighed in troy weight. One ounce in troy weight is 1.09714 ounces in avoirdupois weight. To convert troy ounces to avoirdupois, you simply multiply by 1.097. To convert avoirdupois ounces to troy, multiply by 0.9115.

Table 11-1   Troy Weight

24 grains	= 1 pennyweight (dwt)
20 pennyweights	= 1 troy ounce
12 troy ounces	= 1 troy pound

You must also have the proper type of solder to go with the particular metals that you order. Hard silver solder comes in five grades according to flowing temperatures: IT, hard, medium, easy, and extra easy. Gold solders are graded by color and weight as well as by hard, medium, and easy. Solder should be about the same gauge as the metal to be soldered. Remember to always check the thickness of purchased solder and thin it if necessary. It can be pickled and cleaned before using.

ALLUVIAL GOLD

Alluvial (or "placer") gold is a type of gold panned from riverbeds. It is a 22-karat gold alloy that contains small amounts of fine silver and copper in proportions different from those in commercially made alloys. Commercial alloys may also contain other metals such as zinc and nickel. The ancient Etruscans used alluvial gold for their intricate granulation work. You can make alluvial gold in your studio to use for your own granulation work. You can also take your alluvial gold to a silversmithing shop to have it rolled into sheet or wire, or you can thin it yourself if you have a rolling mill.

Making Alluvial Gold

Alluvial gold contains 22 parts of 24-karat gold, $1\frac{1}{2}$ parts silver, and $\frac{1}{2}$ part copper. If you buy 22 pennyweights of 24 karat gold, you will simplify the weighing process. After adding $1\frac{1}{2}$ pennyweights of silver and 12 grains of copper, you will have 24 pennyweights or $1\frac{1}{5}$ troy ounces of alluvial gold alloy. This amount thins out to a workable size sheet to cut up into strips for bezels or to thin further into wire.

If you cannot begin with just 22 pennyweights of gold, table 11–2 tells exactly how much silver or copper you need for various amounts of gold.

Table 11–2   Amounts of Gold, Silver, and Copper in Alluvial Gold

GOLD	SILVER	COPPER
22 dwt	1 dwt, 12 gr	12 gr
21 dwt, 2 gr	1 dwt, 10.5 gr	11.5 gr
20 dwt, 4 gr	1 dwt, 9 gr	11 gr
19 dwt, 6 gr	1 dwt, 7.5 gr	10.5 gr
18 dwt, 8 gr	1 dwt, 6 gr	10 gr
17 dwt, 10 gr	1 dwt, 4.5 gr	9.5 gr
16 dwt, 12 gr	1 dwt, 3 gr	9 gr
15 dwt, 14 gr	1 dwt, 1.5 gr	8.5 gr
14 dwt, 16 gr	1 dwt	8 gr
13 dwt, 18 gr	22.5 gr	7.5 gr
12 dwt, 20 gr	21 gr	7 gr
11 dwt, 22 gr	19.5 gr	6.5 gr
11 dwt	18 gr	6 gr
10 dwt, 2 gr.	16.5 gr	5.5 gr
9 dwt, 4 gr	15 gr	5 gr
8 dwt, 6 gr	13.5 gr	4.5 gr
7 dwt, 8 gr	12 gr	4 gr
6 dwt, 10 gr	10.5 gr	3.5 gr
5 dwt, 12 gr	9 gr	3 gr
4 dwt, 14 gr	7.5 gr	2.5 gr
3 dwt, 16 gr	6 gr	2 gr
2 dwt, 18 gr	4.5 gr	1.5 gr
1 dwt, 20 gr	3 gr	1 gr
1 dwt, 22 gr	1.5 gr	.5 gr

To make alluvial gold, you need a fine balance scale with ounce, pennyweight, and grain weights, clean fine tweezers, soldering torch with #3 tip, two clean pieces of charcoal without any traces of soldering flux on them, some powdered borax, baking soda, and

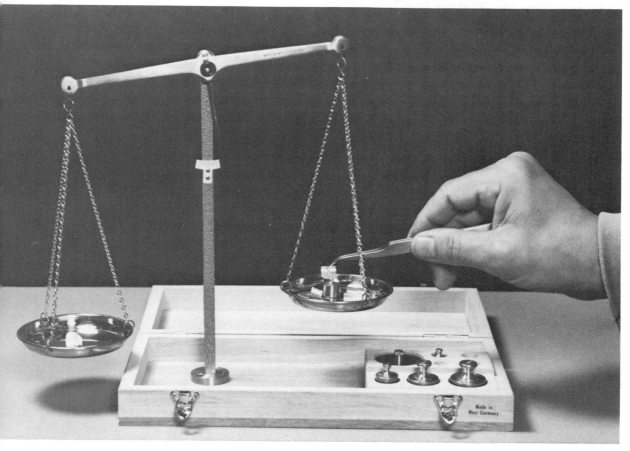

Figure 11–1 Use a balance scale such as this one to weigh gold alloy.

pickle. You will also need, of course, some gold, silver, and copper in the proportions described in Table 11–2. These directions apply to making *any* gold or silver alloy.

1. Place all of the metal in a jar of hot pickle for a few minutes. Rinse the metal in a solution of baking soda and water, then in clean water.

2. With tweezers or some other tool, make a small, shallow, rectangular indentation about ⅛″ (3 mm) deep and about ½″ × 1½″ (1.3 cm × 3.8 cm) big in a clean piece of charcoal block. Sand the surface of the charcoal smooth. This will be your melting surface. A metal ingot mold can also be used for this purpose.

3. Place the gold in the indentation. Heat the gold with a #3 torch tip (figure 11–2). When it becomes molten, drop in the silver and copper. Continue heating.

4. When all the metal is molten, add a pinch of borax to it. To stir the metal, move the torch flame around and make the glob of metal wiggle. Additional stirring can be done with a carbon rod. When mixed, turn off the torch.

138

Figure 11-2 Gold alloy is heated with the torch on a charcoal block until it becomes molten.

5. Press another clean block of charcoal on top of the molten metal glob to flatten it a bit. Then let it cool.

6. Immerse the hardened piece of metal in pickle and then rinse it. To be certain that the alloy is homogenized thoroughly, you can repeat steps 3 to 6 twice. You can now either make the alloy into wire or sheet, or store it as a lump until needed.

Solder for Alluvial Gold

You can use commercial 22-karat solder with alluvial gold, or you can make your own solder, melting together equal amounts of alluvial gold and either hard, medium, or easy silver solder. Follow the instructions for making alluvial gold, then roll out your solder with a rolling mill until it is thinner than the gold you wish to solder. Mark it clearly with the karat and type of solder.

MAKING ALLOY INTO SHEET AND WIRE

To make a lump of alloy into a sheet of metal, you need access to a rolling mill, a forming hammer, a micrometer, the torch, pliers, a steel block, and pickle.

1. Hold the lump of gold with pliers, using your weaker hand. Hold the forming hammer in your stronger hand, and hammer the lump against the steel plate. The gold will begin to flatten. As it becomes work hardened, anneal it with the torch. Continue hammering and annealing until the gold is flat enough to put through the rolling mill.

2. Put the gold once through the rolling mill, then anneal it. Repeat until the gold is as thin as you need. (Check from time to time with the micrometer). The gold sheet will be somewhat oval in shape.

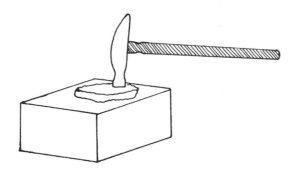

Figure 11–3 Alloyed metal must be flattened with a forming hammer before being made into sheet or wire.

3. When the gold sheet is the right thickness, pickle and clean in baking soda and water solution. It is then ready to use.

To make gold wire rather than sheet, it is a good idea to save the tiny excess pieces cut off from your alluvial gold sheet to remelt and use as wire. To make wire, you need the torch, a clean piece of charcoal block, the wire rolling mill, tweezers, drawplate and tongs, bench vise, a half-round file or 100-grit wheel, beeswax, and a wire gauge.

1. Make a long, narrow indentation in a clean piece of charcoal block. Melt your alloy with the torch, then let it cool. The slug of gold will be long, narrow, and round.

2. Open the rolls of the mill wide enough to accept the gold slug in the largest groove. Put the slug through the mill. Tighten the rolls slightly and insert the slug again. When the rolls meet, it is time to insert the slug into the next smaller groove (figure 11–4). You can usually roll the slug through the mill three or four times before annealing it. Continue annealing and putting the slug through the mill until the wire has gone through the smallest opening you need. It will be thin square gold wire. (See figures 11–4 and 11–5.)

3. If you want to make the wire round, secure an E or F drawplate in a bench vise (figure 11–6). Tighten the vise.

4. File a fine point on one end of your gold wire using a cut 2 hard file (or file it on a 100-grit wheel).

5. Anneal the wire with the torch using a #2 tip. Place the wire on a charcoal block or annealing pan and move the torch back and forth along every part of the wire. Turn the wire occasionally using soldering tweezers, and watch its progress very carefully. If you do this in reduced light, you will be able to see the wire glowing slightly as it reaches annealing temperature in each segment. It is important that every part of the wire be annealed or the wire will be in danger of breaking when pulled through the drawplate. You can also anneal the wire by winding the wire into a coil and putting it into a hot kiln for 20 seconds.

6. Wax the wire with beeswax along its whole length.

7. Place the point of the wire in the largest hole in the drawplate that secures it. Grip the end of the wire that is just peeking through with the drawtongs held in your stronger hand. With your weaker

Figure 11–4 The elongated lump of alloy is put through the largest opening in the rolling mill.

Figure 11–5 Place the wire in successively smaller openings in the rolling mill until it is the thickness you want.

Figure 11–6 Wire is pulled through the drawplate using tongs.

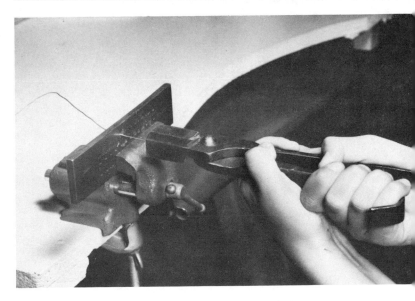

hand, squeeze the jaws of the drawtongs so they pinch the wire tip hard. Now give a short, hard pull on the tongs so the wire moves through about $\frac{1}{16}$" (1.6 mm). Release the tongs and regrab the wire close to the drawplate. Pull through $\frac{1}{16}$" (1.6 mm) again, and repeat until the point filed on the wire has come through the plate. Then pull the rest of the wire through in one continuous, smooth pull (see figure 11–6). Anneal.

8. Repeat this process, pulling the wire through progressively smaller holes in the drawplate. Anneal between each hole. As the wire lengthens, you will need to step further and further back to pull it.

9. Keep checking the diameter of the wire with the wire gauge until the wire is the size you want. If necessary, switch to a drawplate with smaller holes, such as an AK, to make the wire even thinner. Anneal a final time and the wire is ready to use.

ANCIENT GOLD

Ancient 18-karat gold is another gold alloy that can be made in the studio. It can be successfully fused and granulated, whereas 18-karat commercial gold cannot. However, it is not as easy to use as the 22-karat alluvial gold, and it has a paler greenish color that is not as rich looking as alluvial or commercial gold. It is stronger than a higher-karat gold, and this quality may be necessary for some pieces. If this alloy must be used, but a richer color is desired, the whole setting can be gold-plated when finished.

Ancient gold contains 18 parts of 24-karat gold, $5\frac{1}{2}$ parts silver, and $\frac{1}{2}$ part copper. Table 11–3 shows exactly how much of each you will need.

Table 11–3 Amounts of Gold, Silver, and Copper in Ancient Gold

GOLD	SILVER	COPPER
18 dwt	5 dwt, 12 gr	12 gr
17 dwt, 8 gr	5 dwt, 6.5 gr	11.5 gr
16 dwt, 12 gr	5 dwt, 1 gr	11 gr
15 dwt, 18 gr	4 dwt, 19.5 gr	10.5 gr
15 dwt	4 dwt, 14 gr	10 gr
14 dwt, 6 gr	4 dwt, 8.5 gr	9.5 gr
13 dwt, 12 gr	4 dwt, 3 gr	9 gr
12 dwt, 18 gr	3 dwt, 21.5 gr	8.5 gr
12 dwt,	3 dwt, 16 gr	8 gr
11 dwt, 6 gr	3 dwt, 1.5 gr	7.5 gr
10 dwt, 12 gr	3 dwt, 5 gr	7 gr
9 dwt, 18 gr	2 dwt, 23.5 gr	6.5 gr
9 dwt,	2 dwt, 18 gr	6 gr
8 dwt, 6 gr	2 dwt, 12.5 gr	5.5 gr
7 dwt, 12 gr	2 dwt, 7 gr	5 gr
6 dwt, 18 gr	2 dwt, 1.5 gr	4.5 gr

142

Table 11–3 continued

GOLD	SILVER	COPPER
6 dwt,	1 dwt, 20 gr	4 gr
5 dwt, 6 gr	1 dwt, 14.5 gr	3.5 gr
4 dwt, 12 gr	1 dwt, 9 gr	3 gr
3 dwt, 18 gr	1 dwt, 3.5 gr	2.5 gr
3 dwt,	22 gr	2 gr
2 dwt, 6 gr	16.5 gr	1.5 gr
1 dwt, 12 gr	11 gr	1 gr
18 gr	5.5 gr	.5 gr

Ancient gold is made the same way as alluvial gold. Follow the instructions on page 137. You can also make ancient gold sheet and wire, following the instructions given previously in this chapter. Use commercial gold solder with this alloy.

Advanced Metal Techniques

12

The most common way of joining two or more pieces of metal is through soldering. But there are several other methods of joining metals that you should know in order to provide variety and enhance your jewelry settings. This chapter will discuss fusion, which is the joining of metals with heat but without using solder; granulation, or the embellishment of settings by adding tiny balls of silver or gold in decorative patterns; and some cold metal techniques, which include ways of joining metals without heat, such as using rivets, hinges, nuts and bolts.

Note, though, that this book is not intended as a complete course in metalworking. The techniques included here are only those necessary to make settings for simple, classic pieces. Many more intricate techniques could also be included in your designs. The bibliography lists a number of good books that will increase your knowledge of metalworking.

FUSION

Fusion is a way of joining two or more pieces of metal using the heat of the kiln or torch, but without using solder. The metal is heated just enough so the surface of the metal flows, but not so much that the core of the metal melts. Once two adjacent pieces of metal have been heated to this degree, their surface will be joined when the metal cools. Fusion takes practice, but it is not as difficult as it might sound. The trick is to circle slowly and evenly around the outside of the piece with the torch flame to build up an intense "cone" of heat. Only then does the torch flame actually touch the joint to be fused just until the metal flows.

Fusion is a process that has many uses. For example, links of chain that will be shaped or bent after they have been joined should be fused rather than soldered, because solder is too hard and brittle to bend easily. A setting that will eventually include granulation must have all joints fused, because the heat necessary for granulating would melt any solder. In fact, any piece that will undergo intense or prolonged heating should have the first joint, such as the bezel seam, fused rather than soldered.

Fusion is quite successful with fine silver, 24-karat gold, 22-karat alluvial gold, and 18-karat ancient gold. Sterling silver and 14 karat gold can also be fused, but not as easily.

Fusing a Bezel Seam

As an example of fusion, let us say that you wish to fuse the seam of a silver or gold bezel before soldering the bezel to the back. You will need 26-gauge fine silver sheet or 22-karat alluvial gold for your bezel. You also need the torch, a #2 tip, flat-nosed pliers, soldering tweezers, a charcoal block, a glass of water, 220-grit dry sandpaper, the kiln, two steel blocks, ring mandrel, and pickle for cleaning.

1. Prepare the bezel as you would for soldering, but allow a bit of extra height in the bezel as there may be some shrinkage during fusing.

2. The two ends of the bezel must butt together firmly. This is accomplished by "springing" the ends. Once you have formed the bezel into a circle, make the circle even smaller by working the two ends past each other. Do this several times. This develops a spring to the bezel and work hardens it. When you then place the ends together, they will push against each other and form an even seam. Crimp the seam with flat-nosed pliers to further ensure that the two ends meet head-on, not at an angle.

3. Stand the bezel, seam side up, on a charcoal block (see figure 12–1). If necessary, flatten the bezel slightly to make it stand upright. Using the #2 torch tip, play the feather end of the flame around the top of the piece until you have built up a "cone" of heat. Then concentrate the flame on the joint, keeping the flame constantly in motion. The surface of silver will become molten-looking and shiny on both sides of the seam just before it is fused. Watch for a "flash" in the seam. Gold will glow slightly just before it is hot enough to

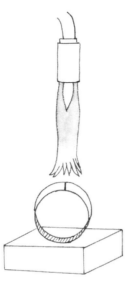

Figure 12–1 Fuse a bezel closed by heating the seam with the torch flame until the metal begins to flow.

fuse, but only the seam itself will actually look molten. Remove the heat as soon as the metal flows.

4. Cool the bezel immediately by dipping it with soldering tweezers in a glass of water. Then test the seam to make sure it is thoroughly fused. If it isn't, repeat the above procedure.

5. Sand the seam with 220-grit dry sandpaper. Also sand the top and bottom edges of the bezel so the bezel sits evenly. If the seam is still visible, it can be filed smooth.

6. Anneal the bezel in a hot kiln for 20 seconds. Put it on the mandrel and roll it gently on a wooden surface to work harden it. Then place the bezel between two steel blocks and press to make sure it is level. The ring mandrel will also reshape it into a circle if necessary. The bezel is now ready to be joined to the back piece of the setting.

Fusing Wires to Sheet

Another practical use for fusing is in attaching gold or silver wire to sheet, either for structural or decorative purposes. These same procedures can also be used for fusing a bezel to a base.

You will need fine silver or 22-karat alluvial gold wire and 26-gauge sheet metal. Also necessary are yellow ochre or typist's correction fluid, soldering flux, water, hide glue, a brush, the heat lamp, the kiln, firing tweezers, the torch with #2 tip, and pickle.

1. Paint a thin coat of yellow ochre or typist's correction fluid on the underside or back of the sheet. This will prevent it from melting in the kiln. Let the coating dry.

2. Mix a solution of one drop of hide glue, one drop of soldering flux, and 15 drops of warm water. Mix well and brush the top side of the sheet with this solution. Place the wires or bezel carefully on the glued surface, making sure the wires or bezel are positioned correctly and that they fit smoothly against the sheet with no air spaces.

3. Carefully move the sheet and wires under the heat lamp to dry. The glue will turn brown when dry. Once the glue is dry, the wires will stay in place during fusion and transportation. Plug in the kiln.

4. Move the piece into the hot kiln and cover. When the piece begins to glow (white for silver, cherry red for gold), uncover the kiln. The glue will have burned off.

5. Play the torch around the outside of the piece, directing the flame toward the kiln floor. This will evenly raise the temperature of the metal.

6. Watch for the metal surface to become shiny and just begin to flow. If there is a spot where the metal has not flowed, feather the tip of the flame over the spot. When all of the metal has flowed, immediately remove the flame and blow on the piece to reduce the temperature in the kiln. Remove the piece with firing tweezers and let cool.

7. Make sure the piece has been fused securely in all spots. If it isn't, repeat the above procedure. Then pickle and clean.

Fusing Sterling Silver

Fine silver is easier to control during fusion than sterling silver, but there is a method by which you can safely fuse sterling. You will need an annealing pan (a tuna fish can would do), pumice chunks, some wire mesh, Prip's flux, a brush, a tiny piece of copper, watchmaker's tweezers, the torch and a #3 tip, and pickle.

1. Place pumice chunks in a shallow pan and center a wire mesh on top of the chunks. Place the pieces to be fused on the wire mesh.

2. Anneal all the metal using a #3 torch tip (a soft flame).

3. Coat all surfaces with Prip's flux (except the bottom on the mesh, to keep it level). The surface will look chalky. Heat with the torch until the surface has turned glassy.

4. Take a copper shaving (about $\frac{1}{16}$" or 2 mm) with the tweezers and dip it in Prip's flux. Place it at the beginning of the seam where the fusion will take place. Keep playing the flame around the work (not directly on the metal). The copper will melt before the silver does. Draw the melting copper along the seam with the torch flame. This contact with copper will reduce the melting point of the silver along the surface of the seam, allowing it to flow. The rest of the silver never reaches melting point. A silver flash indicates that fusion has taken place.

5. Pickle and clean.

GRANULATION

Granulation is a method of embellishing metal by fusing tiny round balls of silver or gold to a metal surface in decorative patterns. It is an ancient technique used by the Etruscans in especially intricate and beautiful patterns. Granulation is a fine way to enhance settings for cloisonné.

Making Granules

To make the individual granules, you will need fine silver or 22-karat alluvial gold, either sheet or wire. You should also have ready the torch with #1 tip, charcoal block, shears, tweezers, a glass of water, paper towel, and an aluminum pie plate.

1. Set the charcoal block on the edge of an aluminum pie plate so that, as the paillons ball up into granules, they will roll off into the pie plate.

2. Using shears, cut as many paillons from your metal sheet or wire as you will need to complete your project. Particles that are $\frac{1}{32}$" to $\frac{1}{16}$" (.8 to 1.6 mm) square will make small to medium-size granules. Marking the metal with dividers will help ensure the paillons are all the same size. Place the particles about $\frac{1}{2}$" (13 mm) apart on the charcoal.

3. Heat the paillons by aiming the torch flame straight down on top of.

4. When all the paillons of metal have been formed into balls,

Figure 12–2 Examples of granulation on a pendant bail, a metal sphere pendant, a griffin brooch, and a tie tack.

pick them up with tweezers and put them in a glass of water to clean off any charcoal residue. Pour the granules onto a paper towel in the pie plate to dry. The granules can be further sized by sifting them through sized wire mesh.

5. The granules are now ready to use or to store for future use. Should any granules discolor before you need to use them, simply dip them in a small glass of hot pickle for a few minutes, then rinse with water. Dry on paper toweling in the pie plate.

Fusing Granules to a Base

Granules must be fused rather than soldered to a base because melting solder would fill in the spaces between the tiny balls and spoil the effect. If you have a soldered piece to which you wish to add granules, it is best to first fuse the granules to a thin base sheet, then cut the sheet around the granule pattern and, lastly, solder the sheet to the setting. Fusing granules directly to the soldered piece is not safe because the heat may melt the solder.

For fusing you will need gold or silver granules, fine silver or 22-karat alluvial gold sheet (26 gauge), yellow ochre or typist's white correction fluid, bobbing and white diamond (two common jeweler's polishing compounds), detergent, hide glue, soldering flux, water, a brush, the heat lamp, the kiln, and your torch with #2 tip, and firing tweezers.

1. Polish the side of the base sheet that will be decorated with granules using bobbing and white diamond. Clean the base sheet with detergent and rinse with water.

2. Brush the underside of the base sheet with a thin coat of yellow ochre or typist's correction fluid. Let it dry.

3. Mix a solution of 1 drop hide glue, 1 drop soldering flux, and 15 drops of warm water. Stir well. Place the base sheet on your worktable, ochre side down.

4. Use a small brush dipped in glue solution to pick up each granule and place it on the base sheet in your predetermined pattern. Use a magnifying glass if necessary. You will find that the granules will want to cling together because of the capillary action of the glue. It is therefore easier to form patterns such as triangles than straight line designs. Plug in the kiln.

5. Let the piece dry thoroughly. You can use the heat lamp to speed the process, and then put the piece directly on the heated kiln top.

6. When the glue turns brown, the piece is dry and can be placed inside the hot kiln with the firing tweezers. Leave the kiln top off.

7. The torch with a #2 tip should be turned on to a warming (small) flame. When the piece in the kiln begins to glow, play the feather tip of the torch flame around the outside of the piece. (See figure 12–3.) You will see the granules and the base begin to shine. If the piece is large you may have to play the flame across the top of the

Figure 12–3 Granules are fused to a bottom sheet by placing the piece in a hot kiln and playing the torch flame around it until the metal becomes shiny.

granules as well. When the piece begins to get shiny and wet looking, remove the heat, blow on the piece to stop the melting process immediately, and quickly take the piece out of the kiln with firing tweezers.

8. Test the granules by tugging on them with tweezers. If any of the granules lift off, repeat the above procedure. Let the piece cool.

COLD METAL TECHNIQUES

Cold metal joining techniques permit you to make whole settings without ever lighting the torch or heating up the kiln. You can also add materials other than metal to settings fabricated with cold metal techniques. Wood, plastic, industrial findings, and leather are just some of the interesting materials that can be used. Cold metal techniques include making rivets, using bolts and screws, nailing, gluing, and the various methods of cutting and shaping metal sheet and wire.

Rivets

A rivet is a small wire rod or thin tube that is inserted into holes drilled in the two pieces of metal to be joined. The rivet is flared at one end, inserted through the holes, then flared at the other end so it is secured in place. Rivets can be large and decorative, or they can be countersunk in the metal so they are hardly noticeable. Rivets that have heads on them are stronger than countersunk ones and should be used if there will be any tension placed on the joint. If the rivet is made to fit very tightly, then the joint will be immobile. If it is slightly loose, then the rivet will act more like a pivot and allow the joined pieces to move, especially if a small washer called a "heishi" is placed between the two metal pieces.

To make a rivet in your setting, you will need the pieces of metal to be joined, a drill with a high-speed twist drill bit, a flexible shaft machine or a drill press, a centerpunch, commercial hard-tempered nickel silver or brass rivet wire (sterling or 14-karat gold wire can also be used if put through a drawplate first for springiness), masking tape, saw, steel block, a chasing hammer, a dapping tool, a #2 cut file, and a small piece of wood.

1. Align the pieces to be joined and adhere them with double-faced tape or rubber cement. Mark the spot where the hole will be drilled for the rivet. Then lightly tap this spot with a centerpunch to make a slight indentation in the metal so the drill bit will not slip.

2. Drill a hole straight down through the metal pieces.

3. Wire for the rivet should have the same diameter as the drilled hole. Saw or snip off a piece of wire that is $\frac{1}{16}$" (2 mm) longer than the thickness of the pieces to be joined. File the sawed edges flat and true or the resulting rivet will be weak.

4. Now you will form one end of the rivet. First wrap a piece of masking tape around the wire rivet, leaving an unmasked tip. Place

the rivet in a vise with the unmasked tip protruding from the top of the vise.

5. File the end flat. Use the ball end of the chasing hammer to form a head by tapping the wire end in a circular pattern. The head can be left mushroom shaped or flattened.

6. Remove the rivet from the vise and take off the tape. Place the rivet in the hole you drilled through the metal pieces, upside-down so the rivet head is at the bottom.

7. If the rivet head you formed is flat, place the piece head-down against the bench plate. If the head is raised, then a piece of wood with a depression gouged into it can serve as a rest.

8. To form the bottom head of the rivet, now that the rivet is in place in the setting, place the tip of a blunt-ended center punch against the rivet and tap the center punch with the flat head of the chasing hammer.

Tube Rivets

You can make rivets from metal tubing as well as from wire. These will cause less pressure on the pieces being joined than solid wire, but they will not be as strong. To form the head of a tube rivet, use a center punch inserted in the end of the tube and tap lightly with a chasing hammer to flare it.

Telescoping Tube Rivets

If you have used an enameling cup, a stone can be set in the enamel, by using telescoping tube rivets. You will need thick-walled, unseamed stone-setting tubing which can be ordered from Delaware Jewelry Supply, a round cabochon or faceted stone, an enameling cup, slide calipers or a degree scale, a tube holding jig, a jeweler's saw, soldering equipment, a flexible shaft, a drill bit, a metal wire, a stone setting burr, oil of wintergreen, a vise, masking tape, a chasing hammer or dapping punch, and medium solder.

1. After making the enameling cup, mark the floor of the cup at the spot where the stone is to go.

2. Measure the diameter of the girdle of your stone with a slide caliper or a degree scale. Choose a piece of tubing whose outside diameter is $\frac{1}{2}$ mm larger than the girdle of your stone. Choose a second piece of tubing which will slide over the first tube and fit snugly.

3. Measure the height of the bezel of the enameling cup with dividers and scribe a length of the outer tube three times the height of the bezel. Saw the tube off in a tube holding jig at this scribe mark.

4. Drill a hole at the marked spot in the floor of the enameling cup. The outer tube should fit snugly in the hole.

5. Put the outer tube in the hole in the cup so that one-third of the tube sticks up and its top is even with the top of the bezel; two-thirds sticks out the bottom of the cup.

Figure 12–4 A Enameling cup with larger tube soldered in place. The narrower tube, in which the stone will be set, is lying next to the cup. On the right is a fired and polished enamel with the tube and stone set in place.

Figure 12–4 B The narrow tube "telescopes" into the larger one, as seen on the left, but first the layers of enamel must be fired in the cup.

6. Set the cup in Carborundum grains and solder the tube in place with medium solder. Pickle and rinse in baking soda solution.

7. Fill and fire, counter enamel (making sure not to plug the tube), and then polish the enamel.

8. You are now ready to set the stone in the narrower tube. Cut off a piece of tube ⅛" (3 mm) longer than the thickness of your enamel and file the end flat.

9. To keep the tube from collapsing while you set the stone, slip a piece of wire that fits snugly into the cavity of the tube. Wrap a piece of masking tape around the bottom of the tube to protect it. Place it in the vise with the unmasked tip up.

10. Choose a burr the same diameter as your stone or slightly smaller and put it on the flexible shaft. Dip the burr in oil of wintergreen and burr out a seat in the tube. Be careful to keep the burr in a vertical position.

11. Set the stone the same way you would an enamel (see Chapter 13).

12. Take the tube out of the vise and remove the wire and tape. Slip the tube, stone side up, through the tube in the enamel and check to be sure it is exactly 1/16" (1.6 mm) longer than the counter enamel. File off any excess.

Figure 12–5 Cloisonné enamels in silver by Felicia Liban and woodwork by Edward Lewand are combined in a jewelry box, a magnifier, a comb with hand-cut tortoise shell, a mirror, and a brush with boar's bristle. The box is walnut; the other pieces are rosewood.

13. Hold the enamel bottom up in the palm of one hand. With your stronger hand, flare the tube end by burnishing it with the ball end of a chasing hammer, dapping punch, or other small round-ended tool. Tape the flared end of the rivet to the counter enamel to keep it from sliding until it is held securely in the setting case.

Bolts and Screws

Bolts and screws can be used for decorative reasons, or for a piece that will have to be taken apart occasionally, such as a picture frame. You can simply buy commercial bolts, nuts, and screws in the sizes you need and then have them silver- or gold-plated, or you can make your own from sterling silver or 14-karat gold. The male and female threads must be formed with a tap and die set. Refer to a good jewelry handbook for instructions.

Bolts are designed to go through both pieces to be joined and then must be secured from behind with nuts. Screws should go through the top sheet and only part way through the bottom sheet. The decision to use either bolts or screws depends both on the function and the desired look of the finished piece.

Nails

There may be occasions when it is necessary to use nails in your jewelry settings, such as when metal must be secured over a wood core. Thin sheets of metal are most easily attached to wood by small nails. These can be purchased in many types of metal, and can be silver or gold plated. Nails can also be made from sterling silver or 14-karat gold wire, but the stems must first be pointed with a file and then work hardened.

Glue

Gluing pieces together is a last resort because the glue will disintegrate over time, but sometimes it is the only thing to do. Glue must be used, for example, to secure an enamel in a depression routed in a piece of wood. If you must use glue, use a good brand of contact cement or epoxy that you mix up right before you use it.

There are many different kinds and brands of glue. Read the labels to get the right glue for the right job. For instance, for materials such as wood or ivory, which expand and contract with temperature and humidity changes, you would need a glue that remains viscous.

Enamel
Settings
13

The size of your enamel is an important consideration in selecting a setting for it. An enamel could be a brooch, stick pin, pendant, ring, hair ornament, buckle, book end, or mirror back, but it should be of an appropriate size and weight for its intended use. The size, shape, and weight of the setting should also be appropriate for the function of the piece. A round enamel does not necessarily need a round setting. Nor does a setting need to be flat. It can be far more interesting to have a three-dimensional setting for a piece.

This chapter will describe a wide variety of settings. All settings, however, begin with a simple setting case designed to hold the enamel. This is no more than a bezel and back just like the original enameling cup, except that it is often made of a harder metal and its appearance is more finished. The enamel sits raised up inside the case, and a lip or rim must be formed around the edge to keep the enamel in place. Then you add whatever is necessary to the cup to make it into a usable piece of jewelry. For example, you would add a shank to make a ring, a bail (the hanging loop) for a pendant, or a catch pin to make a brooch. The final additions would be decorative, such as bits of granulation, wirework, or stones.

Settings can be made with a wide variety of materials—gold, silver, copper, wood, plastic, almost anything that can be fabricated. We will concentrate, however, on the classic enamel settings made from gold and silver. You can vary a setting through color (by combining colors of metals or introducing wood or ivory). You can also add texture with embellishments such as twisted wire or tiny metal granules. Another alternative is to make your setting move or to add other parts through hinges, rivets, and such decorations as dangling beads or stones.

No matter what type of setting you choose to make, it is important to remember that you must fabricate the entire setting *before* putting the enamel into the setting cup. This is because the enamel could be damaged by the heat needed to make the setting. Therefore, instructions for adding the actual enamel do not appear until the end of the chapter.

Whatever design you choose, we suggest you draw your setting on paper first. Then, if needed, you can actually make a model from clay or manila paper. Manila paper can also be used as a template

(pattern). Clay works especially well on a sculptural project because it can be so easily manipulated. When clay becomes leather hard you can also carve into it.

A particular technique may involve some very specialized tools that are not part of the general jewelry-making tools described in Chapter 1. These special tools are described in the sections where they are used, and purchasing them is dependent on whether you wish to try the particular project.

MAKING A SETTING CASE

A setting case is the basis for all pieces of jewelry that will hold an enamel. It protects the enamel from impact and hides the unattractive counter-enameled underside.

A setting case is made in much the same way as an enameling cup, except that its back is generally made of stronger metal and the solder is placed inside rather than outside the bezel for a neater appearance. The bezel should fit loosely around the enamel and should be high enough so its edge can be bent over the enamel to secure it.

To make a setting case you will need 26-gauge (.016" or .4 mm) fine silver or 22-karat alluvial gold for the bezel. Sterling silver or 14-karat gold should not be used because it is not malleable enough. A thinner metal would be too fragile, and a thicker sheet would not bend easily enough. For the back, you should use a metal that is 26 gauge or thicker. Sterling silver, or 14- or 18-karat gold, will be stronger than fine silver or 22-karat gold, but stronger metals are a bit more difficult to solder. The actual thickness of a backing sheet depends on the size of the enamel. The larger the piece, the thicker the back needs to be.

The tools necessary for making a setting case are soldering equipment, bezel shears, set-screw dividers, a pencil and piece of masking tape, firing tweezers, a ring mandrel, two steel blocks, a charcoal block, a ruler, pickle, baking soda and water solution, and 150-grit dry sandpaper.

1. Measure for the height of the bezel by finding the thickness of your enamel with the dividers. Open the dividers to $\frac{1}{8}''$ to $\frac{3}{16}''$ (3 to 5 mm) more than the thickest part of the enamel. (The actual height of the bezel depends on the size of the enamel and how heavy you wish the case to look). Score the metal with the dividers.

2. Determine the length of the bezel by using a piece of masking tape to measure the circumference of the enamel. Make the length of the bezel $\frac{1}{4}''$ (6 mm) longer than the enamel's circumference. Mark this length on the scored metal sheet with a pencil.

3. Cut out the bezel using bezel shears. Then anneal the bezel with the torch for a few seconds.

4. Form the bezel into a circle and fit it around the outside of the enamel. Make sure the bezel fits exactly, then mark the metal where it overlaps with a pencil. Cut off the extra bezel length, making sure the cut is straight. Spring the two bezel ends by working the ends past one another. When you place the two ends together, they should butt up against each other very firmly and form an even seam.

5. The bezel can be closed by fusing or soldering. To fuse, follow the directions in Chapter 12. (Remember it is best to use fusion if you will be adding granules later.) To solder, place the bezel on edge on a charcoal block. Cut a $\frac{1}{16}''$ (1.6 mm) square of IT solder and place it directly beneath the seam of the bezel. Brush a drop of soldering flux on the seam.

6. Light the torch with the #1 tip and run the feather tip of the flame around the bezel to evenly build up heat. When the bezel is hot enough, the solder will flow into the seam. Remove the torch, pick up the bezel with firing tweezers and dip it in water to cool it. Let the bezel dry.

7. Reshape the bezel by placing it on a ring mandrel and rolling it on a steel block. Turn the bezel upside down on the mandrel and roll again so the bezel forms an even circle. Do any further shaping (a square or other shape) with pliers using drafting tools for guides. Then set the bezel aside.

8. Prepare the back piece by placing your enamel on the sheet of metal and penciling a square that is $\frac{1}{8}''$ (3 mm) larger than the enamel

all around. Cut out the square and flatten it between two steel blocks. It is at this point that we stamp our pieces with the appropriate metal classification or logo.

9. Place the bezel on the back to check for fit. Sand the top and bottom edges of the bezel with 150-grit dry sandpaper until there is a perfect seam between the bezel and the back. The bottom edge of the bezel should rest evenly on the back, with no gaps.

10. Place the back, stamp side up, on the steel mesh of the tripod and warm it with the torch. Coat it with Prip's flux and dry until it turns white. Turn it over and center the bezel on the back. Brush soldering flux all around the inside of the seam where the bezel joins the back. Dry the flux by heating it slightly with the torch from underneath the tripod.

11. Cut enough $\frac{1}{16}$" (1.6 mm) pieces of medium solder that they can be placed at $\frac{1}{4}$" to $\frac{1}{2}$" (6 to 13 mm) intervals around the inside of the bezel. The larger your piece of jewelry is, the less distance should be left between solder snippets.

12. Using watchmaker's tweezers, place the bits of solder evenly around the inside of the bezel seam.

13. Using a #2 tip on the torch, heat the bezel and back from underneath the tripod. Use the middle part of the flame and move in a circular motion. When the soldering flux turns brown, then glassy, the solder is ready to flow. Watch for a thin, shiny line to appear along the seam. Press down on the top of the bezel with a soldering pick if there is a spot where the bezel is not touching the back. Then remove the torch.

14. Clean the setting case in hot pickle and rinse in baking soda solution.

15. Add any embellishments you want to the setting cup, such as twisted wire or granulated patterns. When all the necessary soldering has been completed, trim the excess metal from the back sheet with bezel shears or a saw.

16. Sand off any remaining edge on the setting cup with 150-grit dry sandpaper. It is helpful to place the sandpaper on your worktable and to move the setting cup, tipped on its side, along the sandpaper with a swiveling motion. Or you can file off the edge. The setting cup is now ready to be made into the ring, pendant, or other piece of jewelry you have planned.

MAKING A SEATED BEZEL CASE

A seated bezel case is another way of setting the enamel that also reduces the amount of silver or gold needed. The setting cup just described actually holds the enamel, using silver or gold or a combination of both. For the seated bezel case, silver or gold is still necessary to surround the enamel, but the metal on the back of the piece can be eliminated by using other materials such as ivory, slabs of semiprecious stone, bone, exotic woods, leather, plastic, or almost anything that you would like to use. All of these materials are readily

Figure 13–2 Cloisonné enamel pendant with a flower set in a silver seated bezel case.

Figure 13–3 The zebrawood backing to the flower pendant in figure 13–2.

Figure 13–4 Cloisonné enamel pendant with an edelweis, set in a silver seated bezel case.

Figure 13–5 The ivory backing to the edelweis pendant in figure 13–4.

available and lend themselves to embellishment. Both stones and ivory can be purchased at gem and mineral shows or through stone dealers. Ivory can be carved or decorated with scrimshaw; leather can be tooled, wood must be cut and polished. Plastic is easy to cut and comes in a variety of colors. The cost of the setting can be greatly reduced in this way.

A seated bezel case can be used to set two things (an enamel and ivory backing, for example) in order to hide the unsightly back of one of them. It can also be used to set only one thing which has a back worth displaying. This would be true of a cabochon, stone, ivory, or a cloisonné enamel whose counter enamel was a good color and polished.

A seated bezel case consists of a wire bearing that fits snugly inside a bezel. Commercial sterling seated bezel wire is available (it may be called step bezel wire or two-step bezel wire). The commercial wire has a very narrow seat. If you make your own, you can make the sterling seat wider and the outer bezel of fine silver, whose flexibility is advantageous in setting enamels.

To make the seated bezel case, you will need 26-gauge fine silver or 22-karat gold for the bezel. For the bearing you will need square 16-gauge sterling or 14-karat gold wire, depending on which metal you are using for the bezel. You will also need IT, hard, medium, and easy silver solder, or 12-karat medium and 12-karat easy solder if you are working in gold.

Tools needed include bezel shears, set-screw dividers, a pencil, masking tape, double-stick tape, soldering equipment, a ring mandrel, a steel block, a tripod, a charcoal block, a ruler, a small brush, heated pickle, copper tongs, and 150-grit dry sandpaper.

1. Determine the length of the bezel by using a piece of masking tape to measure the circumference of the enamel. (This should have the same circumference as the backing.) Remove the tape and put it on the metal sheet, making the length of the bezel ⅛" (3 mm) longer than the circumference. Mark this length with a pencil.

2. To determine the height of the bezel, take the cut and shaped backing (ivory, stone, wood, etc.) and secure it to the enamel with double-stick tape. Open the dividers ⅛" (3 mm) wider than the sandwiched pieces. Score the metal for the bezel with the dividers.

3. Cut out the bezel using bezel shears. Then anneal the bezel with the torch or in a hot kiln.

4. Fit the bezel around the outside of the enamel. Make sure the bezel fits exactly, then mark the metal where it overlaps. Cut off the extra bezel length, making sure the cut is straight. Spring the two bezel ends by working the ends past one another. When you place the two ends together, they should butt up against each other firmly and form an even seam.

5. The bezel can be closed by fusing or soldering, as described on pages 146 and 159.

6. After soldering, reshape the bezel by placing it on a mandrel and rolling it gently against a steel block. Turn the bezel upside-down on the mandrel and roll it again so it is not cone shaped. Sand the

162

Figure 13–6 Seated bezel case. Square wire is soldered inside the bezel.

top and bottom edges until the bezel sits flat. Do any further shaping (an oval or other shape) with pliers using drafting tools for guides. Then set the bezel aside.

7. To make the bearing, anneal the square wire and cut it to size the same way you did the bezel. You want the square wire to fit *airtight* inside the bezel. When it fits, take it out, spring the ends and butt them like you did with the bezel. Solder the seam with hard silver solder. Pickle, rinse, and dry.

8. Take the bezel, round it out, and place it on a steel block. Fit the shaped and soldered bearing into it so the bottom edges are flush with each other (see figure 13–6).

9. Put the bezel with the bearing or "seat" in it on a charcoal block with the seat up. Cut tiny pieces of medium silver solder. Flux and dry the seat of the bezel. With tweezers, place the solder snippets ¼" (6 mm) apart on the seam between the wire and the bezel. Turn on the torch with tip #2, and run the feather tip of the flame around the bezel to evenly build up heat. When the metal is hot enough, the solder will flow into the seam between the bearing and the bezel. Remove the torch, pickle, rinse, and dry.

10. Add any embellishments or findings to the case that are needed for the jewelry setting.

11. The final step, of course, is setting the enamel and the backing into the seated bezel case. Before doing this, polish and clean the seated bezel. The procedures for polishing and setting are described later in this chapter.

PENDANTS

Pendants deserve particular attention because they are one of the most popular cloisonné settings, and also because they offer a good deal of variation in design and decoration.

To make a pendant, you only need to add a bail to the setting case. The bail is the metal loop on the pendant through which you put the chain. Because commercially available bails are limited in design, we will give instructions for making several different styles. You might begin with a simple half-round wire bail, then move on to more elaborate ones. Whichever you choose, make sure to keep the bail in proportion to the size of the pendant. It should be large enough to accomodate the chain that will go through it, but not so large that it dominates the enamel design.

The chain you choose for your pendant can be a simple link chain, an intricate hand-formed chain (see Chapter 14) or even a silken rope that has graceful silver endings. Many chains can be

Figure 13—7 Pendant by Felicia Liban depicts a thistle, $1\frac{1}{4}$″ × $1\frac{1}{2}$″ (32 mm × 38 mm).

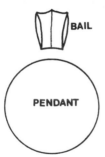

Figure 13—8 The size of planned bail should be in proportion to the setting case (this bail is too large). The bottom of the bail should be shaped to conform to the curve of the setting case.

bought through jewelry finding suppliers. A small pendant might look best on a 15-inch (38 cm) chain worn high at the neck. A larger pendant can take a longer chain, such as one that is 19 inches (48 cm) long, or a forged neckwire. Silk or synthetic cord or rope can be cut to the desired length and knotted or finished with commercial silver finials.

Half-Round Wire Bail

To make the simplest form of bail you will need 10-gauge half-round sterling silver wire, round-nosed or forming pliers, bezel shears, a pencil, a bowl of Carborundum grains, a third-arm with self-locking tweezer, medium solder, the torch with #2 tip, soldering flux, a small brush, pickle, and 150-grit dry sandpaper or a needle file.

Figure 13–9 Simple bails include, from left to right, a half-round wire bail, a loop bail, and a figure-8 bail.

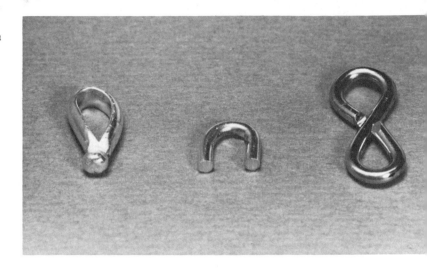

1. Shape the wire bail by placing the middle of the nose of fine round-nosed or forming pliers about $\frac{1}{4}''$ (6 mm) from the end of the wire. With a twisting motion, turn the wire back on itself so it forms a teardrop.

2. Cut the ends of the wire with bezel shears so the two ends of the teardrop are even. Then, holding the bail by the loop, sand the ends with 150-grit dry sandpaper to make sure the ends are straight. The teardrop bail should be able to stand on end.

3. Decide which part of the setting case should be the top, and mark it with a pencil. If necessary try the enamel in the setting case to help you decide.

4. Embed the setting case (without the enamel) straight up in the bowl of Carborundum grains so that just the top with the pencil mark shows. Place the flat end of the teardrop bail in the tweezers of the third arm.

5. Brush some soldering flux on the pencil mark at the top of the setting case and dry it. Cut a $\frac{1}{16}''$ (1.6 mm) square of medium solder and place it on the soldering flux. Light the torch with #2 tip and heat the case with the middle of the flame until the solder melts. Remove the torch.

6. Put another drop of soldering flux on the melted solder. Then lower the third arm until the ends of the bail are centered over the melted solder. Make sure the bail is straight and touching the solder. Relight the torch and wave the feather end of the flame over the back of the setting case (not on the bail). Make sure the bail is securely soldered on. If it isn't secure, clean off oxidation, rinse in pickle, reflux, and reheat. Only add more solder if it seems it's really needed. Once the enamel has been set, it will be more difficult to repair the bail.

7. Clean the setting in hot pickle, rinse with baking soda and water, and dry. Sand off any solder marks with 150-grit dry sandpaper or with a flat, blunt needle file. The bail and setting case is now ready to be polished.

Loop Bail

A loop bail is made with round wire. It can be attached to the back of the setting case so as not to be seen, or it can be attached to the top of the case, where it will be visible. Attached vertically, as in figure 13–10, a loop bail can accommodate a small chain. Attached horizontally, a figure-8 bail can be hooked into it to accommodate a larger chain.

The loop bail is made with 18-gauge sterling silver or 14-karat gold round wire (do not anneal it before use). The tools you will need are a mandrel (for a vertical bail), round-nosed pliers, bezel shears, a pencil, a bowl of Carborundum grains, a third-arm with self-locking tweezer, medium solder, the torch with #1 and #2 tips, soldering flux, a soldering pick, a small brush, pickle, and 150-grit dry sandpaper or a needle file.

1. Shape the wire into a U if it is to be attached to the back of the case or the bezel. For a graceful vertical bail, shape the wire into a round using a mandrel so the ends almost, but don't quite, meet. If you have made a U shape, sand the ends flat (see figure 13–9).

2. With a pencil, mark the point on the setting case where you will attach the bail. To solder the bail onto the bezel, embed the setting case in a bowl of Carborundum grains so that just the part to be soldered shows. Set the loop with the ends facing up into the third arm (see figure 13–11). Flux the ends and the part of the case to be soldered and dry.

3. Point solder two $\frac{1}{32}$" (.8 mm) squares of medium solder onto the two flat ends of the loop using the #1 torch tip.

4. Reverse the bail in the tweezer so the ends are pointing down, then lower the bail into the desired position on the setting case. Sweat solder the bail onto the setting case using the #2 tip on the torch. Wave the flame back and forth on the case beneath the bail, keeping the heat away from the bail itself, and remove the torch as soon as the solder flows.

5. Pickle and clean the bail and setting case. Sand or file off any solder marks, then polish.

Figure 8 Bail

This bail is designed to hook into a loop bail that has been attached horizontally, so the pendant swings freely (figure 13–9). It can also be used in place of a jump ring on the end of a chain. Like your loop

Figure 13–10 A loop bail can be soldered to the setting case in this position.

166

Figure 13–11 Place the loop bail in the tweezers of the third arm for soldering. Two paillons of solder will be point soldered on the ends.

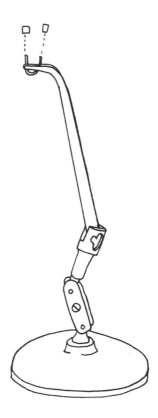

bail, it is made from either 18-gauge sterling silver or 14-karat gold round wire that is left unannealed. The tools you will need are chain-nosed pliers, round-nosed or forming pliers, a mandrel if needed, a file, and your soldering tools if desired.

1. To shape the figure 8, place one end of the wire in the middle of the round-nosed or forming pliers. With the chain-nosed pliers, turn the end until it forms a loop and meets the side of the wire. Form another loop in the reverse direction, and cut off the wire where it meets the side. File both wire ends so they lie flat against the sides of the wire.

2. Open one of the loops sideways to hook the bail into the loop. Close the loop again and you have a free-swinging device to slip a chain through. This figure 8 is strong enough to hold a chain without being soldered because it has been left unannealed and therefore is hard. You could solder the ends to make it more secure.

Simple Flared Bail

A flared bail does more than just hold the chain—it adds elegance to any pendant. The simplest flared bail is made by cutting out a pattern in 26-gauge (.015" or .4 mm) sterling silver or 14-karat gold sheet.

To make it you will also need your soldering tools, round-nosed pliers, pencil and paper, double-stick tape, scissors, bezel shears, pickle, and a half-round needle file.

Figure 13–12 The simple flaired bail.

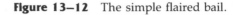

Figure 13–13 An enlarged pattern for a simple flaired bail. A is the widest point and B notes where a lip should be made.

1. Cut your paper into the shape shown in figure 13–13. Make sure to keep the size of the bail in proportion to the size of the enamel.

2. Place the paper pattern on the metal sheet with double-stick tape. Then cut the metal around the pattern; remove tape and pattern. Leave the metal unannealed to avoid oxidation and to improve its strength.

3. Using round-nosed pliers, bend the bail in half at the widest point (point A in the diagram). Near the narrow end of the bail, bend up a lip until the two ends meet (point B).

4. Brush flux on the joint and point solder it with medium solder. Pickle and clean.

5. Shape the bottom of the bail with a half round file so it fits snugly on the top of the setting case bezel (see figure 13-8).

6. Point solder the bail to the top of the setting case with easy solder. Pickle, clean, and polish.

Repoussé Flared Bail

The repoussé flared bail (figure 13–14) is more decorative than the simple flared bail, and making it involves a metal-shaping technique called repoussé. Special repoussé tools are pressed into the metal, which is placed face down on a soft surface. This bail is much more

168

Figure 13–14 The repoussé flaired bail.

complicated than the previous ones, but the results are well worth the effort. It is a beautiful and classical accompaniment to a cloisonné enamel. If you want to make a number of these bails, it may be worth your while to make one perfect one from which you can make a mold and cast duplicates.

To make the repoussé flared bail you will need 26-gauge fine silver or 22-karat alluvial gold sheet, and some 22-gauge fine silver or 22-karat alluvial gold wire. You will also need soldering tools, the kiln, bezel shears, two steel blocks, a center punch or ring mandrel, pickle, 150-grit dry sandpaper,a repoussé tool and piece of felt, a flat needle file, forming pliers, the third arm, a charcoal block, and a bowl of Carborundum grains.

1. The finished bail should be about one-fourth as wide as it is long. Cut a rectangle from the metal sheet that is sufficiently long to make your bail and about ⅛″ (3 mm) wider than the planned finished measurement. This excess will be cut off later.

2. Cut three pieces of wire the same length as the metal rectangle. Anneal these and the rectangle in the kiln for about 10 seconds.

3. Flatten the rectangle between two steel blocks. Roll the wires between the blocks to straighten them.

4. Gently curve two of the wires by pressing them around the largest part of a mandrel.

5. Place the rectangle on the tripod. Arrange the wires on the rectangle so the straight wire is in the center and a curved wire is on either side. The three wires should all touch each other at each end of the rectangle (see figure 13–15). The bail can now be fused, as described in Chapter 12, or soldered, as described in the following steps.

6. Flux the wires and the rectangle. Make sure the wires are exactly in position. Then dry the flux by lightly heating the piece from underneath with the torch.

7. Cut two tiny pieces of IT solder and place one at each of the wire ends. The solder should curve down over the wire ends as shown in figure 13–15. Run the middle of the torch flame (#1 tip)

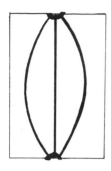

Figure 13–15 Position the wires on the sheet in this way. The solder is placed over the ends of the wires as shown here.

back and forth along the piece from underneath the tripod until the solder flows.

8. Remove the torch. Pickle and clean the piece. Next trim off the excess metal sheet from around the outside of the curved wires. Sand the sides and the ends of the piece with 150-grit dry sandpaper until they are smooth.

9. Place the bail, with wires facing down, on a piece of felt that has been folded into several layers. Using the large ball of the repoussé tool or a small dapping punch make two indentations along the length of the bail between the wires. Anneal in the kiln for 10 seconds. Make another indentation along each of the first ones with the smaller ball of the repoussé tool or a smaller dapping punch. Anneal again in the kiln. Trim away the excess metal from the width of the bail.

10. Hold a center punch in your weaker hand, wrap the bail around it with the wires against the center punch and squeeze the ends together with your fingers. Remove the center punch and press tightly with forming pliers. File the ends with a flat needle file or 150-grit dry sandpaper so they make a beveled joint (see figure 13–16).

11. Embed the bail, ends up, in a bowl of Carborundum grains, and flux. With a #1 torch tip, heat a piece of medium solder on a charcoal block until it forms a ball. Heat the ends of the bail with the torch until the flux turns brown. Pick up the warm ball of solder with a soldering pick. Then touch the solder on the pick to the joint between the ends of the bail. The solder will flow into the joint. Quench the bail in a glass of water to cool it.

12. File a shallow curve across the soldered end of the bail with a half-round file, as shown in figure 13–17. This groove will hold a small ball of metal that will then be soldered to the pendant. Return the bail to the bowl of Carborundum grains, soldered end up.

Figure 13–16 File the edges of the bail ends so they form a beveled joint.

170

Figure 13–17 File a circular groove in the edge of the bail with a half-round file to accommodate a ball.

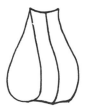

Figure 13–18 Solder the ball into the groove bail.

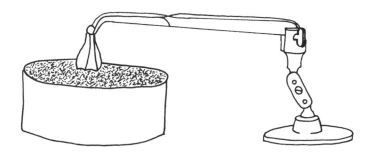

13. Cut a $\frac{1}{4}$″ (6 mm) square of fine silver or 22-karat alluvial gold. Place it on a charcoal block and heat with the torch until the metal forms a ball. When cool, flux the ball.

14. Cut a $\frac{1}{16}$″ (1.6 mm) square of medium solder, and place it on the charcoal block. Pick up the solder with the soldering pick and sweat solder it down on top of the ball by heating the ball until the solder melts.

15. Turn the tweezers of the third arm so the piece of solder on the ball faces down. Lower it so it touches the curved end of the bail (figure 13–18). Flux the groove and the solder, then heat the area with the feather tip of the torch flame until the solder flows. Pickle, clean, and polish the bail.

16. Using 150-grit dry sandpaper, file a flat area on the bottom of the ball where it will attach to the bezel of the setting case.

17. With a pencil mark the top of the setting case where it will be soldered and embed it in a bowl of Carborundum grains.

18. Place the bail in the third arm with the ball end up. Sweat solder a $\frac{1}{16}$″ (1.6 mm) piece of easy solder onto the flattened end of the ball, using a #1 torch tip.

19. Lower the bail, ball end down, onto the pencil mark on the setting case. Make sure the bail is straight, then flux the joint. Play the torch (#2 tip) around the setting case and ball, but not directly on the bail, until the solder flows. The bail will then seat itself onto the setting case. Pickle, clean, and polish the entire piece.

Repoussé Straight Bail

A straight bail can be made in the same basic design as the repoussé flared bail. Simply omit the center wire and keep the side wires straight instead of curved. The wires can be affixed either inside or outside the bail. Otherwise, follow the same directions as for the repoussé flared bail.

Figure 13—19   The repoussé straight bail.

Wire-Embellished Bail

A strong-looking geometric bail can be made easily from a rectangle of sheet metal covered with wires in a simple pattern (figure 13–20).

To make it you will need 26-gauge fine silver or 22-karat alluvial gold sheet, 22-gauge fine silver or 22-karat alluvial gold wire, and 16-gauge square gold or silver wire the same thickness as your bail. Also necessary are shears, the kiln, two steel blocks, a tripod, 150-grit dry sandpaper, a center punch or forming pliers, a pencil, pickle, and soldering equipment.

1. From the metal sheet, cut a rectangle that is in proportion to your enamel. Cut four wires that have the same length as the rectangle. Anneal all five pieces in the kiln for about 10 seconds.

2. Flatten the sheet between two steel blocks. Roll the wires between the blocks to straighten them.

3. Set the rectangle on a tripod. Position the wires on top of it lengthwise so the wires lie side by side touching each other and a little space is left before the edge on the long sides of the sheet. Flux the wires and sheet all over, then dry from underneath with the torch.

4. Cut two pieces of IT solder that are each about $\frac{1}{16}$" (1.6 mm) wide by $\frac{1}{8}$" (3 mm) long. Curve these pieces of solder around both

Figure 13—20   The wire-embellished bail.

ends of the rectangle and wires. Heat from underneath with the #1 tip on the torch. The solder will flow under the lengths of wire. Remove the heat. Pickle and clean the bail.

5. Make sure all the wires are firmly attached. If not, resolder. Then cut away the excess sheet metal from the sides of the wires and sand the sides of the bail until they are smooth.

6. Using a center punch or forming pliers as a shaping tool, form the bail into a circle. Make sure the ends butt against each other firmly.

7. Embed the bail, ends up, in a bowl of Carborundum grains. Flux and dry. Cut a piece of medium solder and point solder the joint. Pickle and clean.

8. To shape the bail into a teardrop, put it on a center punch and press the sides of the bail together with your fingers on either side of the seam. File a flat seat at the seam the width of your square wire.

9. Cut a $\frac{1}{8}$" (3 mm) piece of the 16-gauge square wire and file it flat. Put it in the self-locking tweezer of the third arm. Sweat solder a $\frac{1}{32}$" (1 mm) piece of easy solder onto the filed end of the wire.

10. Place the bail, flat end up, in a bowl of Carborundum grains. Turn the tweezer in the third arm so the soldered end of the wire faces down. Lower the wire so it touches the flat end of the bail. Heat with a #1 torch tip until the solder flows. Pickle and clean.

Spherical Bail

This is perhaps the most beautiful type of bail (and it can be used as a base for granulation), but it is quite difficult to make. It requires some specialized equipment including a circle cutter, a dapping block, and dapping tools, and it involves fusing (described in Chapter 12).

In addition to the tools mentioned above, the spherical bail requires 26-gauge fine silver or 22-karat alluvial gold sheet, and 20-gauge fine silver or 22-karat alluvial gold wire. You will also need 220-grit dry sandpaper, the kiln, a drill, two steel blocks, soldering equipment, iron binding wire, a mandrel, a charcoal block, a flexible shaft machine with a bud burr, oil of wintergreen, a half-round file, third arm, and self-locking tweezers.

Figure 13–21   The spherical bail.

173

If you don't have dapping tools, or if you just want to save yourself some work, you can purchase a gold or sterling silver bead and start with step 7 below.

1. Place your metal sheet in a circle cutter and make two $\frac{1}{2}$" (13 mm) diameter circles (see figure 13–22). Anneal the circles in a hot kiln for 10 seconds.

2. Place one of the circles in the largest hole in the dapping block. Use the dapping tool to form a slight dome in the metal (figure 13–23). Anneal the metal. Continue to use successively smaller holes until the circle becomes a hemisphere. Anneal the metal after it is removed from each hole to soften it. Repeat the same procedure with the second circle.

3. Check to make sure the two hemispheres form a perfect sphere when placed together. If not, anneal and redap until they are shaped properly. Then sand the rim of each hemisphere until they are smooth and flat.

4. Drill an 18-gauge hole in the center of the top of each of the hemispheres (figure 13–24). Hold the two pieces so they form a sphere (figure 13–25), and thread binding wire through the two holes. Twist the ends of the wire together so the pieces become immobile.

5. To avoid crushing the sphere, secure it in the third arm, by placing either the whole sphere (seam parallel to tweezer arms) or just the ends of the binding wire in the tweezers. Using the #1 tip on your torch, fuse the two hemispheres together.

6. Sand the fused seam with 220-grit dry sandpaper until the surface is smooth. You can also buff the sphere with a rouge stick if desired.

7. Make two $\frac{1}{4}$" (6 mm) diameter circles out of 20-gauge fine silver wire. Put the circles on the charcoal block and fuse the ends using the #1 torch tip.

8. Reshape the circles by placing them on the end of a center punch and rolling it on a steel block. Then flatten each circle by pressing it between two steel blocks.

9. Place the sphere on a charcoal block with one of the holes facing up. Place one of the rings of wire around the hole. Flux the ring and area around the hole and dry. Cut four $\frac{1}{32}$" (1 mm) squares of medium solder and carefully place them on the sphere inside the wire ring.

10. Using the feather tip of the torch flame (#1 tip), heat the sphere with a circular motion until the solder flows.

11. Repeat this process on the other hole of the sphere with the second wire ring.

12. Put a small bud burr on the flexible shaft machine and lubricate it with oil of wintergreen. Hold the sphere securely and rout out first one hole, then the other, almost up to the wire rings. Be sure to hold the piece tightly; if it slips from your hand, it may be badly dented by the machine.

13. To make a large granule, cut a piece of fine silver or alluvial gold about $\frac{1}{4}$" (6 mm) in diameter. Heat the silver or gold on a

Figure 13–22 Cut a circle from the sheet metal with a circle cutter.

Figure 13–23 Form the circle into a hemisphere in the dapping block.

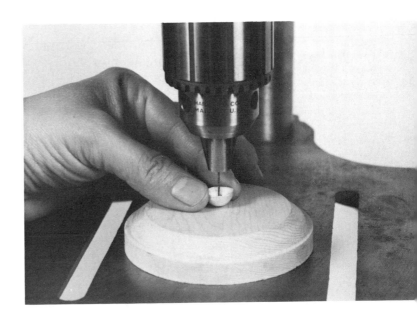

Figure 13–24 Drill a hole in the center of each hemisphere.

175

charcoal block with the torch until it forms a ball. Rinse with water, then use a half-round file to make a flat spot where the ball will be attached to the sphere.

14. Set the sphere in a bowl of Carborundum grains so the two holes are on the sides and the "belly" of the bail is facing up. Heat the sphere with the torch, then touch the spot where the granule will be attached with a drop of flux. Cut a $\frac{1}{16}$" (1.6 mm) piece of medium solder and place it on a charcoal block. Heat it with the torch and pick it up with a soldering pick. Place the solder on the fluxed spot on the bail, and continue to heat the bail until the solder melts in place. Add more flux to the top of the solder and dry.

15. Place the granule in the tip of self-locking soldering tweezers in the third arm. Touch the flat side of the granule down on the solder on the top of the bail. Heat with the torch from above until the solder flows. Pickle and clean the bail.

16. Put the setting case, front facing forward, in a bowl of Carborundum grains and put the bail in the tweezers of a third arm with the granule facing down. Flux the spot on the case where they will join and place a small square of easy solder on it. Melt the solder using a #2 torch tip. Lower the bail until the ball is touching the solder on the case. Brush flux on the joint. Heat the case, moving the flame under the bezel, until the solder flows. Pickle, clean, and polish before setting the enamel.

RINGS

A ring setting can be the perfect way to display a small enamel. The enamels that work best are circles that are no more than about $\frac{1}{2}$" (13 mm) in diameter, and ovals, squares, or rectangles of a similar size. Depending on its design, a ring can look strong and heavy or quite delicate, so when designing the ring, keep in mind the person who will wear it.

The part of the ring that goes around the finger is called the shank. Making a ring for a cloisonné enamel can be as simple as attaching a commercial ring shank to a setting case, then adding your

Figure 13–25 Silver ring with moss agate, made by Felicia Liban, has a flat wire shank and granulation on each side.

176

enamel. Shanks that have been cast from metal can be purchased from a jewelry findings supplier in a wide range of ring sizes. Most craftspeople, however, prefer to make their own ring shanks.

This chapter will detail five different ring shanks representing various degrees of complexity. First, you must make your setting case, then the ring shank. After finishing and polishing the entire ring setting, you put in your enamel.

Half-Round or Flat Wire Shank

The simplest ring shank is made from heavy wire soldered to the sides of the setting case. You will need either 14- or 16-gauge half-round sterling silver wire, or 16- or 18-gauge rectangular sterling silver wire. Eighteen- or 14-karat gold wire can also be used. Tools include a ring sizer, ring mandrel, bezel shear, pencil, bobbing and white diamond (jeweler's polishing compounds), soldering equipment, charcoal block, third arm with self-locking tweezers, and 220-grit dry sandpaper.

1. Measure the size of the finger that will wear the ring with a ring sizer or with iron binding wire. Make sure the ring will be able to slide off over the knuckle. Slip the ring sizer or wire onto a ring mandrel. If the mandrel is calibrated, note the correct ring size where the sizer has stopped. If uncalibrated, mark the spot where the sizer stopped by wrapping a piece of tape around the mandrel.

2. Hold one end of the half-round or flat wire against the spot on the mandrel that is one size smaller than the planned ring size. Wrap the wire around the mandrel until it overlaps (figure 13–26). When you release the tension on the wrapped wire it should drop down on the mandrel to the correct ring size. Double-check the loop size by placing it on the finger, if possible, or comparing it to the ring sizer or measuring wire.

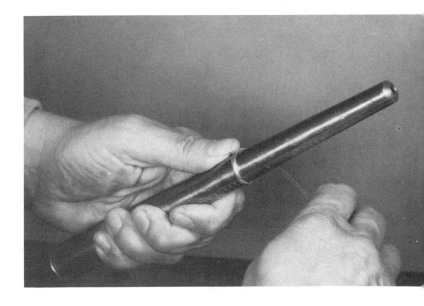

Figure 13–26 Bend the ring shank around a mandrel.

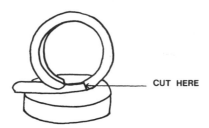

CUT HERE

Figure 13–27 Position the shank on the setting case and mark the spot where the wire is to be cut.

3. The wire will be soldered near the edge of each side of the setting case. To determine where to cut the wire, place the wire loop against the back of the setting case. The spot where the wires overlap should be at one spot where the shank will be soldered. With a pencil, mark the spot where the other end of the wire will be soldered (see figure 13–27). Cut the wire at this mark. You will now have a U-shaped piece of wire.

4. Place a piece of 220-grit dry sandpaper on your worktable. Hold the shank so the two ends touch the sandpaper. Sand until both ends are perfectly flat.

5. Polish the back of the setting case with bobbing and white diamond compound. Once the shank is soldered on, it is difficult to polish around it.

6. Place the setting case face down on a charcoal block. Place the shank, ends down, in the tweezers of a third arm. Move the arm so the ends are positioned on the back of the case. Prip's flux the ends and all areas of the setting case that have been polished and dry.

7. Cut two $\frac{1}{16}"$ (2 mm) pieces of medium solder. With a #2 tip and a low flame, point solder the ends to the case, placing the solder on the inside of both joints so the solder marks will not show. Pickle and clean.

Twisted Wire Shank

Making twisted wire is not a difficult process, and it can enhance many types of settings. It is especially attractive when used as the shank of a ring that is intended to look delicate and feminine.

You will need one foot (30.5 cm) of 18-gauge sterling silver wire, a vise, an empty thread spool or a heavy cardboard circle with a hole in the center, a large (6 or 8 penny) nail, 220-grit dry sandpaper, a third arm, charcoal block, and soldering equipment.

1. Bend the length of wire in half. Secure the two ends together in the jaws of the bench vise.

2. Slip the thread spool over the loop at the other end of the wire, and slip a nail through the loop (figure 13–29). Twist the nail in one direction until the wire actually looks beaded rather than just twisted. The resulting wire is stronger and more decorative than a single wire. You can also twist wire using a hand drill with a hook attached in place of a bit (see figure 13–29).

3. Proceed to form a shank and solder it to the setting case as described for the half-round or flat wire shank.

Figure 13–28 The twisted wire shank.

Figure 13–29 Make twisted wire either with a drill (top) or with a spool and a nail.

Wire-Embellished Shank

If the plain flat wire shank is not as decorative a style as you like, this wire-embellished shank may provide the right alternative. The technique used to make this shank is similar to that for the wire-embellished bail.

You may use sterling silver or 22-karat gold. You will need 30-gauge sheet and 24-gauge wire. Tools include shears, two steel blocks, a tripod, soldering equipment, 150 grit dry sandpaper, ring sizer and mandrel, and pickle.

Figure 13–30 The wire embellished shank.

1. Determine the ring size using a ring sizer and a mandrel as in step 1 of the half-round wire shank. From the metal 30-gauge sterling sheet cut a rectangle that is about ¼" (6 mm) wide and long enough to make the ring. Cut four pieces of wire the same length as the rectangle. Anneal the sheet and wires in a hot kiln for 10 seconds.

2. Flatten the sheet metal between two steel blocks. (At this point you can stamp the shank with the metal classification or logo.) Roll the wires between the blocks to straighten them.

3. Set the sheet on the tripod. Position the wires on the rectangle so they lie side by side touching each other down the center of the sheet. There should be space between the outside wires and the edges of the sheet. Flux the wires and sheet all over, then dry from underneath with the torch.

4. Cut two pieces of hard solder that are each about ⅛" (3 mm) long. Curve these over both ends of the rectangle and wires. Heat from underneath with the torch until the solder flows. Pickle and clean. Cut away the excess sheet and file or sand the sides.

5. Form the shank and, using medium solder, solder it to the setting case in the same way as described for the flat wire shank.

Split Wire Shank

A delicate feeling can be given to a ring by making a split wire shank. The shank can be made with two, three, or four wires.

You will need 18- or 20-gauge sterling silver or 14-karat gold wire. Tools include a ring sizer and ring mandrel, shears, soldering equipment, two steel blocks, iron binding wire, chain-nosed pliers, and pickle.

1. Determine the ring size with a ring sizer and mandrel, or with a length of iron binding wire. Cut three pieces of gold or silver wire this length.

2. Anneal the wire in a hot kiln for 10 seconds, then roll each wire between two steel blocks to straighten them. The wires should be work hardened before they are soldered together, and rolling them will accomplish this.

3. Bind the wires together tightly with iron binding wire in three places as shown in figure 13–32. Use chain-nosed pliers to twist and tighten the closings of the binding wires. Spread the ends of the gold or silver wires so they are not touching, then place them on a charcoal block.

4. Flux the areas between the wires and dry. Cut $\frac{1}{16}$" (1.6 mm) squares of medium solder and place them along the length of the inside seams between the binding wires as shown in figure 13–32. Use the #1 tip on the torch, and play the feather part of the flame back and forth along the shank wires until the solder flows.

5. Secure the shank in a third arm, with one end of the wires hanging down. With the #1 tip on the torch, heat the ends of the wires. The metal will melt and form a ball. Reverse the tweezers so the other side hangs down and repeat.

6. Remove the binding wires. Pickle and clean. Form the ring

Figure 13–31 The split wire shank.

Figure 13–32 Bind the wires of the split shank together and place on a charcoal block for soldering. Position the solder as shown by the dark spots on the drawing.

shank around the mandrel, and spread the ends of the wires apart to fit your setting case.

7. File the balls so they fit the setting case smoothly. Solder the balls to the case following the directions for the half-round or flat wire shank.

Sheet-Metal Shank

It is also possible to form a ring shank from a flat piece of metal sheet (see figure 13–33). Such a shank forms its own bezel, so the enamel does not require a setting case. The resulting ring is solid and regal in appearance. It works very well with a large rectangular or square enamel.

To make it you will need copper foil or manila paper, double-stick tape, 18- or 20- and 26-gauge sterling silver sheet, a bench pin and jeweler's saw with 2/0 blade, a hammer and anvil, a ring mandrel, flat-nosed pliers, a file, soldering equipment, shears, a small brush, micrometer, #2 cut file, and pickle.

1. Make a pattern from copper foil or manila paper that conforms to figure 13–34 and fits the finger that will wear the ring. (The copper foil is better than a paper pattern because it will stay on the finger for sizing.) Cut out the pattern and stick it to your 18- or 20-gauge sterling silver sheet with double-stick tape.

2. Place the silver and pattern on a bench pin and cut around the pattern with a jeweler's saw, using a 2/0 blade. Remove the pattern and tape.

3. Place the shank on a ring mandrel and shape it to fit the appropriate ring size. Then, with flat-nosed pliers, bend the shank

181

just a little at points A and B (see figure 13–34). Remove the shank from the mandrel, and use the hammer and anvil to gently bend the metal at points A and B until the sides form a right angle to the curve of the shank (figure 13–35). Recheck the fit of the shank on the finger or mandrel. Sand all the edges.

4. Bend the shank at 90° angles at points C, D, E, and F. A hammer and anvil will help with bending.

5. Butt end G to end I and end H to end J, springing the ends past each other so they form a tight joint (figure 13–36). Use hard solder and the #2 tip on the torch to solder the ends together. This forms a bezel for your enamel.

6. Next you will make a floor for the bezel from 26-gauge sterling sheet. It is best to make a paper pattern first. Cut the floor a bit larger than the actual opening, then file the edges for a perfect fit. The floor should be shaped so it fits snugly, meets the shank smoothly, and appears to be part of the shank itself.

7. When the floor fits the bezel exactly, embed the shank in Carborundum grains and place the floor inside the shank. Flux the seam and let dry. Place tiny squares of medium solder all along the seam and point solder with the #2 tip on the torch.

8. The bezel is too thick as is to bend easily over the enamel. To remedy this, file the rim at a 45° angle until the edge of the rim is only .012" to .015" (.3 to .4 mm) thick. Pickle, clean, and polish. Set your enamel directly into the bezel following the directions at the end of this chapter.

A variation of this shank is to solder a bearing of square wire into the bezel, instead of a floor. This is especially effective with a stone set into the ring, or with an enamel that has a pleasing counter enamel on it.

PINS, EARRINGS, TIE TACKS, AND CUFF LINKS

You can turn your enamel into a brooch, earring, or other small piece of jewelry by adding commercial findings. These attachments include pin catches, earring posts and wires, cuff link backs, and stickpin posts with end covers. Most commercial findings are strong and readily available, so we recommend that you purchase rather than make these items.

Pins or brooches provide an ideal setting for large enamels. Use very small enamels with cuff links, earrings, stickpins, and tie tacks. As always, you must make the setting case before adding the necessary findings.

Pins or Brooches

The setting for a brooch or pin can be left plain or can be elaborately embellished. But no matter what the decoration, you must add a pin back finding. This item has three parts: the joint, the catch, and the pin stem. Pin backs are available in a variety of lengths. You can also add a loop bail to the back of the setting case, so the enamel can

Figure 13–33 Felicia Liban made this ring shank from silver sheet.

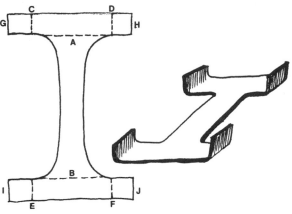

Figure 13–34 A pattern for a ring with bezel included.

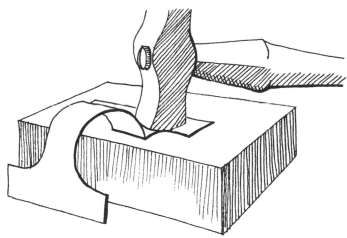

Figure 13–35 Shape the ring using a hammer and anvil.

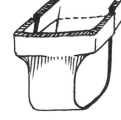

Figure 13–36 The edges of the bezel must butt perfectly.

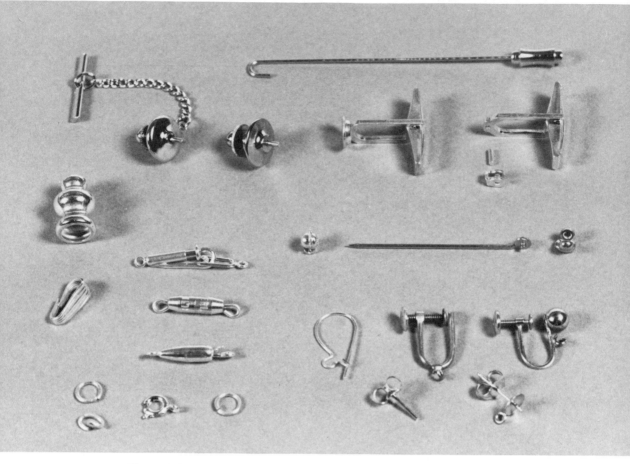

Figure 13–37 A selection of the commercial findings that are available for earrings, pins, cuff links, tie tacks, etc.

function as both a pin and a pendant, or you can slip a convertible bail made out of tubing over the pin stem (see figure 13–38).

To attach a commercial pin back to your setting case you need a pencil, a charcoal block, soldering equipment, two self-locking tweezers, pickle, bobbing, white diamond, chain-nosed pliers, and riveting tools.

1. Determine the placement of the pin stem, joint, and catch on the back of the setting case. Offset the position of the hinge slightly so the pin stem will be under tension when it is closed (see figure 13–39). Mark the positions of the joint and catch on the case back with a pencil.

2. Place the setting case upside down on a charcoal block. Flux the entire back with Prip's flux. Cut two $\frac{1}{16}$" (1.6 mm) pieces of easy solder and place them on the two marked spots on the case. Sweat the solder down.

3. Place the joint in a self-locking tweezer in a third arm. Flux

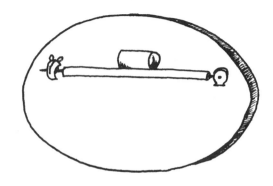

Figure 13-38 A convertible bail made out of tubing slips over the pin stem of a brooch.

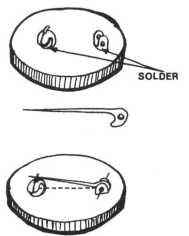

Figure 13-39 Position the joint and clasp so they are slightly out of line with the pin stem so the stem will be under tension when held in the clasp.

SOLDER

and dry. Holding the torch in your weaker hand (#2 tip), and moving the flame in a circular pattern, heat the setting case (not the findings) until the solder flows. If you are skilled enough, you can eliminate the third arm. With your stronger hand, pick up the self-locking tweezer with the joint in it and set it on one blob of melting solder, and remove the heat and tweezer. Repeat the process for the catch. Pickle and clean.

4. Before adding the pin stem to the joint, polish the setting case with bobbing and white diamond (see the end of this chapter). The last step is to rivet the joint closed. Then set the enamel.

Stickpins, Earrings, and Tie Tacks

The enamels for these pieces of jewelry have to be quite small—about a half inch (13 mm) in diameter— and the setting case should be kept simple. The basic procedure for soldering any of these findings to a setting case is the same for all. You will need soldering equipment, a charcoal block, a third arm, and pickle.

1. Place the setting case face down on a charcoal block. Place the earring post, stickpin, or tie tack post in the self-locking tweezer of the third arm with the part that will be soldered to the setting case facing up.

185

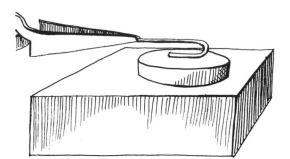

Figure 13–40 Solder the stickpin finding to the setting case in this position.

2. Cut a $\frac{1}{32}''$ (.8 mm) piece of easy solder. Flux the end of the finding that will be attached to the setting case, then sweat the solder down on the finding, using a #1 torch tip.

3. Reverse the tweezer so the soldered end of the finding can be lowered onto the exact spot where it will be soldered to the setting case. With the stickpin, make sure the curved end does not extend beyond the edge of the case or it will show when worn (see figure 13–40).

4. Prip flux the back of the setting case and dry. Using the #1 tip on the torch, with a circular motion, heat the setting case (not the finding) until the solder flows. Then pickle, clean, and polish before setting the enamel.

Cuff Links

The standard cuff link finding has three parts: a joint similar to that of the pin back, a stem that is attached to the joint by a rivet, and a swiveling arm at the end of the stem. Stem and swiveling arm together are called the counter swivel.

You will need two small enamels with setting cases and findings, as well as the soldering equipment, shears, a hammer and anvil, a center punch, a small brush, tripoli, rouge, and a charcoal block.

1. Place both setting cases face down on a charcoal block. Prip flux and dry the back of the setting case. Cut two $\frac{1}{16}''$ (1.6 mm) pieces of easy solder and sweat solder the joint to the case (figure 13–41). Pickle and clean.

2. Polish the cases with bobbing and white diamond.

3. Position each counter swivel in a joint and insert the rivets through the holes (figure 13–41).

4. Turn one cuff link on its side on a small anvil. Place a center

Figure 13–41 Sweat solder the cuff link joint to the setting case, then add the swivel and rivet.

punch on top of the rivet and use a hammer to carefully hammer the end of the rivet flat. Do the same with the other end of the rivet.

5. Repeat the hammering process with the second cuff link. Check to make sure the cuff link swivel works properly and that the joints are secure. Then set the enamels (see the end of this chapter for instructions).

BELT BUCKLES

A belt buckle is an ideal setting for a large or unusually shaped enamel. It also works well with enamels and settings that are quite vibrant or intricately patterned. One point to remember is that there are "male" and "female" belts. Men's clothes fasten from the right to the left, whereas women's clothes fasten from left to right. The belt, of course, can be made from a great number of materials, such as leather, fabric, or woven yarn.

Figure 13—42 Belt buckles, clockwise from lower left: ritulated quartz set in silver and gold by Dick Pritz; "Coffee and Cake" cloisonné by Felicia Liban; jasper set in silver by Louise Mitchell; abstract cloisonné on black background by Felicia Liban; and cloisonné landscape set in silver by Felicia Liban.

The following instructions are for the simplest type of belt buckle. It is made from a regular bezel-and-back setting case. To this is soldered a loop to attach the buckle to the belt and a hook that will go through a hole in the other end of the belt. The setting case should be made from a heavy gauge silver, for example 18- to 20-gauge sterling for the back sheet, and 24- to 26-gauge fine silver sheet for the bezel.

You will need 10-gauge sterling silver round wire for the hook and 10-gauge sterling half-round wire for the loop. You will also need the soldering torch with #3 tip, shears, medium solder, the bench vise and a rawhide or horn mallet, a half-round file, the third arm, a charcoal block, a bowl of Carborundum grains, flux, a small brush, and pickle.

1. To determine the length for the loop on the back of the buckle, add the width of the buckle to four times the thickness of the belt. Cut the half-round wire to this measurement.

2. Next, bend the ends of the loop wire. Place one end of the wire in a vise so that a piece of wire equal in length to twice the thickness of the belt protrudes from the vise jaws. Hammer this end with the rawhide mallet until it forms a right angle to the rest of the wire. Repeat this process with the other end of the wire.

3. File the ends of the wire flat so the loop can stand on its own.

4. To shape the hook, cut a length from the round wire that is four times the thickness of the belt. Place half the length in the jaws of the vise, then hammer the other half to a right angle using the rawhide mallet.

5. File one end of the hook so it is flat. With the file, shape the end of the hook that will go into the belt hole until it is rounded at the tip.

6. Place the setting case face down in a bowl of Carborundum grains. Cut three paillons of easy solder. Place the hook in the tweezers of the third arm, flat end up, and place the loop, ends up, on a charcoal block. Sweat solder the squares of solder to the ends of the loop and the hook.

7. Prip flux and dry the entire back of the setting case. Position the loop on the case so it stands on its own and position the hook (still in the third arm) on the case. Use the #3 tip on the torch to heat the whole case in a circular motion, being careful to avoid the

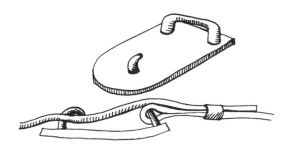

Figure 13–43 Top: hook and loop positioned on a belt buckle. Bottom: buckle attached to belt.

188

findings themselves. Watch for the solder to flow. Pickle, clean, and polish the case before setting the enamel.

POLISHING THE SETTING

The setting can be polished to a bright shine or to a dull or satin finish. You can polish a piece by hand using steel wool, tripoli, and rouge. First go over the whole setting with 220-grit wet and dry sandpaper, then progress to 320, 400, and 600 grit, always sanding in the same direction. The setting now has a satin finish. For a high gloss finish, polish the case with white diamond compound. Then polish with rouge, if desired. Wash off each polishing compound with a soft sponge or brush in a mixture of ammonia and detergent and warm water. Fingerprints can be removed with a rouge cloth.

A buffing machine with muslin buffs makes polishing much easier and faster (figure 13–44). First, remove by hand all scratches and oxidation using successively finer grades of wet or dry sandpaper (220 to 400 grit). Then machine polish the case with bobbing compound or tripoli. Do not overload the bobbing compound or it can leave black marks. After polishing the piece, wash in ammonia, detergent, and warm water and dry. Repeat the process with white diamond compound on a muslin buff. If it has a stand and a chuck to

Figure 13—44 Polish the finished piece on a polishing machine.

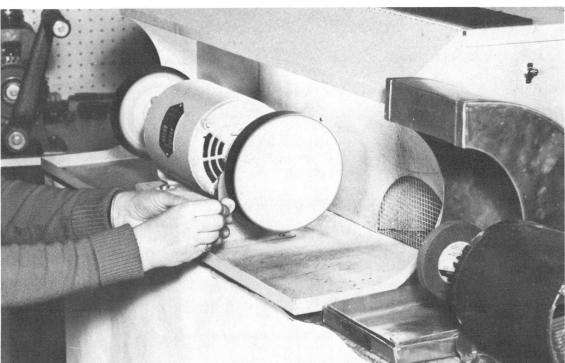

hold the buffs, an electric hand drill can be used instead of a polishing machine, but be sure to keep separate buffing wheels for the bobbing and the white diamond.

SETTING THE ENAMEL

Putting the enamel into the setting case is the last thing to be done to complete your piece. All soldering must be completed on all parts of the setting before the enamel is secured, as the heat from further soldering would damage the enamel.

Putting the enamel into the setting case is a relatively easy procedure. First some cushioning material, such as sawdust, is placed in the case to raise the enamel off the floor of the case to about $\frac{1}{16}''$ (1.6 mm) below the top of the bezel. The enamel is inserted, and the bezel edge is pushed down over the edge of the enamel to secure it and to hide the rim of the enameling cup.

There are many things you can use as cushioning material. Cardboard discs or layers of rag paper will work, although rag paper is preferable because it holds up better with time. The problem with both is that finding the exact height and the correct level for the enamel can be difficult. Some people use epoxy putty, which is soft and pliable, but it sets very fast and it can be difficult to remove the enamel if it has not been positioned correctly. Also, it is possible that the epoxy putty will crumble inside the case eventually. We prefer to use sawdust as a cushioning material. It is soft, easily shaped, and does not deteriorate. We suspect it was used in the ancient world for the same purpose.

To set your enamel, you will need some fine sawdust, masking tape, a small wood block covered with a piece of felt, a rocker pusher or stone pusher (a standard jeweler's tool), and a curved burnisher.

1. Cover the inside of the setting case with a thin layer of sawdust and level it with the back of a flat tool. Place the enamel in the case and check the distance between the edge of the enamel and the top of the bezel. The enamel should come to within $\frac{1}{16}''$ (1.6 mm) of bezel top, all around. Remove the enamel and add more sawdust if necessary. If the enamel is hard to remove, press a loop of masking tape on the face and pull up (a toy dart that has a rubber plunger works very well for removing enamels).

2. Place the setting case with the enamel facing up on the felt-covered wood. Position the case so you will not put pressure on any findings, for instance, with the bail extending over the side. It is a good idea to cover the face of the enamel with masking tape to within about $\frac{1}{8}''$ (3 mm) of the rim.

3. Press down hard on the face of the enamel with your thumb. Then, with a rocker pusher, press against the outside edge of the bezel (figure 13–45). Press down with the rocker at a 45° angle, first on the north side of the bezel, then the south, east, and west. This will secure the enamel in the proper position.

4. Press with the rocker pusher at the points between the first

190

Figure 13–45 Push the edge of the setting case over the edge of the enamel using a rocker pusher held at a 45° angle.

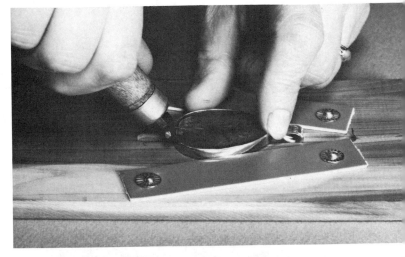

Figure 13–46 Burnish the sides of the bezel as shown.

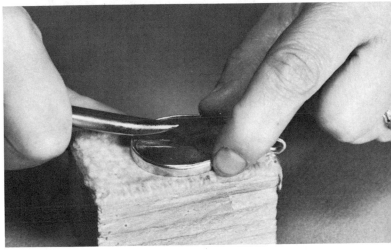

four. Continue in this manner until the rim of the bezel is pushed down snugly against the enamel. Continue pressing as you rotate the setting slowly in one direction, until the metal rim is flattened against the enamel.

5. Smooth out the bezel rim with a curved burnisher (figure 13–46). Press with the convex side (point facing up), using the same motion as you would to pare an apple. If the bezel needs further smoothing, use a rubber pumice wheel on a flexible shaft. This wheel will not harm the enamel if it inadvertently touches it.

Chains
14

There are many types of mass-produced chains available that look very nice when combined with small, simple enamels. Handmade chains, however, usually have a quality that is much closer to that of a cloisonné piece and setting. This is especially important when the enamel is large or elaborate. Manufactured chains simply look stamped out of a mold. They are often much "harder" looking, whereas handmade chains have a softness and fluidity. Also, if you make your own chain, you can control the entire artistic process. For example, the chain closure can be designed to match the enamel setting case, or the chain might include beads in the same color as the enamel. Design possibilities become much greater.

This chapter will describe how to make a variety of chains, both simple and complex. We suggest the easiest size to work with for each one. Once you learn how to make the particular type of link for each chain, making the whole length of chain becomes an easy but repetitive process. You then add whatever type of closure, or terminal, that you feel is most appropriate, and your chain is ready to be worn by itself or with an enamel pendant.

EQUIPMENT

Basically, chains are made by forming links around dowels, shaping the links, fusing or soldering them closed or together in groups, and joining them in the required pattern. The equipment needed is simple, but a few of the necessary tools are unique to chainmaking.

Wire

Fine silver, sterling silver, and gold wire are all available in a variety of shapes such as round, half-round, flat, square, and triangular. The chains in this chapter use round wire in various gauges, especially 18, 20, 22, and 24 gauge. Except for the bird's nest chain, the links for all chains we describe are fused. Only fine silver, alluvial gold, and ancient gold can be fused. Alluvial gold and ancient gold wire can be made in your studio by following the instructions in Chapter 11.

Figure 14–1 Sailor's knot necklace by Felicia Liban made from a handmade 22-gauge 22-karat gold chain, enameled Chinese beads, and a $\frac{1}{2}''$ (1.3 cm) diameter cloisonné clasp. Collection of Louise Boland.

Dowels

Links are formed by wrapping wire over a rod. Pencils or large nails can be used, but it is most convenient to have a supply of wooden dowels in a variety of diameters. They are available in any lumberyard and at some hardware stores or hobby shops. It is a handy idea to drill a small hole near the end of each dowel. The end of the wire can be secured through this hole, which will make wrapping easier. We suggest obtaining dowels in the following diameters: $\frac{3}{32}''$, $\frac{1}{8}''$, $\frac{3}{16}''$, $\frac{1}{4}''$, $\frac{5}{16}''$, $\frac{3}{8}''$, $\frac{7}{16}''$, $\frac{1}{2}''$, $\frac{5}{8}''$, and $\frac{3}{4}''$ (or 2 mm to 18 mm).

194

You can also purchase a jump ring winder, which comes with steel mandrels ranging in diameter from $\frac{3}{32}''$ to $\frac{1}{4}''$ (2.4 mm to 6 mm).

Tools

Making the chains in this chapter will require round-nosed and chain-nosed watchmaker's pliers, bezel shears, needle files, a rawhide mallet, a small metal forming pliers, two scribers (small pointed tools), a hat pin or tapestry needle, a jeweler's saw, and a bench vise. You will also need the kiln, soldering tools, a new charcoal block that is kept just for chainmaking, yellow ochre, a third arm, a tripod, iron binding wire, pickle and white correction fluid.

It is also a good idea to have a flexible shaft machine, a chasing hammer and anvil, epoxy glue, a hand drill, and a burnisher, although these are only necessary for a few of the chains included here.

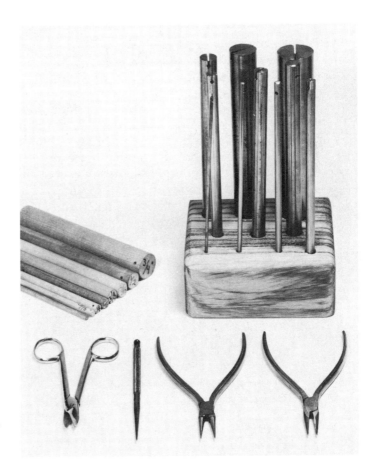

Figure 14–2 The tools for chainmaking include wooden and metal dowels, bezel shears, scriber, round-nosed pliers, and chain-nosed pliers.

Beads and Stones

Small beads made from semiprecious stones can be very effective interspersed between chain links.Stones can grace the terminals on a chain, perhaps in a color that matches or enhances the enamel pendant. You can purchase beads and stones from a gem or mineral supplier. Some of the loveliest types are garnet, carnelian, ruby, topaz, amethyst, jade, lapis or sodalite, coral, and onyx. Check each bead and stone for lack of flaws, uniform size, and good color, and make sure the holes in the beads have uniform diameters.

WIRE GAUGES

Naturally, the first step in the chainmaking process is to choose the type of chain you wish to make. Next you must determine the link size for the chain and how many links will be required to complete the chain. The number of links per inch varies slightly from dowel to dowel (even among those supposedly of the same diameter) and with the tightness of your winding. Make up a small sample, and then count the number of links you use per inch.

Table 14–1 will help you decide, for each chain described in this chapter, what gauge your wire should be, and which dowel size is required to make the links. Keep in mind that the smaller the diameter of the link, the harder it is to weave the pattern.

MAKING CHAIN LINKS

1. Wind the wire into a coil and anneal in a hot kiln for a few seconds (30 seconds on each side is good). Or anneal with the torch on a charcoal block, but be careful not to melt the wire.

2. Place one end of the wire in a bench vise and secure the other end through the hole in the dowel. Pull the wire taut. Holding the dowel horizontally, rotate it slowly as you move toward the vise. The wire will wind onto the dowel evenly and tightly. (See figure 14–3.)

3. Pull the wire free from the hole and slide the wire off the dowel. It will look like a long spring. Hold the spring in one hand

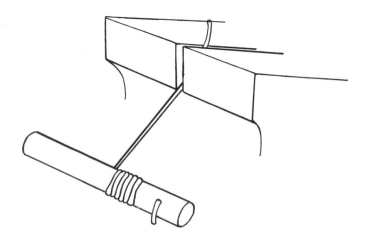

Figure 14–3 To make links, place one end of the wire in a vise, put the other end through the hole in the dowel, and wind.

196

Table 14–1   Wire Gauges and Dowel Sizes for Chains

CHAIN	WIRE GAUGE	DOWEL DIAMETER inches (mm)
Fused Silver or 22-Karat Gold Chains		
Sailor's Knot	24	$\frac{5}{16}$(8)
	24	$\frac{1}{4}$ (6)
	22	$\frac{5}{16}$(8)
	22	$\frac{7}{16}$(11)
	20	$\frac{1}{2}$ (13)
	20	$\frac{3}{4}$ (19)
Single Loop-in-Loop	24	$\frac{3}{16}$(5)
	22	$\frac{1}{4}$ (6)
	22	$\frac{5}{16}$(8)
	20	$\frac{3}{8}$ (9.5)
Double Loop-in-Loop	24	$\frac{1}{4}$ (6)
	24	$\frac{3}{16}$(5)
	22	$\frac{5}{16}$(8)
	22	$\frac{1}{4}$ (6)
	20	$\frac{3}{8}$ (9.5)
	18	$\frac{7}{16}$(11)
Quadruple Loop-in-Loop	24	$\frac{1}{4}$ (6)
	22	$\frac{5}{16}$(8)
	22	$\frac{3}{8}$ (9.5)
	20	$\frac{3}{8}$ (9.5)
	18	$\frac{7}{16}$(11)
Heracles' Knot	20	$\frac{1}{2}$ (13)
	20	$\frac{7}{16}$(11)
Sterling Silver or 14-Karat Gold Chains		
Bird's Nest	20	$\frac{3}{32}$(2)
	18	$\frac{1}{8}$ (3)
Fine Silver or 22-Karat Mesh Chains		
7 links per 1 inch	22	$\frac{3}{4}$ & $\frac{5}{16}$(19 & 8)
7 links per $\frac{7}{8}$ inch	24	$\frac{3}{4}$ & $\frac{5}{16}$(19 & 8)
4 links per $\frac{5}{8}$ inch	22	$\frac{5}{8}$ & $\frac{5}{16}$(16 & 8)
5 links per $\frac{5}{8}$ inch	24	$\frac{5}{8}$ & $\frac{5}{16}$(16 & 8)
4 links per $\frac{1}{2}$ or $\frac{9}{16}$ inch	26	$\frac{1}{2}$ & $\frac{5}{16}$(13 & 8)
3 links per $\frac{1}{2}$ inch	22	$\frac{1}{2}$ & $\frac{5}{16}$(13 & 8)

and carefully cut down the length of the spring with shears. You could also put the spring in the vise and saw down its length to make your links.

4. Repeat the winding and cutting process until you have enough links to make your chain. It is a good idea to make more than enough, because some links can get spoiled in forming. Extra links can always be labeled and stored for the future.

5. Spring the ends of the links by pushing the ends past each other with pliers. When the ends are placed together they should butt firmly. File any rough edges if necessary.

6. Place some of your links $\frac{1}{2}''$ (13 mm) apart on a clean charcoal block. Fill the entire block with links, and turn all the joints toward you.

7. Use the #1 tip on the torch to fuse the links. Aim the torch straight down and run the flame around the first link until it glows. Then aim the flame at the joint until you see a flash of molten metal. Do the same with the rest of the links.

BIRD'S NEST CHAIN

The bird's nest chain is a good one to begin with because it is easy to make (no soldering or fusing is required) and it is suitable for large-gauge wire. It is sometimes called the idiot's delight chain because of the repetitiveness involved. The result is a rope-like chain that glitters like a faceted stone. We suggest 18-gauge sterling silver wire on a $\frac{1}{8}''$ (3 mm) dowel for the beginner.

1. Make the links as described in the previous section. These heavy links have better joints if they are sawed. Do not fuse the ends together. File off any rough edges with a needle file.

2. On two links, spring the ends to form a tight join. Tie a small length of iron binding wire to them. This forms a tail to hold on to and identifies the beginning of the chain.

3. Open up two more links. (To open, twist the ends apart sideways.) Slip these two open links through the two closed ones. Close each link tightly and file any rough edges at the joints. Then, using the same method, add two more links to the second pair. You now have three pairs of links hooked together in a row.

4. With the tail down, hold the tail and the two sets of end links between your forefinger and thumb. Let the top links fall to the sides (figure 14–5).

5. Slip a hat pin or needle between the middle set of links to pick up and lift the inside edges of the top links (that are now on either side of the middle links) as shown in figure 14–6.

6. Slip two new open links through the links you have just lifted, then close the new links. (These two links take the place of the hat pin.) Treat these two links like your original two links—that is, spring the ends closed and add four links, as described in step 2. Continue as you did with the first series of six links until the chain is the desired length. (Note that the hat pin is inserted once for each set of six links.)

7. Add a simple terminal to the chain, such as a hook and jump ring (described later in this chapter). Polish, and the chain is finished.

SINGLE LOOP-IN-LOOP CHAIN

This chain is light, airy, and easy to make. It is a flexible chain that is especially good for a small pendant. Because it is an open weave, it uses relatively little silver or gold. We recommend using 22-gauge fine silver or 22-karat alluvial gold on a $\frac{5}{16}''$ (8 mm) dowel.

Figure 14–4 A bird's nest chain.

Figure 14–5 Let the top two links fall to the side.

Figure 14–6 Slip a hat pin or large needle between the middle set of links to pick up the inside edges of the top links.

1. Make the correct number of links as described under "Making Chain Links" and fuse them closed.

2. Form each link into an elongated shape by inserting the ends of chain-nosed pliers, with the seam on the outside, and opening the pliers as far as possible. (See figure 14–8 B.) If a link has not fused properly it will come apart, but it is better to have this happen now than when the chain is woven. Pinch the center of each link with pliers so a figure 8 is formed, as shown in figure 14–8 C.

3. With round-nosed pliers, bend one link into a U shape (figure 14–8 D). Insert a scriber or round-nosed pliers into the circular ends of the U to round them out. Slip one of the flat figure 8 links through the circular ends of the first U. Bend this flat link into a U shape and round its ends as you did with the first (see figure 14–9). Continue this process until the chain is the length you want.

4. Use a scriber to round out each of the links on all sides of the finished chain so it is smooth and even. Add a hook and jump ring as described later, then polish.

DOUBLE LOOP-IN-LOOP CHAIN

This chain is a more substantial one than the single loop-in-loop, but it uses basically the same technique. The result is a squarish, rope-

199

Figure 14–7 A single loop-in-loop chain.

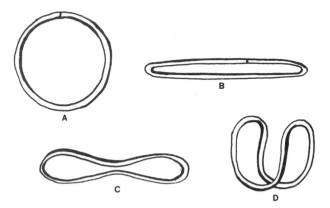

Figure 14–8 Shape each link for a loop-in-loop chain in the order shown here.

Figure 14–9 A single loop-in-loop chain in progress.

like chain. Use 22-gauge fine silver or 22-karat alluvial gold on a $\frac{5}{16}$" (8 mm) dowel.

1. Make your flat figure 8 links in the same way as you did for the single loop-in-loop chain.

2. Bend one link into a U shape and round out the ends with a scriber. Slip a flat figure 8 through the end loops of the first, bend it into a U shape, and round out its ends as you did in the single chain.

3. Now, take another flat figure 8 loop and slip it through the circular end of both the previous two links. Bend it into a U shape and round the ends. Continue to slip new links through the two previous links until the chain is the desired length. (See figure 14–11.)

4. Push the scriber through each of the links of the chain to smooth and round them further. Anneal the chain in a hot kiln for a few seconds, then gently hammer the four sides of the whole chain with a rawhide mallet to accentuate the squarish shape. If the chain is stiff, anneal it again and then flip it around like a jump rope to loosen it up. Add a terminal to complete the chain.

Figure 14–10 A double loop-in-loop chain.

Figure 14–11 A double loop-in-loop chain in progress.

QUADRUPLE LOOP-IN-LOOP CHAIN

This chain takes the loop-in-loop system one step further for a heavy chain that uses a great deal of metal. It looks like a round, tightly woven rope. Use 20-gauge fine silver or 22-karat alluvial gold wire on a ⅜" (9.5 mm) dowel. (Using 22-gauge wire would result in a square instead of round rope.)

1. Make your links and fuse them closed. Form them into figure 8 shapes as for the single loop-in-loop chain. Make plenty of links, as this chain uses four times as many as the single loop-in-loop chain.

2. Place one flat figure-8 link on the charcoal block. Flux the middle section and place another link across it to make a cross. Point solder the centers of the links together with medium solder, using a #1 torch tip.

3. Use round-nosed pliers to bend up the ends of the soldered links so they form U shapes. Shape the ends into circles with a scriber. Slip a flat figure-8 link through the upright ends of one of the soldered links. Press it down in the center, bend its ends up, then shape the ends into circles with the scriber. Slip another flat figure-8 link through the other soldered link's ends. Press it down, bend up the ends, and shape the ends into circles.

4. There are now four shaped and opened links, one pair crossing the other pair at a 90° angle (figure 14–13). Add two more links, one through the ends of one pair of links, and one through the

Figure 14–12 A quadruple loop-in-loop chain.

Figure 14–13 To begin the quadruple loop-in-loop chain, two figure-8 links are soldered together at right angles. Then each new link goes through the rounded ends of the two previous links.

other pair of links. Press the links down and shape them. Continue in this way, passing each new link through the ends of the previous *two* links, as for the double loop-in-loop chain, until the chain is the length you want. Be sure to bend up the four ends of each pair of links equally, or else your chain will be crooked.

5. Anneal the chain in a hot kiln for a few seconds. Then, to emphasize the squarish shape, hammer the sides of the entire length with a rawhide mallet. Roll it between two pieces of wood if necessary to make it even. Anneal again and flip it around like a jump rope to loosen it up. Add a cylinder terminal as described later and polish.

FLAT MESH CHAIN

Although a mesh chain takes an enormous amount of silver, it makes a striking choker or bracelet, especially if you use an enamel in the terminal. You could even make a belt with a stupendous enamel buckle. Use 24-gauge fine silver on $\frac{3}{4}''$ (19 mm) and $\frac{5}{16}''$ (8 mm) dowels.

1. Make both long and short fused links, as described earlier under "Making Chain Links." It takes 35 short links and 5 long links to make $\frac{1}{2}''$ (13 mm) of mesh chain. Form the links into figure 8s, as in figure 14–15 A and B.

2. Lay one of the long links on a charcoal block and flux along its length. Place seven short links, evenly spaced, across the long one as shown in figure 14–15 C. Point solder each link with medium solder.

Figure 14—14 A flat mesh chain.

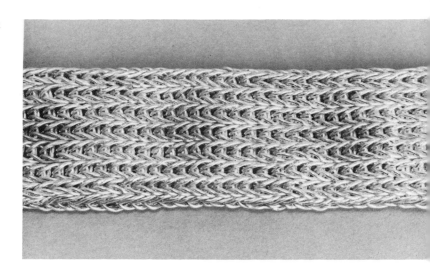

Figure 14—15 The steps in making a mesh chain.

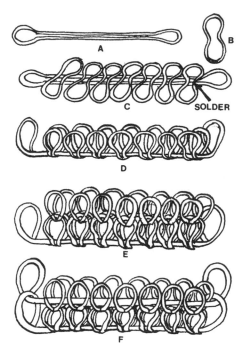

3. Bend the ends of the long link up. Then bend the ends of the short lengths into U shapes (figure 14–15 D). Slip a short figure-8 link through each of the seven U-shaped links. Press down on each link and bend their ends into U shapes. Using the scriber, open up the ends of the bottom row of links and form circular shapes. Also run the scriber along the lengths of the channels to make sure the links are evenly spaced and formed and to make room for the next long link.

4. Slip a second long link through the ends of the first long link as shown in figure 14–15 F. Turn its ends up.

5. On the third row, begin using the same method of weaving the links as described in step 3 of the double loop-in-loop chain. Repeat this process, alternating rows of long and short links, until the chain is as long as you want. Gently hammer the chain with a rawhide mallet to even out the shape. Then add a square terminal such as the one on page 214.

SAILOR'S KNOT CHAIN

This simple chain is light and delicate and does not require much metal to complete. It is especially attractive if you add beads every three or four links. Use 22-gauge fine silver or 22-karat alluvial gold wire on a $\frac{3}{8}$" (9.5 mm) dowel.

1. Make your links and fuse them closed. Elongate the links by inserting the tip of flat-nosed pliers and opening the pliers as far as possible. Each link should be a long, skinny oval, as shown in figure 14–8 B. Then bend the ends of the links up into U shapes (figure 14–8 D).

2. Place a scriber in a vise with the point facing up. Slip the two loops of one link over the point. Slip another scriber, perpendicular to the first, through the loops that are extending and pull on it to even out the shape. Using round-nosed pliers, pinch together the loops in the middle. Turn the pliers and pinch again in a perpendicular direction. Switch the loops on the scriber to check that they are the same size.

3. To join the links, begin by prying open two links with your fingernail, then slip one inside the other. Close both links with pliers. Open a third link and the other end of the second link. Slip the new link inside. Close the links each time. Continue in this way until the chain is the desired length.

4. Add a simple hook and jump ring terminal as shown later, then polish. If beads are desired, add them as described with the Heracles' knot chain.

HERACLES' KNOT CHAIN

The Heracles' knot is the most open of all the chains, and it is quite easy to make and uses very little metal. The links are fused together rather than woven, and they are held together by beads and wire. You will use 20-gauge fine silver or 22-karat alluvial gold round wire on a $\frac{3}{8}$" (10 mm) dowel for the links. Use annealed 24-gauge wire to thread through the beads and to tie the links together.

1. Make your links and fuse the ends closed. You should only use perfectly smooth links in your chain.

2. Prepare to shape the links by slipping a $\frac{15}{64}$" (6 mm) circle template hole over a ring mandrel. Mark the spot where it stops with masking tape. Slip a link on the mandrel to the spot with the tape and hold it there with your thumb. With pliers, pinch the link so a tiny loop is formed in one end, as shown in figure 14–19 A.

Figure 14–16 A sailor's knot chain.

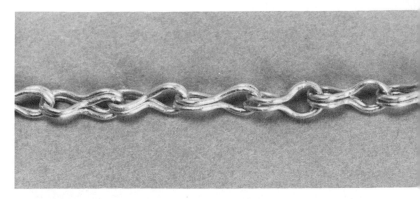

Figure 14–17 Pinch the middle of the link with chain-nosed pliers.

3. Put a scriber in the vise, pointed end up. Slip the tiny loop of the link on the scriber, and mark this spot with tape so that all the links will be the same size.

4. Shape another link in the same way.

5. Using your fingers, curve the links slightly as shown in figure 14–19 B. Line the two links up so the small loops face each other. Slip the links together so the small loop of one is covered by the large loop of the other (see figure 14–19 C).

6. Place the links on a steel block and tap them with the hammer until they lie flat. Try not to disturb the way they are placed together.

7. Transfer the links to a charcoal block. Run the torch with #3 tip over the links until they fuse. Turn the links over and repeat the fusing on the other side. Test with tweezers to make sure all points are fused.

8. To join the links, cut a 2″ (5 cm) piece of annealed 24-gauge wire and slip it through a bead. Put one end of the wire through the small loop of a link. Twist the wire around itself twice. Cut any excess wire at this end. Use pliers to help twist and make the wire secure. Repeat this procedure with the other end, pulling the wire so the bead sits tightly between the two twists. Cut off any excess wire.

9. Add a figure-8 jump ring and hook terminal.

Figure 14–18 The Heracles' knot chain.

Figure 14–19 Shape the links on the mandrel, then connect the links as shown.

Figure 14–20 The fused links are joined with wire and beads.

TERMINALS

When your chain is completed, you need to add a closure, called a terminal. This can be fashioned from commerical findings such as locking clasps, spring rings, sister hooks, and jump rings. However, just as you handmade a chain to go with your enamel, it is far more effective to make your own terminals for your chains. The terminals described in this section range from simple findings to elaborate closures that incorporate stones or enamels.

Jump Rings

Jump rings are circular links that can be used at one or both ends of a chain. Combined with a simple hook, it can make a perfectly

Figure 14–21 Assorted chain terminals, hooks, and a clasp.

adequate closure for a chain. They require less heat to solder than some other chain terminals, and this is one of their advantages.

Use 18- to 20-gauge sterling silver of 14-karat gold round wire for strength in your jump rings. To make them you also need a dowel or jump ring winder, pliers, shears, soldering equipment, a charcoal block, a third arm, a file, and pickle.

1. Make jump rings around a dowel in the same way as you formed links for a chain. (If you are only making a few rings, you can form them with pliers, but you will not achieve the uniform roundness that a dowel provides.) Spring the ends closed. A figure-8 jump ring is stronger and more elegant than a simple round one. Form a figure-8 jump ring in the same way as the figure-8 bail described in Chapter 13. (See figure 14–23.)

2. You can solder jump rings closed instead of just springing the ends for a tight fit and a more secure joint. If you need a soldered ring on the end of a chain, put the jump ring through the last link of the chain, and spring the ends closed. Place the jump ring, joint facing up, in the tweezer of the third arm. Flux the joint and point solder it closed with a very tiny amount of easy solder. File the joint smooth. Pickle and polish the jump ring.

Figure 14–22 A simple jump ring and hook closure.

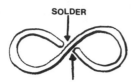

Figure 14–23 A figure-8 jump ring can be soldered together.

A Simple Hook

A handmade hook lends a touch of elegance to even the plainest chain. Considerable variation is possible in the size and curves of your hooks. The simplest hook is used with a jump ring to finish a chain. This hook uses 18-gauge sterling silver or 14-karat gold round wire. You also need a torch, charcoal block, easy solder, and pliers.

1. With forming pliers, form a small circle at one end of a short (1 ½" or 4 cm) piece of wire. This circle will act as a jump ring.

2. Put the wire vertically in a self-locking tweezer with the jump ring on top. Using a #2 torch tip, heat the bottom end of the wire until it forms a ball. This is the hook end.

3. Form the hook by bending the wire into whatever shape you find most pleasing.

4. Open the small loop and slip it through the last link of the chain. Spring the ends, secure the loop in the third arm, and point solder the loop closed using easy solder.

Double-Loop Hook

The double-loop hook is slightly more difficult to make than a simple hook, but it has a lovely appearance that is worth a little extra effort. Use 18-gauge sterling silver or 14-karat gold round wire. Also needed are the kiln, shears, a file, round-nosed pliers, chain-nosed pliers, forming pliers, a planishing hammer and anvil, and a burnisher.

1. Cut a 2" (5 cm) length of wire. File ¼" (6 mm) of one end of the wire to a gradually tapered point. (Or you can ball this end, as shown at A in figure 14–24.) Anneal in a hot kiln for a few seconds.

2. Using round-nosed or forming pliers, bend the wire into two loops, as shown in figure 14–24, loops A and B.

3. Taper ½" (13 mm) of the other end of the wire to a point and anneal again.

4. Use round-nosed or forming pliers to shape a large loop at this end of the wire. Slip this loop (loop C in figure 14–24) through the last link of the chain. Grasp the pointed end of the wire with chain-nosed pliers and wrap the wire tightly around the shank of the loop (figure 14–25). Use chain-nosed pliers or a small hammer to gently press or tap the wire against the shank.

5. Cut off any extra wire at point A and file the end smooth. You can further work harden the hook by rubbing it with a burnisher against the steel block. If you want to flatten the hook for decorative purposes, hammer it against the steel block with a planishing hammer.

Figure 14–24 Begin making the double-loop hook by bending the wire at points A, B, and C.

Figure 14–25 Wrap the end of the wire around the shank of the hook.

A Fused Clasp

Another simple clasp (figure 14–26) has the effect of intricate openwork, but it is easy to make and requires very little metal. This clasp is a basic style that can be changed in numerous ways. For example, a tiny stone could be set in a bezel in the center.

Use 18-gauge and 20-gauge fine silver or 22-karat alluvial gold round wire. Also needed are a rolling mill, a mandrel, the kiln, the torch with #1 tip, flux, easy solder, yellow ochre, fine sandpaper, roundnosed pliers, a file, a charcoal block, and pickle.

1. For the large circle, cut one piece of 18-gauge wire that is 2" (5.1 cm) long; for the side loops, cut two pieces that are ⅜" (9.5 mm) long.

2. Cut one piece of 20-gauge wire that is 4" (10 cm) long. Flatten the wire in a rolling mill until it is .017" (.4 mm) thick. Cut four pieces from this, each 1" (2.5 cm) long, for the interior wires.

3. Form the 2" piece of 18-gauge wire into a circle using a mandrel. Spring the ends of the circle. To fuse the joint closed, place the circle on a charcoal block. Use a torch with #1 tip to build up the

Figure 14–26 A fused clasp with hooks and undecorated cylinder terminals.

209

Figure 14–27 Patterns for an oval and a circular fused clasp.

heat around the circle, then briefly direct the flame toward the joint until it fuses.

4. Use round-nosed pliers to shape the interior wires according to either pattern in figure 14–27. Fit these wires inside the circle so all the wires are touching. The shapes will be held firm by tension inside the circle. Fuse the wires to the circle in the same way that you fused the circle joint. Turn the piece over and fuse on the other side. Check each joint with tweezers, then pickle and clean.

5. To make the side loops, bend the two remaining pieces of 18-gauge wire into semicircles, using round-nosed pliers. Sand the ends of each semicircle flat against fine finishing sandpaper. Flux and dry the pieces, then sweat solder them to each side of the openwork circle with easy solder. Paint the first soldered piece with yellow ochre or typist's white correction fluid before soldering the second to prevent the first from remelting. Pickle and clean. Use two hooks at the ends of the chain to secure the clasp.

6. An alternative to the semicircle loop closing is to make two hooks and solder them to each side of the clasp (see figure 14–26).

Setting Cup Clasp
Setting a small enamel or stone into a clasp makes a beautiful closure (see figure 14–21). It is not even necessary to add a pendant to the chain if the clasp is decorative enough. The first step is to make a setting cup for the enamel or stone. Wire hooks will be soldered to the cup, and the hooks will go through jump rings or other terminals on the chain. To complete the clasp you will need the setting cup, 18-gauge sterling silver or 14-karat gold round wire, shears, a drill, soldering equipment, a third arm, a tripod, and a flexible shaft machine.

1. Drill two holes that have the same diameter as the wire in opposite sides of the setting case (see figure 14–28). The holes should actually touch the floor of the case as shown in figure 14–28C. Cut a length of wire that is 2" (5 cm) longer than the space between the two

Figure 14–28 Drill holes in the bezel near the base of the setting cup (as shown in C) and slip a wire through to make a double hook. Holes can be drilled above center (A) so the clasp hangs as a pendant, or they may be drilled directly opposite each other (B) so the clasp is centered on the chain.

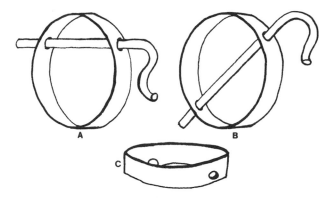

holes of the cup. Feed the wire through the holes so there is an equal length of wire extending from each hole.

2. Place the cup on a charcoal block. Flux the holes and wire inside the cup and dry. Use a #1 tip on the torch to point solder the joints with easy solder. Keep the flame away from the wire and concentrate on the holes from outside the cup.

3. Set the cup in a third arm so one end of the wire is facing straight down. Heat the end of the wire until it forms a ball. Repeat this process with the opposite end of the wire.

4. Cut off the wire inside the cup, then clean away any excess wire using a burr on a flexible shaft.

5. Set the enamel in the setting cup as described in Chapter 13. Polish the clasp and form the wire ends into hooks.

A Cylinder Terminal

The thickness of your chain, such as the double loop-in-loop chain, may require a different type of terminal than a hook and jump ring. A pair of cylinders makes an attractive solution. One cylinder has a loop attached (figure 14–29) and the other has a hook. They can be decorated with granules or with wires. The cylinder described here is fused, but if there is to be no granulation, it could be soldered.

Figure 14–29 A cylinder terminal with wire loop.

211

Use 26-gauge and 24-gauge fine silver or 22-karat alluvial gold sheet, 22-gauge fine silver or 22-karat alluvial gold wire, and 18-gauge sterling silver or 14-karat gold round wire. You also need a mallet, a felt-tip pen, paper for a pattern, shears, round-nosed pliers, soldering equipment, yellow ochre or white correction fluid, a charcoal block, the kiln, a scriber, a forming hammer, sandpaper, a needle file, a third arm, and pickle.

1. With a felt-tip pen mark each end of your chain about ¼" (6 mm) from the end. Gently mash the chain with a mallet from the marks to the ends. The cylinders will fit over these flattened ends and will seem to "grow" from the chain.

2. Make a paper pattern having the same length as the flattened chain ends and wide enough to wrap around the chain. Cut a piece of metal sheet the same size. Anneal the cut piece, then form it around the chain end. Cut the edge of the piece if necessary to get a really tight fit around the chain.

3. Place the cylinder on a charcoal block. Fuse the seam by heating with the #1 tip on the torch. Reshape the cylinder around a small center punch if necessary for a perfect fit, then file the ends until they are flat and smooth. Make a second cylinder in the same way.

4. Cut two squares of 26-gauge fine silver or 22-karat alluvial gold sheet that are slightly larger than the diameter of the cylinders. Anneal and flatten the squares. Coat the bottom of each with flux and let dry. Then coat the other sides with yellow ochre or white correction fluid and let dry.

5. To fuse the cylinder to the square sheet, put one square in a hot kiln, ochre side down, and stand a cylinder on top of it. Use the #2 tip on the torch and build up the heat evenly all around the cylinder until the metal flashes along the seam. Pickle, then trim off any excess sheet from around the cylinder and file the edge smooth. Fuse the other square and cylinder in the same fashion.

6. If you want to fuse any embellishments onto the cylinders, you must do it now before any soldering takes place. In figure 14–29, 22-gauge fine silver rings were added. (You could also use 22-karat alluvial gold.) After a careful airtight fitting, the ring joints were

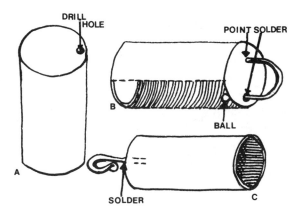

Figure 14–30 Drill a hole in each cylinder and make a loop on one cylinder and a hook on the other.

212

fused closed, and then the rings were fused to the cylinders one at a time. To add granules to the cylinders, see Chapter 12.

7. Place a 1¼″ (3.2 cm) piece of 18-gauge sterling silver or 14-karat gold wire in a third arm with one end of the wire hanging down. Heat the end until it forms a ball. Drill a hole the same size as the diameter of the 18-gauge wire in the center of the top of one cylinder. Thread the wire up through the bottom of the cylinder until the ball stops it. Secure the wire in a third arm so the cylinder hangs in mid-air. Flux and point solder the spot where the wire comes out of the hole with medium silver solder or 12-karat gold solder, using a #1 torch tip. Reverse the wire in the third arm so that the cylinder is on top. Apply heat to the other end of the wire hanging down until it forms a ball.

8. Use forming pliers to bend the wire into the shape of a hook (figure 14-30 C). Lay the hook flat on a steel block and tap it gently on the curve with a planishing hammer to flatten it slightly and work harden it.

9. Using a ½″ (1.3 cm) piece of the same wire, use the same method to make a loop on the second cylinder, but drill the hole $\frac{1}{16}$″ (1.6 mm) from the top edge (figure 14–30A). After the wire is point soldered in the hole, file it flat on the opposite end. Then bend it with forming pliers until it forms a loop. The end should be $\frac{1}{16}$″ (1.6 mm) from the edge, opposite the soldered point. Cover the soldered joint with yellow ochre or typist's correction fluid and dry. Then point solder the loose end down with medium silver solder or 12-karat gold solder (figure 14–30 B).

10. Press one flattened end of the chain into one of the cylinders so it fits tightly. Stand the cylinder up on a charcoal block and support the chain straight up in a third arm. Using a #1 torch tip, heat up the cylinder, keeping the flame away from the chain, and point solder with easy solder the four spots where the chain wire touches the cylinder rim (figure 14–31). Repeat on the other end of the chain.

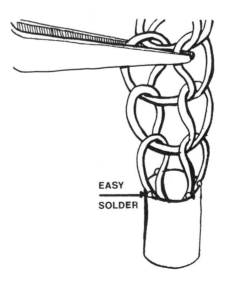

EASY
SOLDER

Figure 14–31 Solder the chain to the terminal at the points shown.

Rectangular Terminal

Because of their shape the quadruple loop-in-loop chain and the flat mesh chain both require a rectangular terminal. It is made like the cylinder terminal, but it uses a rectangular instead of a cylindrical tube. Like the cylinder terminal, this type is especially beautiful when decorated with granules, wires, or small stones.

Use 20-gauge fine silver or 22-karat alluvial gold sheet for the terminal walls, 26-gauge sterling silver or 14-karat gold sheet for the bottom, and 18-gauge sterling silver or 14-karat gold round wire for the hooks and rings. You will also need manila paper for a pattern, a felt-tip pen, a mallet, round-nosed and flat-nosed pliers, shears, a charcoal block, torch and soldering equipment, sandpaper, the kiln, a bowl of Carborundum grains, and pickle.

1. Determine the dimensions of the rectangular tube that works best with your chain and make a paper pattern for it. With a felt-tip pen, mark the area on both ends of the chain that will be covered with the terminal. Gently mash the ends to that mark using a mallet. This will insure a tight fit for the terminal.

2. Cut a piece of metal sheet according to the pattern. Wrap it around the chain, square the corners, and cut away any excess metal. Spring the joining sides so they butt together firmly. Fuse the seam by placing the terminal in a hot kiln and playing the torch around and around until the metal flows. File the seam and both ends of the tube until the edges are smooth.

3. Cut a rectangle of 26-gauge sheet for the bottom that is slightly larger than the open end of the terminal. Lay the metal sheet on a tripod and place the terminal on top of the sheet. If you will be

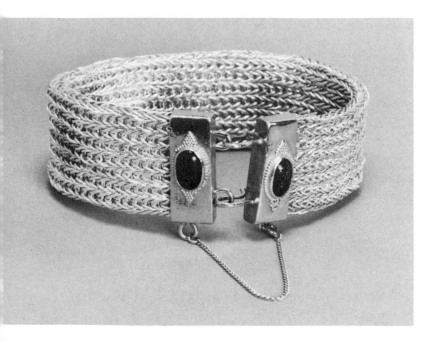

Figure 14–32 Bracelet by Felicia Liban in handwoven fine silver mesh. The terminals are 22-karat gold, embellished with granules and lapis gems. Collection of Etty Geier.

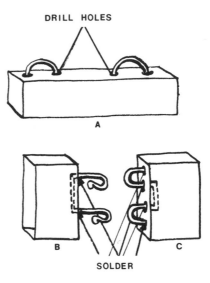

Figure 14–33 Solder the loops and hooks to the rectangular terminals. See steps 6 through 11.

adding any granulation, the bottom sheet must be fused instead of soldered. To fuse, see step 5 for the cylinder terminal, above. To solder, flux on inside and dry from underneath. Place four small pieces of medium solder along the inside of the seam and heat from under the tripod with the torch and #1 tip until the solder flows.

4. Make another terminal in the same way.

5. Add any embellishment at this point, such as decorative wires, or settings for stones.

6. To make the hook (see figure 14–33), first drill two holes the same diameter as your wire, in the top of one terminal. Position both holes an equal distance from all three edges.

7. Cut a piece of 18-gauge wire long enough to make two hooks plus the distance between the holes. Measure the distance between the holes. Mark the center of your wire and measure out from it half the distance between the holes. With flat-nosed pliers make 90° bends at these two marks, so the wire is bent like a square-cornered U. Thread wire ends through the holes from inside the terminal.

8. Secure the wire in a third arm so the cylinder hangs in mid-air. Flux and point solder the spots where the wire comes out of the holes with medium silver solder or 12-karat gold solder and a #1 torch tip.

9. Reverse the wire in the third arm so that the cylinder is on top. Apply the heat to the end of each protruding wire until it forms a ball. Use forming pliers to bend the wire end into the shape of a hook (figure 14–33 B). Put each hook on a steel block and tap it gently on the curve with a planishing hammer to flatten it slightly and work harden it.

10. To make the loops, drill two holes the same diameter as your wires in the top of the second terminal. Position the holes so that the centers of the loops will be exactly opposite the hooks on the first terminal.

215

11. Cut a piece of 18-gauge wire the same length you cut for the hooks. Follow the directions in step 7 to measure, bend and thread the wire through the holes. With forming pliers, bend the wire into loops of the height desired. Cut off the excess wire with bezel shears and file the end flat. Position the wire ends to align with the holes, as indicated in figure 14–33 C.

12. Set the terminal on a charcoal block with the loops facing up. Flux, and point solder the wire ends with medium silver solder or 12-karat gold solder, using a #1 torch tip. (Heat the terminal, not the wire.)

13. Attach the terminals to the chain with solder in the same way as the cylinder terminals. Pickle, clean, and polish.

POLISHING A CHAIN

You can polish a chain with a polishing wheel, but even this can be tricky because the chain can easily slip from your hands and be damaged. To prevent this, wrap the chain around a piece of wood and tack the ends down securely with staples or nails. Polish the terminals by holding them between thumb and forefinger with the rest of the chain in your palm. When polishing, use bobbing first, clean the chain, then use white diamond and clean again. The easiest and best device for cleaning a chain is a tumbler with steel shot and detergent. A tumbler is a machine designed to burnish the surface of stones, but will also polish difficult items, such as chains.

REPAIRING A BROKEN LINK

Occasionally you will break a link in your chain and only discover it after the chain is completed. To fix it, you need a charcoal block, soldering equipment, a third arm, and a needle file.

1. Spring the ends of the broken link together. Isolate the link in a third arm by setting it up so the rest of the chain is behind it in the tweezer.

2. Flux the joint and let dry. Cut a minuscule piece of easy solder and place it on a charcoal block. Heat the solder with the torch (#1 tip) and pick it up on a soldering pick. Heat the joint, and touch the solder to the joint.

3. With the link still positioned on the third arm, file the soldered joint smooth with a needle file.

Boxes
15

Next to jewelry, boxes have historically been the most popular setting for enamels. Many museums boast such treasures, and you will see some lovely examples of modern boxes in the craft galleries.

A box can be any shape: cylindrical, cubical, rectangular, or irregular. The lid can be flat or contoured. It can overlap the sides or be an extension of the sides. The lid can be secured by friction, a metal sleeve inside the box, a hinge, a catch, or any combination of these. An enamel can be set into the box lid, sides, or bottom. The most common setting, of course, is the lid. A bezel can be attached to the lid to hold the enamel, or the lid itself could form the bezel.

This chapter will give instructions for two simple boxes, both round. They are simple because their lids double as bezels. The lid setting for the enamel is very similar in effect to a seated bezel case (there will be no sheet metal supporting the back of the enamel), so these boxes are especially appropriate for setting enameled domed discs.

One box is made from 2" (5 cm) diameter brass or copper tubing that can later be silver plated; the other is made from silver sheet. If you wish to use gold, we suggest you use it as an accent on your box, such as in the catch, or as decoration in the form of granules or wire. Boxes can also be made from wood, leather, ivory, or clay. If you are using commercial tubing, the box should be made before the enamel so that the base can be custom fitted inside the box lid.

COPPER TUBE BOX

Using manufactured tubing eliminates soldering a seam on the side of the box. This easy box is made from 1" to 2" (2.5 to 5 cm) diameter copper or brass tubing. In addition to the tubing, you will need 24- and 26-gauge copper sheet, soldering equipment, yellow ochre or typist's correction fluid, pickle, a file, shears, and a plumber's tube cutter. A tube cutter not only holds a large tube, but it includes a cutting device and a reamer. It can be bought at a plumbing supply store or hardware store.

1. With a tube cutter cut two pieces of copper tube. One should be 1" (25 mm) high (for the box) and the other ½" (13 mm) high (for the lid) as shown in figure 15–3, #1.

Figure 15–1 Boxes by Felicia Liban, clockwise from left: Great Wave design on a copper tube box, a copper cup and lid with figures sketched by daughter Claudia, portraits of children Julia and David, a peacock feather on a rectangular box, and an enamel set into a walnut box by Edward Lewand. The walnut box is in the collection of Alice Gottlieb.

2. Now you will make a sleeve to fit inside the lid. The sleeve provides a ledge for the enamel at one end and, at the other, an extension that pressure-fits into the box. Make the sleeve just like you make a bezel. From 26-gauge copper or brass sheet cut a strip that fits airtight inside the smaller copper ring. Solder the sleeve seam closed using hard solder. Place the sleeve inside the $\frac{1}{2}''$ (13 mm) copper ring so it extends $\frac{1}{4}''$ (6 mm) beyond the bottom edge of the lid. These dimensions will accommodate the thickness of an enameled disc on top of the sleeve (figure 15–3, #2). Flux the seam from the inside and solder the sleeve to the lid with easy solder.

3. For the bottom of the box, cut a square of copper or brass sheet the same gauge as the tube. Coat one side of the square with Prip's flux and let dry. With a #3 torch tip and hard silver solder (on the outside of the tube), solder the square to the bottom of the larger tube. Pickle and rinse in baking soda and water. Trim away any excess metal.

220

Figure 15–2 Box by Felicia Liban, made of 1½" (4 cm) copper tubing set with a champlevé enamel.

4. File any rough edges. The top of the box, which acts as a bezel, is too thick as is to bend easily over the enamel. To remedy this, file the rim at a 45° angle until the edge of the rim is only .012" to .015" (.3 to .4 mm) thick. Then polish the box. If desired, send the box to be silver or gold plated. Set your enamel disc into the lid with epoxy cement.

A ROUND SILVER BOX
Like the copper box, this box is essentially a tube with an enamel set into the lid. It is very simple to make because the lid acts as the bezel.

Figure 15–3 Constructing a copper tube box.

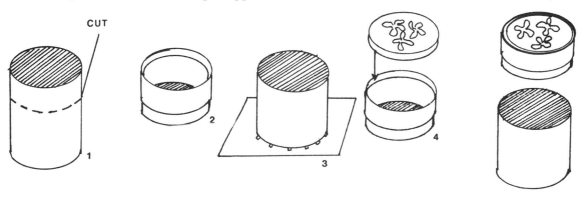

221

Figure 15–4 Silver box, $1\frac{1}{2}''$ × 2″ (4 × 5 cm) by Felicia Liban. Sleeve is constructed from sterling; cloisonné enamel on copper is set in the lid.

A 1″ to $1\frac{1}{2}''$ (2.5 to 4 cm) diameter box is a good size to start with. The larger the box, the heavier the gauge of silver that should be used. Any box larger than 1″ (2.5 cm) across should be made from at least 18-gauge sterling. 20-gauge fine silver can be used if the box is quite small, but even in small boxes it is a good idea to make at least the bottom surface of the box from sterling.

Tools needed include manila paper for a pattern, silver sheet, shears, set-screw dividers, the kiln, soldering equipment, annealing pan, two steel blocks, a rawhide mallet, large mandrel, a tripod, file, pickle, baking soda solution, and polishing materials.

1. Determine the circumference of your enamel by wrapping masking tape around it. Use this measurement to cut a rectangle of manila paper as a pattern for your box, tailoring the box height to its purpose. Draw a horizontal line on the pattern for the most pleasing division between the body of the box and its lid (figure 15–5 A).

2. Use the pattern to cut a rectangle of silver sheet. Open the dividers to the distance between the drawn line and one edge of the pattern. Score the piece of silver sheet along its length and cut it apart. Open the dividers to the planned height of your enamel and lightly score the piece for the lid.

3. Spring the ends into cylinders of both the body of the box and the lid (scored line on inside) and set them up on a charcoal block. Solder the seams with a #2 torch tip using hard solder.

222

Figure 15–5 Begin a silver box by (A) cutting the lid and body from sheet metal. (B & C) Spring the ends and solder the seam. (D) Shape the cylinders on a mandrel. (E) Solder the body to the base. (F) Solder the sleeve to the lid. (G) Set the enamel in the lid, as in a seated bezel.

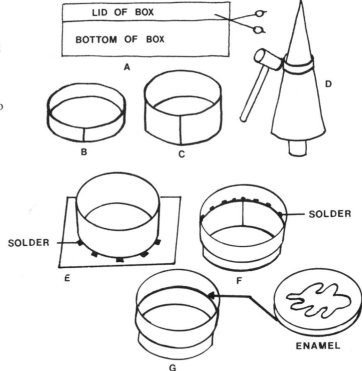

4. Round out the cylinders for the lid and box body using a rawhide mallet and a large mandrel. Reverse the cylinders on the mandrel so that they come out straight. Make sure they have exactly the same diameter. If they don't, stretch the smaller one by further forming around the mandrel. Anneal if necessary when forming.

5. Cut a square of sterling silver sheet for the base of the box and set it on the tripod. Stand on it the cylinder that is the body of the box. Prip flux and dry both sides of the seam and place pieces of medium solder along the outside (since cleaning off excess solder inside a box is rather difficult) of the seam until the solder flows (figure 15–5 E). Heat from underneath the tripod with a #3 torch tip until the solder flows. Pickle, trim the excess metal, and file the joints and edges smooth.

6. If your box is to have a hinge, now is the time to file the grooves for it, as described in the next section, "Hinges and Catches."

7. To determine the height of the sleeve that goes inside the lid, add $\frac{1}{4}$" (6 mm) to the height of the lid and subtract the height of the enamel to be set in the lid. Use the manila paper pattern to determine the length of sheet to cut for the sleeve.

8. Form the sleeve into a cylinder that fits air tight inside the lid. Make sure it also fits into the box itself for a pressure fit. Solder or fuse the seam closed, then pickle and rinse in baking soda solution.

9. Insert the sleeve so its top edge aligns with the scored line in the lid. The sleeve will protrude about ¼" (6 mm) from the bottom of the lid. Set the lid with the sleeve protruding downward on a charcoal block in an annealing pan. Cut about twelve pieces of medium solder $\frac{1}{32}$" (.8 mm) square onto another charcoal block. Protect the soldered joint in the sleeve with yellow ochre or typist's white correction fluid. Prip flux and dry the lid inside and out. Using a #2 torch tip, point solder the seam between the sleeve and lid, turning the pan as you solder (figure 15–5 F). Pickle and clean in baking soda solution. File and sand away any excess solder.

10. Polish the box as described in Chapter 13.

11. Set the enamel according to the instruction in Chapter 13, using the top lip of the lid as a bezel.

HINGES AND CATCHES

You may want to add a hinge alone or a hinge and catch to your box. If you wish to make a hinge, the box body and lid should be filed before adding the sleeve. A catch should be added after the box is completed and the hinge is soldered, but before the hinge is riveted together. The diameter of the tubing used to make the hinge and catch can vary depending on the size of the box. Our instructions call for $\frac{3}{32}$" (2.4 mm) tubing.

Making a Hinge

To form a simple tube and rivet hinge, you will need tubing with a diameter of $\frac{3}{32}$" (2.4 mm), made of sterling silver, 14-karat gold, copper, or brass. You also need rivet wire of a diameter that will fit through the tubing, a jeweler's saw, a tube-holding jig, binding wire, sandpaper, soldering equipment, yellow ochre or typist's correction fluid, a small brush, a file, a bowl of Carborundum grains, masking tape, a vise, a small dapping tool, a chasing hammer, and an anvil or steel block.

1. Determine the length of the hinge according to the proportions of the box and curve of the sides. Mark this length on the correct position on the rims of the box and its lid.

Figure 15–6 A closeup of a handmade box hinge.

224

2. Set your dividers to the length of the hinge and score the tubing. Divide the length by three and score the tubing in thirds. If the box is large enough, it is better to make the middle piece of tubing longer than the two outer pieces.

3. Cut the tubing into the three pieces with a saw in a tube-holding jig. Sand the edges smooth and paint the ends of the tubes with yellow ochre or typist's correction fluid. Slip a piece of heavy iron binding wire through all three tubes so the tubes form a straight line and are held together tightly.

4. When making the box (at step 6), file grooves in the body and lid of your box that equal the combined length of all three tubes. File at a 45° angle as shown in figure 15–7A.

5. Make the sleeve and solder it into the box lid according to the directions given above for the silver box, steps 7 through 9.

6. Tie the lid and bottom of the box together tightly with binding wire so the grooves are exactly aligned. Set this into a bowl of Carborundum grains so the box is half covered and the grooves are facing up.

7. Paint yellow ochre or typist's correction fluid at the points marked with an X in figure 15–7B, and brush flux on the areas marked with an 0. (Do not get any flux near the seams where the tubes meet each other). Point solder the tubes to the box at the spots marked X using easy solder. Remove the binding wire, clean off the yellow ochre or correction fluid, pickle, and clean in baking soda solution.

8. Add the catch at this point if there is to be one. Then make a flat rivet following the instructions in Chapter 12. When the rivet is secure, polish the box and set the enamel.

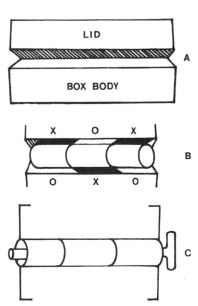

Figure 15–7 Making a hinge for a box from tubing includes filing a groove (A), soldering the tubes (B), and adding the rivet (C).

Figure 15—8 A closeup of a handmade box catch.

Figure 15—9 Brass box, 3″ (7.6 cm) square and 3½″ (9 cm) high, by Felicia Liban. Constructed from a square tube, hinged in the back and secured with a sterling clasp. Cloisonné enamel on copper sheet depicting Jonah and the whale is set in the lid.

Making A Catch

There is an infinite variety of catch designs, but the one provided here is simple to make and pleasing to look at. A catch should be soldered to the box after the hinge is soldered but before it is riveted.

You will need $\frac{3}{32}$″ (2.4 mm) diameter silver or gold tubing and 18-gauge sterling silver or 14-karat gold, copper, or brass round wire the diameter of the inside of the tubing. You also need soldering equipment, a saw, a pencil, a small brush, yellow ochre or typist's correction fluid, a bowl of Carborundum grains, shears, round-nosed pliers, and pickle.

1. Cut a piece of tubing of the desired length to hold the catch. Position it on the lid and mark the position with a pencil. Set the lid in Carborundum grains with this mark facing up. Flux and point solder the tube to the lid with easy solder (#1 torch tip), then pickle.

2. With a pencil, mark the body of the box at the point under the tube where the ball will go. Make a ball by heating a small piece of the wire with the torch until it forms a ball. Point solder it to the marked spot with easy solder, pickle, and rinse in baking soda solution.

3. Hold the unriveted hinge together with binding wire. Place the box on a charcoal block with the tube and ball facing up. Coat the tube with yellow ochre or typist's correction fluid. Slip a piece of the round wire through the tubing and bend it into the shape of a keyhole. The wire must fit securely around the ball and the ends must form a tight butt.

4. Lift the catch wire up into a vertical position and point solder the joint with a #2 torch tip using easy solder. Clean off the yellow ochre or correction fluid. If the wire is not in the exact shape you desire, reshape it now. Pickle, rinse in baking soda solution, and polish.

STANDARD B & S SHEET AND WIRE GAUGES

GAUGE	THICKNESS (inches)	THICKNESS (mm)
9	.114	2.9
10	.102	2.6
12	.081	2.05
14	.064	1.6
16	.051	1.3
18	.040	1.0
20	.032	.8
22	.025	.6
24	.020	.5
26	.016	.4
28	.013	.3
30	.010	.25

Thomas Thompson Enamel Colors

Each enamel available from the Thomas C. Thompson Company is listed below by number. Following the number is an abbreviation for opaque (O), transparent (T), or Opalescent (Opal), and the name of the color. A color chart showing their complete line of enamels can be obtained with their catalog by writing the Thomas C. Thompson Company, P.O. Box 127, 1539 Old Deerfield Road, Highland Park, Illinois 60035.

Thomas Thompson enamel colors are arranged on the chart according to type and hue, and on the price list by hue alone. This makes it awkward to translate the number backward into the name and color. To solve this problem for you, we are including this chart which lists the enamel colors in numerical progression. For making notes, it is easiest to use color numbers, rather than names; it is also more specific, since the name of a color may change, but the number always remains the same.

5	O	Hard Fusing White	124	O	Medium-Fusing Black
W10	O	Soft Fusing Black	124A	O	Hard-Fusing Black
100	O	Pea			
101	T	Pigeon	129	T	Khaki
106	T	Allspice	130	T	Champagne
107	O	Horizon	131	T	Tan
108	T	Forsythia	132	T	Toast
109	T	Lilac	137	O	Rejane
110	T	Bluebell	140	O	Hyacinth
111	T	Sapphire	147	O	Slate
112	T	Hazel	150	T	Wineberry
113	T	Dresden	154	T	Amulet
116	O	Middy	160	T	Lawn
118	O	Medium-Fusing White	162	O	Colonial
			166	O	Lettuce
120	T	Ultramarine	167	O	Chinese
121	T	Emerald	175	O	Flame
122	T	Imperial	179	T	Tobacco
123	T	Meadow	191	T	Seal

195	O	Cardinal	450	T	Flux for Silver Plated Steel
196	O	Tangerine			
198	O	Princeton	459	O	Goldenrod
200	T	Aquamarine	463	O	Charcoal
207	O	Sky	478	O	Emerald
208	O	Indian	487	O	Pastel
217	O	Calamine	503	O	Robin Egg
226	O	Marigold	506	T	Citron
230	O	Briarwood	531	T	Burnt Orange
234	T	Evergreen	595	O	Dove
238	T	Cocoa	603	T	Bluebird
239	O	Bittergreen	604	T	Copen
240	T	Mauve	610	O	Daphne
241	O	Larkspur	621A	O	White Undercoat for Transparents
248	O	Heliotrope			
254	O	Myrtle	635	O	Porcelain
261	O	Parchment	638	T	Cerise
265	O	Pearl	643	O	Copen
267	T	Tea Rose	644	O	Soft-Fusing White
277	T	Delft	655	O	Wedgewood
279	O	Royal	657	T	Dark Tyrolian
287	O	Periwinkle	659	T	Turquoise
288	O	Delphinium	664	O	Ochre
291	T	Regal	667	O	Civette
301	O	Carmel	674	T	Ruby
304	O	Mauve	676	T	Raspberry
305	O	Clover	688	O	Spruce
308	T	Chestnut	689	O	Evergreen
313	T	Chinchilla	690	O	Chrome
316	O	Mist	691	O	Elk
317	O	Hunters	707	O	Brick
320	O	Nude	709	O	Geranium
321	O	Geneva	715	O	Bluejay
324	O	Aquamarine	724	T	Gold
326	O	Arcadian	728	T	Amber
328	O	Pastel	736	O	Chartreuse
332	O	Pastel	741	O	Cream
333	T	Hard-Fusing Flux Undercoat	750	T	Peach
			755	T	Mikado
334	O	Ivory	757	T	Flux for Silver
339	O	Sandalwood	760	O	Offwhite
340	T	Bluejay	777	O	Concord
356	T	Concord	798	O	Cordova
358	O	Cornflower	813	O	Cocoa
387	T	Midnite	834	T	Smoke
399	O	Light Brunswick	835	Opal	White
404	O	Delft	837	Opal	Petal
405	T	Mulberry	839	T	Dark Olive
426	T	Soft-Fusing Flux	841	O	Petal

231

843	O	Carnation	938	O	Peacock
844	O	Dark Orchid	942	O	Cactus
849	Opal	Hunters	943	O	Light Turquoise
850	Opal	Elephant	967	O	Sapphire
851	Opal	Periwinkle	976	O	Mouse
852	Opal	Beige	977	O	Dark Slate
853	Opal	Mauve	985	O	Rifle
854	Opal	Chartreuse	986	T	Goldenrod
855	Opal	Turquoise	997	T	Palm
856	Opal	Raisin	1000	O	Background White
857	Opal	Ultramarine			
858	Opal	Flame	1005	T	Medium-Fusing Flux
859	Opal	Goldenrod			
866	Opal	Cerulean	1013	T	Old Silver
904	O	Coral	1035	O	Olive
931	T	Pastel Aqua	1066	T	Garnet
932	T	Shamrock	1067	O	Lemon
933	T	Orchid	1068	O	Citron
934	T	Chrome	1069	O	Canary

Sources of Supplies

It is always a good idea to check your local area for supplies before ordering through the mail. A jewelry supply store or local craft or art store will carry some materials essential to your work, as will some hardware stores. If you still need suggestions about possible sources, you might try contacting a local art center or school art department.

TOOLS AND EQUIPMENT

Abbey Materials Corp.
116 West 29th St.
New York, NY 10001

Allcraft Tool & Supply Co.
100 Frank Rd.
Hicksville, NY 11801

Allcraft Tool & Supply Co.
California Salesroom & Mail Order
204 North Harbor Blvd.
Fullerton, CA 92632

Anchor Tool & Supply Co.
P.O. Box 265
Chatham, NJ 07928
(231 Main St. on Route 24)

Baskin & Sons, Inc.
732 Union Ave.
Middlesex, NJ 08846

Bergen Arts & Crafts
P.O. Box 381
Marblehead, MA 01945

Bluemound Crafts
Division of Valley School Supplies,Inc.
Box 1579
1000 N. Bluemound Rd.
Appleton, WI 54911

Bourget Brothers
1626 11th St.
Santa Monica, CA 90404

Brookstone
127 Vose Farms Rd.
Petersborough, NH 03458

C. R. Hill Co.
2734 W. 11 Mile Rd.
Berkley, MI 48072

D. R. S., Inc.
15 West 47th St.
New York, NY 10036

Enameling Supply Co., Inc.
P.O. Box 119
Albertson, NY 11507
(trinket kilns, heat lamps,
trivets, porcelain tiles
to fire enamels on)

Gamzon Brothers
21 West 46th St.
New York, NY 10036

Gesswein & Co.
255 Hancock Ave.
Bridgeport, CT 06605

Heat Systems Ultrasonics, Inc.
38 East Mall
Plainview, NY 11803

Kassoy, Inc.
30 West 47th St.
New York, NY 10036

Kay M. Co.
Division of The Price Corp.
3729 No. Ravenswood Ave.
Chicago, IL 60613

Metal Crafters Supply Co.
One Concord Rd. (Rear)
Sunbury, MA 01776

Minatec Tools
Division of Hammer, Riglander &
      Co.
435 Hudson St.
New York, NY 10014

Sax Arts & Crafts
Box 2002
Milwaukee, WI 53201

Seaire Mfg. Co.
17909 South Hobart Blvd.
Gardena, CA 90248

Swest, Inc.
10803 Composite Dr.
Dallas, TX 75220

Swest, Inc.
1725 Victory Blvd.
Glendale, CA 91201

Technicraft Lapidaries Corp.
2248 Broadway
New York, NY 10024

Tervo's Lapidary Equipment
14 Nassau Blvd.
Garden City South, NY 11530

Travers Tool Co.
P.O. Box 878
25-26 50th St.
Woodside, NY 11377

T. W. Smith
545 West 59th St.
New York, NY 10019

Woodstock Craft Tools, Inc.
21 Tinker St.
Woodstock, NY 12498

METALS

American Metalcraft, Inc.
4100 Belmont Ave.

Chicago, IL 60641
(aluminum)

ARE
Box 155
Plainfield, VT 05667

Ballard Bay State Refractories
454 Bridge St.
Box 3092
Springfield, MA 01101

T. E. Conklin Brass & Copper Co.
322-324 West 23rd St.
New York, NY 10011

Delaware Jewelers Supply
1114 Greentree Road
Newark, NJ 19713
(silver tubing for stone setting)

T.B. Hagstoz & Son, Inc.
709 Sansom St.
Philadelphia, PA 19106

Handy & Harman
1900 Estes
Elk Grove Village, IL 60622
(gold and silver only)

Hauser & Miller Co.
4011 Forest Park Blvd.
St. Louis, MO 63108

Immerman's Crafts, Inc.
21668 Libby Rd.
Cleveland, OH 44137
(silver-coated steel)

The Maisel Co.
P.O. Box 1333
Albuquerque, NM 87103

Myron Toback
23 West 47th St.
New York, NY 10036

Rio Grande Jewelers Supply Co.
6901 Washington NE
Albuquerque, NM 87109

Rodman & Yaris Refining Co.
17 West 47th St.
New York, NY 10036
(gold and silver only)

Shteinshleifer Co.
40-42 Elizabeth St.
New York, NY 10012
(gold and silver only)

Swest, Inc.
10803 Composite Dr.
Dallas, TX 75220

Swest, Inc.
1725 Victory Blvd.
Glendale, CA 91201

ENAMELS

Allcraft Tool & Supply Co.
100 Frank Rd.
Hicksville, NY 11801
(Thomas Thompson enamels)

Allcraft Tool & Supply Co.
204 North Harbor Blvd.
Fullerton, CA 92632
(Thomas Thompson enamels)

AMACO
4717 W.16th St.
Indianapolis In 46222
(Thomas Thompson enamels,
painting enamels, decals)

Enameling Supply Co., Inc.
P.O. Box 119
Albertson, NY 11507
(Vitrearc enamels)

Kranzberg
4850 Kendall Ct., NE
Atlanta, GA 30342
(Schauer enamels)

Metal Crafters Supply Co.
1R Concord Rd.
Sudbury, MA 01776
(Schauer enamels)

Thomas C. Thompson Co.
P.O. Box 127
1539 Deerfield Rd.
Highland Park, IL 60035

Vitrearc
Division of Ceramic Coating Co.
P.O. Box 370G
Newport, KY 41072
(lead-free enamels)

STONES

A & S Gems
711 Broadway
New York, NY 10012

Baskin & Sons Inc.
732 Union Ave.
Middlesex, NJ 08846

Eidos
5 Larsen La.
Woodstock, NY 12498

Emaco
48 West 48th St.
New York, NY 10036

Globus Gifts, Inc.
1140 Broadway
New York, NY 10001

Golay Buchal USA Ltd
1180 Ave. of Americas
New York, NY 10036

Manning Opal, Inc.
22 West 48th St.
New York, NY 10036

Ross C. Altman
15 Seaview Lane
Port Washington, NY 11050

WOOD

Robert M. Albrecht
8635 Yolanda Ave.
Northbridge, CA 91324
(veneers and precious woods)

Albert Constantine and Sons Inc.
2050 Eastchester Rd
Bronx, NY 10461
(veneers and precious woods)

Craftsman Wood Service Co.
2727 S. Mary St.
Chicago, IL 60608
(veneers and precious woods)

CUSTOM CASTING AND PLATING

JNH Casting
866 Sixth Ave.
New York, NY 1001

Additional Resources

By joining the American Crafts Council, you will automatically receive their magazine *American Craft*. It will keep you up to date with the whole world of crafts. The Council's address is 44 West 53rd Street, New York, NY 10019.

The Society of North American Goldsmiths publishes *Metalsmith*, which contains a wealth of information about current jewelry and metalworking. Write to SNAG, 8589 Wonderland NW, Clinton, Ohio 44216 for their subscription rates.

If you have not already taken a class or workshop in cloisonné enameling, metal fabrication, or jewelry making, we recommend that you do so. The ACC directory, *Contemporary Crafts Market Place*, provides information on courses offered by schools and guilds across the country. It can be ordered from the R. R. Bowker Co., P.O. Box 1807, Ann Arbor, MI 48106. Additionally, joining a local guild is an easy way to meet other craftsmen, and you will find them generous with their knowledge.

Examine as many good examples of historical and contemporary cloisonné as possible. You can find them in museums (most likely those in larger cities) and in public art galleries that specialize in crafts. You may find works of contemporary cloisonné in some high-quality retail jewelry shops and at some of the larger craft fairs. Look in the *Contemporary Crafts Market Place* for retail shop listings.

Finally, remember that your public library is an invaluable source of information on local organizations and crafts in general.

Glossary

Acid (pickle): A solution used to clean oxidation (firescale) and soldering flux from metal. Sparex #2, a noncorrosive pickling solution, and sulfuric acid are two examples.

Alloy: To melt two or more different metals together in a crucible. Also, the metal created by this process.

Anneal: To make metal malleable by subjecting it to intense heat, then cooling it.

Annealing pan: A metal pan, filled with lumps of pumice, which rotates on ball bearings. It is used as a base for soldering and annealing.

Basse-taille: A decorating technique in which a metal surface is engraved, etched, gouged, or hammered, then completely covered with transparent enamels.

Bench plate: *See* Steel block.

Bench vise: A small, smooth-jawed vise that easily screws on and off the worktable.

Bezel: A metal ring used to surround and secure objects such as gems, stones, and enamels.

Bobbing: A fast-cutting compound used on a buff or felt wheel to remove firescale.

Borax: (Also called sodium borate.) An ingredient combined with silicates in the manufacture of enamels. Also used in soldering flux.

Burnisher: A tool of highly polished steel used to smooth metal in hard-to-reach places or to press a bezel around a stone.

Cabochon: A smooth-polished, unfaceted round or dome-shaped stone, usually flat on the bottom.

Carat: A unit of weight for precious stones. One carat is equal to 200 milligrams.

Carborundum: An abrasive used to level enamel surfaces and to polish metal edges. Large grains of Carborundum set in a bowl can be used as a soldering surface.

Carborundum stone: An abrasive stone used under running water on fired enamel surfaces.

Champlevé: A technique in which areas are depressed in metal, then filled with enamel.

Circle cutter: A device consisting of two steel blocks with holes of various sizes in them, and a series of corresponding-sized metal punches. Metal sheet is sandwiched between the blocks and the punches are hammered through.

Cloisonné: An enameling technique in which thin metal wires, forming a design, are attached to a metal or enameled surface. The areas defined by the wires are then filled with enamel colors.

Cloisons: Enclosures, formed with thin wires, which are filled with enamel colors in the creation of a cloisonné enamel.

Counter enamel: Enamel fired onto the back of an enameled piece to prevent warping of the metal.

Dapping block: A steel block with circular depressions in graduated sizes used with dapping punches to form domes in sheet metal.

Dopping: Using dopping cement to attach a short dowel to a metal or enameled piece to provide a temporary handle so the piece can be polished easily.

Drawplate: A flat steel plate with graduated holes in various shapes through which wire is pulled with tongs to reduce its size or change its profile. Also used in forming small tubing.

Feathering: A method of clipping the top of cloissonné wires to produce a look of fur or fringe.

Findings: Functional attachments for jewelry, such as backs for earrings and bails for pendants.

Fine gold: Pure gold; 24 karat.

Fine silver: Pure silver; 999.

Firescale: A copper oxide that forms on unprotected metal upon heating.

Firing tweezers: Nickle-plated soldering tweezers, 7" (18 cm) long, which are kept clean and used only for the kiln.

Flexible shaft: A power tool that can be equipped with a variety of burs, buffs, and files for polishing, grinding, or drilling.

Flux: A commercial preparation used in soldering to prevent firescale and help solder flow. Available in paste and liquid form.

Flux enamel: A colorless, transparent enamel used as a base coat under transparents or to mix with enamels to lighten their color. Also used as a top layer to protect undercoats.

Frit: Enamel in coarse particles.

Fusing: The merging or joining of metals with heat but no solder.

Gauge: A measurement that indicates thickness of metal or wire; the higher the gauge the thinner the metal.

Glass brush: Spun glass bound with cord, used to clean metal and enamel. It can be unwound to expose additional brush fill.

Granulation: A decorative process in which small balls of metal are joined to a metal surface by fusion.

Grisaille: White and gray shades of enamel fired on a dark background.

Hard-fusing enamel: Enamel that fires at high temperatures, from 1420°–1510°F (770°–820°C).

Hazing: Laying a thin coat of enamel one grain deep with a brush.

Iron binding wire: Soft, annealed iron wire, available in standard wire gauges, used to bind metals together for soldering.

Karat: A measure of the purity of gold. Pure gold has 24 karats; 18 karat gold is 18 parts pure gold and 6 parts of another metal. Alloy golds may also be 22 karat, 20 karat, 14 karat, 12 karat, and 10 karat. Those below 10 karat cannot legally be stamped with a karat mark. (Not to be confused with carat, which is a unit of weight for gemstones.)

Kiln: A furnace or heating chamber lined with refractory material, such as firebrick.

Klyr Fire: A water-based adherent used to bind enamels to metal prior to firing.

Lapidary: Pertaining to cutting, grinding, and polishing stones and enamels.

Liver of sulfur: Potassium sulfide, used in a water solution to oxidize (darken) a metal surface to achieve a decorative or antique finish.

Malleable: Capable of being shaped easily; not brittle.

Mallets: Rawhide, horn, plastic, etc., used to shape metal without marring it.

Mandrel: A solid or hollow metal rod, often tapered, used for shaping wire and metal rings.

Matte salt: A chemical applied in paste form to produce a matte finish on an enameled surface.

Medium-fusing enamel: An enamel which fuses at a temperature of 1350°–1420°F (730°–770°C). Most enamels are in this category.

Mica: A transparent sheet-like mineral not affected by heat, used as a base on which to fire enamels, as it does not adhere to the melted enamel.

Mortar and pestle: A vessel, and a club-shaped implement, both made of agate or high-fired porcelain, used for grinding enamels.

Oxidation: Discoloration of metal because of exposure to air, heat, or chemicals.

Paillon: A snippet of metal or solder.

Pickling: Subjecting metal to a warm acid bath to remove oxidation, grease, and dirt.

Pipecutter: A small hand tool; pipe is clamped into it, then turned against a sharp wheel to shear it off.

Plique-à-jour: Transparent enamels fired without a backing to give a stained-glass effect.

Repoussé: Design on metal made by hammering the reverse side, as well as by chasing on the top surface.

Rolling mill: Usually a hand-operated machine with highly polished hard steel rollers, turned by a system of gears, used to reduce the thickness of metal sheet or wire.

Rouge: A polishing compound used on a muslin buff or on a cloth or stick to give a mirror finish to gold or silver.

Scotch stone: A very mild abrasive stone used under running water to remove scratches from enamels or metal.

Self-locking tweezers: Tweezers that are spring constructed to open when squeezed and then lock shut to hold parts together during soldering.

Shot: Small pellets of metal.

Soft-fusing enamel: An enamel that fuses at low temperatures, from 1290°–1350°F (700°C–730°C).

Soft-fusing flux: A clear, soft-fusing enamel used for attaching cloisonné wires to a base. It is also often added to and over enamel colors. It is interchangeable with Vitreac LF 302.

Soldering: Joining two pieces of metal with an alloy (solder) that melts at a lower temperature than the metals being joined.

Soldering pick: A thin steel rod used as an aid in soldering.

Steel block: A heavy block of hardened steel with a highly polished surface which provides a worksurface for hammering and flattening metal. Also called a bench plate, bench anvil, or surface plate.

Sterling silver: An alloy which is a combination of 925 parts pure silver and 75 parts copper.

Surface plate: *See* Steel block.

Third arm: A holding device with self-locking tweezers, used to hold pieces during soldering.

Transite: A hard, heatproof composition board.

Tripoli: A coarse, fast-cutting compound used on a muslin buff for removing scratches from metal by machine. It is coarser than white diamond but finer than bobbing compound.

Tube-holding jig: A device for holding tubing or wire of $\frac{1}{16}$ to $\frac{3}{8}''$ (1.5 to 9 mm) diameter for cutting. Slot for saw blade assures true cuts.

Tumbler: A motorized plastic tub containing metal shot and detergent in which rocks, chains, and small, intricate castings are burnished smooth and shiny.

Undercoat: A fired coat of enamel over which additional layers of enamel will be fired.

Underglaze: Opaque enamel, painted on a piece, over which transparent enamel is to be fired.

Vise: A device having two movable jaws to firmly hold objects being worked on, usually fastened to the edge of a bench or table.

Warping: Distortion of metal usually caused by heat and uneven stresses.

Wet inlay (also **wet pack** and **wet charge**)**:** To lay on moist enamels with a small tool or brush.

White diamond: A compound, used on a muslin buff on a polishing machine, which cuts and polishes in one operation. It is often used as a final polish.

Yellow ochre: A paste applied to areas of metal that prevents the flow of solder to those areas. It is also used to protect metal from melting during prolonged heating. After heating, yellow ochre forms a hard surface which is difficult to clean off. Typist's white correction fluid does the same job and is easier to remove.

Suggested Reading

ENAMELING

Ball, Fred. *Experimental Techniques in Enameling.* New York: Van Nostrand Reinhold, 1972.

Bates, Kenneth F. *Enameling Principles and Practices.* New York: Crowell, 1974.

Bates, Kenneth F. *The Enamelist.* New York: World, 1967.

Chu, Arthur, and Chu, Grace. *Oriental Cloisonné and Other Enamels and a Guide to Collecting and Repairing.* New York: Crown, 1975.

Harper, William. *Enameling Step by Step.* New York: Golden Press, 1973.

Newble, Brian. *Practical Enameling and Jewelry Work.* New York: Viking Press, 1968.

Rothenberg, Polly. *Metal Enameling.* New York: Crown, 1969.

Seeler, Margaret. *The Art of Enameling.* New York: Van Nostrand Reinhold, 1969.

Untracht, Oppi. *Enameling on Metal.* Radnor, Pa: Chilton, 1962.

JEWELRY AND METAL WORKING

Bovin, Murray. *Jewelry Making for Schools, Tradesmen, Craftsmen.* Rev. ed. Forest Hills, NY: Bovin, 1979.

Bowie, Hamish. *Jewelry Making.* Chicago: Regnery, 1977.

Choate, Sharr, and De May, Bonnie C. *Creative Gold and Silversmithing, Jewelry, Decorative Metalcraft.* New York: Crown, 1970.

Coyne, John, ed. *The Penland School of Crafts Book of Jewelry Making.* New York: Bobbs-Merrill, 1975.

Dipasquale, Dominic; Delius, Jean; and Eckersley, Thomas. *Jewelry Making.* Englewood Cliffs, NJ: Prentice-Hall, 1975.

Edwards, Rod. *The Technique of Jewelry.* New York: Charles Scribners, 1977.

Garrison, William E., and Dowd, Merle E. *Handcrafting Jewelry Designs and Techniques.* Chicago: Regnery, 1972.

Gentille, Thomas. *Jewelry Step by Step.* New York: Golden Press, 1974.

Maryon, Herbert. *Metalwork and Enameling.* Rev. ed. New York: Dover, 1971.

Morton, Philip. *Contemporary Jewelry: A Studio Handbook.* Rev. ed. New York: Holt Rinehart & Winston, 1976.

Rose, Augustus F., and Cirino, Antonio. *Jewelry Making and Design.* Rev. ed. New York: Dover, 1967.

Untracht, Oppi. *Metal Techniques for Craftsmen.* New York: Doubleday, 1975.

von Neumann, Robert. *The Design and Creation of Jewelry.* Rev. ed. Radnor, Pa: Chilton, 1972.

241

GEMSTONES

Quick, Lelande, and Leiper, Hugh. *Gemcraft: How to Cut and Polish Gemstones.* Rev. ed. Radnor, PA: Chilton, 1977.

Schumann, Walter. *Gemstones of the World.* New York: Sterling, 1977.

Index

246